Naval Diplomacy in the

This book offers a detailed investigation of naval diplomacy, past and present, and challenges the widely accepted Anglo-American school of sea power thought.

Despite the acknowledgement of the importance of the threat or use of force in the pursuit of policy since the dawn of strategic thought, the utility of sea power in operations other than war is poorly understood and articulated. Theorists have invariably viewed sea power in peacetime through the lens of hard power effects such as coercion and deterrence. Commentaries on engagement, interoperability and the forging of friendships are largely conspicuous by their absence. This book considers how all these strands of international politics can be better understood for use in the 21st century.

The book explains and defines naval diplomacy, with existing theoretical frameworks being critically analyzed. It reviews over 500 incidents from the post-Cold War era, drawing on this empirical evidence to determine that naval diplomacy remains a potent means of 21st-century statecraft. It finds that existing understanding of naval diplomacy is insufficient and offers an alternative model, drawing on basic communication and stakeholder theories. The implications of the book relate directly to national security: naval deployments could be more effectively targeted; foreign activity at sea could be better understood and, if necessary, countered; finally, the ability of non-state actors to support national interests from the sea could, potentially, be better harnessed.

This book will be of much interest to students of naval power, maritime security, strategic studies and international relations.

Kevin Rowlands is Captain in the Royal Navy. He was awarded a PhD in war studies from King's College London and is the author of *21st Century Gorshkov* (2017).

Corbett Centre for Maritime Policy Studies Series

Series Editors: Greg Kennedy, Tim Benbow and Jon Robb-Webb
Defence Studies Department, Joint Services Command and Staff College, UK

The Corbett Centre for Maritime Policy Studies Series is the publishing platform of the Corbett Centre. Drawing on the expertise and wider networks of the Defence Studies Department of King's College London, and based at the Joint Services Command and Staff College in the UK Defence Academy, the Corbett Centre is already a leading centre for academic expertise and education in maritime and naval studies. It enjoys close links with several other institutions, both academic and governmental, that have an interest in maritime matters, including the Developments, Concepts and Doctrine Centre (DCDC), the Naval Staff of the Ministry of Defence and the Naval Historical Branch. The centre and its publishing output aims to promote the understanding and analysis of maritime history and policy and to provide a forum for the interaction of academics, policymakers and practitioners. Books published under the aegis of the Corbett Centre series reflect these aims and provide an opportunity to stimulate research and debate into a broad range of maritime related themes. The core subject matter for the series is maritime strategy and policy, conceived broadly to include theory, history and practice, military and civil, historical and contemporary, British and international aspects. As a result, this series offers a unique opportunity to examine key issues such as maritime security, the future of naval power, and the commercial uses of the sea, from an exceptionally broad chronological, geographical and thematic range. Truly interdisciplinary in its approach, the series welcomes books from across the humanities, social sciences and professional worlds, providing an unrivalled opportunity for authors and readers to enhance the national and international visibility of maritime affairs, and provide a forum for policy debate and analysis.

Early Naval Air Power
British and German Approaches
Dennis Haslop

Naval Diplomacy for the 21st Century
A Model for the Post-Cold War Global Order
Kevin Rowlands

For more information about this series, please visit: www.routledge.com/Corbett-Centre-for-Maritime-Policy-Studies-Series/book-series/CCMPSS

Naval Diplomacy in the 21st Century

A Model for the Post-Cold War Global Order

Kevin Rowlands

Routledge
Taylor & Francis Group

LONDON AND NEW YORK

First published 2019
by Routledge
2 Park Square, Milton Park, Abingdon, Oxon OX14 4RN

and by Routledge
52 Vanderbilt Avenue, New York, NY 10017, USA

First issued in paperback 2020

Routledge is an imprint of the Taylor & Francis Group, an informa business

British Library Cataloguing-in-Publication Data
A catalogue record for this book is available from the British Library

Library of Congress Cataloging-in-Publication Data
Names: Rowlands, Kevin, author.
Title: Naval diplomacy in the 21st century : a model for the post-cold war
    global order / Kevin Rowlands.
Other titles: Naval diplomacy in the twenty-first century
Description: First edition. | London ; New York, NY : Routledge/Taylor &
    Francis Group, 2019. | Series: Corbett centre for maritime policy
    studies series | Includes bibliographical references and index.
Identifiers: LCCN 2018025978 | ISBN 9781138624245 (hardback) |
    ISBN 9780429460951 (e-book)
Subjects: LCSH: Sea-power. | Diplomacy.
Classification: LCC V25 .R69 2019 | DDC 359/.03—dc23
LC record available at https://lccn.loc.gov/2018025978

ISBN 13: 978-0-367-58636-2 (pbk)
ISBN 13: 978-1-138-62424-5 (hbk)

Typeset in Times New Roman
by Apex CoVantage, LLC

MIX
Paper from
responsible sources
FSC
www.fsc.org
FSC® C013985

Printed in the United Kingdom
by Henry Ling Limited

Contents

Figures

Abbreviations

A2AD	Anti-access/Area Denial
AAW	Anti-air Warfare
ADIZ	Air Defence Identification Zone
AGI	Auxiliary General Intelligence (spy ship)
ALTBMD	Active Layered Theatre Ballistic Missile Defence System
APS	Africa Partnership Station
ASEAN	Association of South East Asian Nations
ASUW	Anti-surface Warfare
ASW	Anti-submarine Warfare
AU	African Union
BMD	Ballistic Missile Defence
BRICS	Brazil, Russia, India, China, South Africa
CIS	Commonwealth of Independent States
CNA	US Center for Naval Analyses
CSI	Container Security Initiative
CVN	Nuclear-Powered Aircraft Carrier
DEA	US Drug Enforcement Agency
EEZ	Exclusive Economic Zone
EPAA	European Phased Adaptive Approach to BMD
EU	European Union
EW	Electronic Warfare
FN	French Navy
FPDA	Five Power Defence Arrangement
FS	French Ship
GCC	Gulf Cooperation Council
GDP	Gross Domestic Product
GFS	Global Fleet Station
HADR/HADRO	Humanitarian Assistance Disaster Relief/Operations
HMAS	Her Majesty's Australian Ship
HMCS	Her Majesty's Canadian Ship
HMNZS	Her Majesty's New Zealand Ship
HMS	Her Majesty's Ship
HSV	High Speed Vessel

IAEA	International Atomic Energy Authority
ICBM	Intercontinental Ballistic Missile
IMO	International Maritime Organization
INS	Indian Naval Ship
INTERFRET	International Force East Timor
IR	International Relations
JMSDF	Japanese Maritime Self Defence Force
LeT	Lashkar-e-Taiba (group behind 2008 Mumbai terror attacks)
LST	Landing Ship Tank
LTTE	Liberation Tigers of Tamil Eelam (or 'Tamil Tigers')
MCM	Mine Counter Measures
MCMV	Mine Counter Measures Vessel
MEND	Movement for the Emancipation of the Niger Delta
MEU	US Marine Expeditionary Unit
MIOPS	Maritime Interdiction Operations
MSO	Maritime Security Operations
NATO	North Atlantic Treaty Organization
NEO	Non-combatant Evacuation Operation
NGO	Non-governmental Organization
PfP	Partnership for Peace
PLA	Chinese People's Liberation Army
PLAN	Chinese People's Liberation Army Navy (sometimes PLA(N)
PRC	People's Republic of China
PSO	Peace Support Operation
RAF	Royal Air Force
RAN	Royal Australian Navy
RFA	Royal Fleet Auxiliary
RIMPAC	Rim of the Pacific (US-led maritime exercise)
RN	Royal Navy
RNLN	Royal Netherlands Navy
RNZN	Royal New Zealand Navy
RoC	Republic of China (Taiwan)
ROK	Republic of Korea (South Korea)
RSN	Republic of Singapore Navy
SADC	South African Defence Community
SAR	Search and Rescue
SEATO	South East Asian Treaty Organization
SLNS	Sri Lanka Naval Ship
SLOCs	Sea Lines of Communication
SSBN	Nuclear Powered Ballistic Missile Firing Submarine
SSGN	Nuclear Powered Guided Missile Firing Submarine
SSN	Nuclear Powered Submarine
STANAVFORLANT	NATO Standing Naval Force Atlantic
STANAVFORMED	NATO Standing Naval Force Mediterranean
TAGOS	Tactical Auxiliary General Ocean Surveillance

TLAM	Tomahawk Land Attack Missile
UN	United Nations
UNCLOS	United Nations Convention on the Law of the Sea
UNSCR	United Nations Security Council Resolution
USN	United States Navy
USNS	United States Naval Ship
USS	United States Ship
WEU	Western European Union

Introduction

Though not the raison d'être of navies, naval diplomacy has an enduring role to play in the exercise of sea power. From Thucydides' accounts of the coercive power of the Athenian Fleet to the hegemonic stability delivered by the Royal Navy in 19th-century Pax Britannica, great powers have used their naval forces to shape the world according to their vision. Rising powers have followed suit. Germany, the United States, the Soviet Union, China and India all staked a claim for global status, in part through their fleets and their activities at sea. The Cold War may have seen a different pattern of naval diplomacy from that which went before, primarily based on the might of the Eastern and Western blocs, but it was all, in the main, a state-centric understanding of effect.

But what of now? Is coercive diplomacy involving the threat and actual use of naval force alive and well? The two Koreas or China and Japan might believe that it is. Are alliances and coalitions built at sea? It is certainly an expectation, because states invest substantial amounts of time, effort and money pursuing them. Does naval diplomacy even have to be carried out by the uniformed forces of a recognized state? The Gaza Freedom Flotilla's interaction with Israel in 2010 certainly made news and grabbed the attention of powerful states, as do Greenpeace's environmental campaigns at sea today. Perhaps getting the message across is a good enough outcome in what is essentially a communicative process.

Is naval diplomacy merely a subset of coercive diplomacy? Not necessarily, because there are myriad 'soft' power initiatives from capacity building to the cultivation of friendships, the reassurance of allies, humanitarian assistance and disaster relief, just 'being there' for nationals abroad and providing venues for defence sales which might fall under the umbrella of the topic. To echo the comment made by one former practitioner, naval diplomacy is about what navies actually do, rather than what they train for. One can add to that statement that it is certainly what navies do, but what naval theorists tend not to write about.

Mahan in America and Corbett in England – the writers with the greatest lasting impact on naval strategy – had much to say about sea power, but any reader must look hard at their work to find anything more than an oblique reference to the utility of navies in the pursuit of national political goals when not fighting wars. In the Cold War, economist, game theorist and Nobel laureate Thomas Schelling published *Arms and Influence*, which set out the principles of a coercive strategy and its effect on decision makers. Much of his work informed that which was to come later, but it was general in nature. Only in the 1970s did naval diplomacy begin to be studied as a subject in its own right. In the East Sergei Gorshkov, the man who shaped the Soviet Navy, wrote about it in his classic work, *The Sea Power of the State*. Simultaneously, in the West naval presence became a core mission of the US Navy and the American Edward Luttwak wrote of 'naval suasion', but scratch the surface and the political motivations of those works quickly become apparent.

Ken Booth set out what navies were for (the trinity of military, constabulary and diplomatic roles) and his thoughts were later subsumed into the official doctrine of numerous Western powers. But it was the seminal study by Sir James Cable, *Gunboat Diplomacy*, first published in the 1970s and running to three editions, which most influenced the understanding of the topic for the rest of the century. However, post-Cold War commentators such as Joseph Nye provided a fresh understanding of power, and naval practitioners and academics such as Mike Mullen and Geoffrey Till looked at old ideas through a new, 'post-modern' lens.

This book looks at each of these to determine what the old ideas were and to ask if they are still relevant in the 21st century. That question is important because after the end of the Cold War the purely military war-fighting role of navies, particularly Western 'post-modern' navies, has diminished as their principal focus. With no peer competitors, the combined fleets of the West effectively exercised command of the oceans for a quarter of a century. It is only now, with Russia reasserting its global influence and with the rising powers in the East, particularly China and India, militarily increasingly active in the maritime environment that physical confrontation might once again take centre stage.

However, this shift in emphasis between war fighting, constabulary tasks and diplomatic mission may be more nuanced than initial conjecture implies and it is not necessarily a new phenomenon. Navies have always been peacetime policy instruments of the state and the tools of grand strategy, as well as the fighters of wars at sea. Oliver Cromwell famously declared that 'a man-o-war is the best ambassador'; a 21st-century equivalent shows the US Navy depicted in posters and on T-shirts as an aircraft carrier over the caption '90,000 tons of diplomacy'. The images may be different but the message is the same. So perhaps the opening sentence of this introduction should be revisited – perhaps the advancement of political and economic goals *is* the raison d'être of navies.[1]

Gunboat diplomacy is an instantly recognizable term, probably conjuring thoughts of 19th-century coercion and unwelcome, strong-arm tactics. It is also inaccurate. Not all diplomatic activity carried out at and from the sea is done by ships with guns. And not all diplomatic activity carried out at and from the sea is coercive. Co-operation, collaboration and mutual assistance are increasingly common in the globalized, interdependent world of today. A far better term is *naval diplomacy*, but that lacks a universally accepted definition. Indeed, is it *naval* (of ships) or is it *maritime* (of the sea)? Is it *diplomacy* at all, in the sense of codified discourse between recognized states, or is it part of a wider wielding of influence by a multitude of state and non-state actors? It is, of course, all of the above and more.

Whatever it is, the topic certainly deserves attention.

The purpose of this book and its working hypotheses

The purpose of this book is to address a series of questions about the place of naval diplomacy in the post-Cold War global order and to understand whether macro-level issues from terrorism to climate change, from financial instability to ungoverned spaces, are subject to political influence from the sea. Interagency co-operation and multinational coalitions and alliances are features of contemporary maritime strategy and these too must be taken into consideration when trying to make sense of the uses of sea power today. The broad questions it asks are:

1   What is naval diplomacy? How does it differ from or build upon other forms of military/defence diplomacy?
2   What are the traditional models of naval diplomacy? Who conducts it, how, with what aim and against whom?
3   What, if anything, is new in the post-Cold War era? Have 'globalization' and the perceived increasing importance of non-state actors affected naval diplomacy? Has the incidence of naval diplomacy changed over time?
4   Are the existing models for naval diplomacy still valid? To what extent do they require revision? Do they appropriately encompass likely target audiences (potential adversaries, potential allies and domestic constituencies)?
5   Can a new model be constructed? If so, what should be its key tenets?

In attempting to answer these questions a series of working hypotheses have been framed which are implicitly tested and refined through the course of the book. The hypotheses relate to the nature of naval diplomacy itself and its correlation to the exercise of power in international relations.

The first hypothesis is that naval diplomacy is a subset of general diplomacy and not simply a 'free good' of military capability. Of course, there is a direct relationship between capability and credibility and this too must be acknowledged. Diplomacy is the formal and informal means of communication between international actors on the world stage; any communication can be carried out in innumerable ways and actors will seek to communicate via the means which they have at their disposal. Maritime states with naval forces will, therefore, engage in naval diplomacy.

> **Hypothesis**: naval diplomacy is a subset of general diplomacy and will be used as a means of communication by maritime states in pursuit of their national interest.

Since most states experience varying degrees of peace more frequently than all-out war then, logically, armed forces are more often used in peaceful modes than for fighting an enemy. Ken Booth's widely accepted 'trinity' of naval roles (military, policing and diplomatic)[2] is a useful theoretical model for the understanding of naval power but it can be misinterpreted. The roles are not equally balanced, nor are they mutually exclusive. The prime reason to create and maintain a navy (as opposed to a coastguard) is for its military role. However, a navy may rarely or even never exercise its *military* role in full. The use of limited force and policing or constabulary responsibilities to maintain 'good order at sea'[3] therefore become a navy's day-to-day, year-to-year employment – employment which inevitably has a communicative dimension. Nevertheless, for understandable reasons, the war-fighting role is the focus of most historical and theoretical writing on sea power.

> **Hypothesis**: the diplomatic role of naval forces is more prevalent than the academic literature suggests.

To many, naval diplomacy is synonymous with coercive 'gunboat diplomacy'.[4] Coercion is certainly a possible use of naval power short of war but it is not the whole. Joseph Nye's 'spectrum of behaviour' between international actors, in which power is classified from 'hard' to 'soft',[5] offers a simple framework for situating naval diplomacy. At the 'hard' end, naval forces can be used to inflict punitive damage on an actor in order to secure behavioural changes. At the 'soft' end, they can make friendly port calls and open their doors to visitors to impress, educate and influence, to foster relationships with partners and to build their capacity. In between are countless possibilities for interaction which in some way further the interests of their state.

> **Hypothesis**: naval diplomacy spans a broad spectrum from hard to soft power.

Few if any dedicated studies of naval diplomacy were undertaken until the 1970s, when the study of limited war and military influence became of interest to both East and West. The works published in that decade became a privileged discourse on naval diplomacy and in the main complemented each other. However, they were written by academics and practitioners living with the political realities of the day and should be viewed with that in mind.

> **Hypothesis**: existing models of naval diplomacy were conceived in the Cold War and are products of their time.

The existing models of naval diplomacy assume bilateral, mechanistic relation-ships; that is, one party carries out an action against another party in order to produce a reaction which it calculates will be favourable to its own interests. This action-reaction model, described by James Cable in terms of an 'assailant' and a 'victim', need not be limited to coercion and is applicable across the spectrum of naval diplomacy. However, it is limited. The reality of international relations is far more complex; multiple audiences and stakeholders exist within every com-municative relationship.

Hypothesis: existing models of naval diplomacy are limited by generally assuming a bilateral, mechanistic relationship between the actors involved.

Different levels of communication in naval diplomacy can be explained by use of a sporting analogy. If Team 'A' were playing against Team 'B', then the two teams are clearly the primary competitors in the game. The approach of previous theorists to the sporting analogy would examine the action of 'A' and the reaction of 'B' and declare one a winner, one a loser or an equal draw. There are, however, many more interested parties, all of whom are stakeholders in the wider competition. Both teams will have supporters and, potentially, sponsors. There will be other teams not involved in that particular fixture but who are competing in the same league; they will be interested in the game, as will their supporters and sponsors; the game could affect their own standing. Relative positioning and context is important, as a draw for one team may mean the maintenance of its place in the league, while for the other a draw may result in relegation. Importantly, the result for either team may determine who they play next. Returning to the military dimension, one side can win a battle but lose the war.

Hypothesis: a revised model of naval diplomacy should not be solely event based but take into account different levels of communication and the multitude of stakeholders involved.

Acknowledging that, though not the raison d'être of navies, naval diplomacy is a fundamental role has implications for politicians, planners and practitioners. Force structures, capabilities, deployments and training could be adapted to maximize the potential benefits to be gained. The requirements for naval platforms to perform constabulary tasks are well understood and are fuelling debate, as the words of the former US Secretary of Defense Robert Gates demonstrate: 'You don't necessarily need a billion dollar guided missile destroyer to chase down and deal with a bunch of teenage pirates wielding AK47s and rocket propelled grenades'.[6] A similar level of debate on the subject of naval diplomacy is needed.

Hypothesis: an understanding of contemporary naval diplomacy can aid the development of appropriate force structures and capabilities of maritime states.

Book structure and findings

The book is made up of three parts. The first part (Chapters 1 and 2) explores the theoretical approaches taken to naval diplomacy over time. After defining the place of naval diplomacy in the context of international relations and sea power, the historiography is told through three broad phases: pre-Cold War, Cold War and post-Cold War, where Western, Eastern and non-aligned writings are evaluated alongside more recent contributions of contemporary commentators. As might be expected, the development of ideas has been evolutionary; hard power concepts such as coercion and deterrence feature heavily throughout, but it is the later writers who place the greatest emphasis on the 21st-century soft power concepts of co-operation, assistance and persuasion.

The second part (Chapters 3–6 and the book's Appendix) attempts to provide a reality check. It considers what has actually happened at sea since the end of the Cold War. The Appendix is a chronological database of over 500 incidents of naval diplomacy along with two 'control' periods from the Cold War itself, which can be used by present and future practitioners and scholars for their own purposes. A brief, thematic analysis of the data is conducted, which includes discussion of the forging of amity and enmity between the actors involved, the role of international engagement and disengagement, prestige and symbolism and the numerical incidence of naval diplomatic events.

The second part then expands on the lived experience by drawing on a series of specific examples of incidents of naval diplomacy since the end of the Cold War for a more in-depth case study. Each example considers a different aspect of the topic during a time in which the global order underwent drastic and rapid change. Fragmentation and the uncertain security situation in the immediate aftermath of the fall of Communism, nationalism and opportunism, Pax Americana and resistance to US hegemony, and the return of great power rivalry are all considered. It also includes examples of the political use of the sea by non-state actors attempting to further their own agendas.

Finally, the third part (Chapters 7 and 8) attempts to do something new. It concludes that existing mechanistic 'assailant-victim' models are not appropriate to the 21st century, and instead it proposes an alternative based on an interdisciplinary application of communication and stakeholder theories. This new 'foundational' model is then applied to a different series of case studies drawn from both the Cold War and post-Cold War periods.

The main findings and conclusions may be broken down into six key areas. First, the book defines naval diplomacy as the use of naval and maritime assets as communicative instruments in international power relationships to further the interests of the actors involved.

Second, it reports that only around a quarter of the incidents of naval diplomacy in the post-Cold War period could be described as indicative of enmity between the parties involved. Conversely, some 90 per cent have some degree of amity, or relationship building, in their purpose. The sum is more than the whole because the two are not mutually exclusive and purposes are rarely binary; in complex relationships signals of enmity and amity can be, and are, made concurrently.

Third, it shows that there are varying degrees of engagement and disengagement within naval diplomacy and the state of a relationship can often be assessed by the type of activity practiced. At the lowest end of the scale, goodwill visits can be a means of ongoing 'relationship maintenance' between established allies or symbolic first forays for those with a more adversarial connection. Complexity and interoperability progressively increase until only the very closest allies are capable of fully integrated operations in difficult scenarios.

Fourth, the book identifies that the incidence of non-state actors making use of the seas to exert influence is increasing. Fifth, and closely linked, it identifies that the incidence of naval forces being used for humanitarian assistance is also on the rise. These two findings offer confirmatory evidence to support assumptions that have become widely held since the end of the Cold War.

Finally, the book concludes that existing models and frameworks for naval diplomacy are, essentially, event-based approximations of state actors' use of the 'spare capacity' inherent in military navies when not at war to influence other state actors. They are therefore insufficient for the 21st century.

Notes

1 Patalano defines naval diplomacy as the use advancement of naval assets to secure or advance political or economic goals. Patalano, Alessio. 'Commitment by Presence: Naval Diplomacy and Japanese Defense Engagement in Southeast Asia.' In Brown, James & Kingston, Jeff (Eds.). *Japan's Foreign Relations in Asia.* (Abingdon: Routledge, 2018).
2 Ken Booth. *Navies and Foreign Policy.* (London: Croom Helm, 1977), pp. 15–16.
3 Till, Geoffrey. *Seapower: A Guide for the Twenty-First Century, 2nd Ed.* (Abingdon: Routledge, 2009), p. 286.
4 James Cable. for example, limits his study to incidents of coercion. Cable, James. *Gunboat Diplomacy 1919–1991: Political Applications of Limited Naval Force, 3rd Ed.* (Basingstoke: Macmillan, 1994), p. 3. Ian Speller, however, suggests that naval diplomacy is a wider concept, inclusive of more 'benign applications.' Speller, Ian. *Understanding Naval Warfare.* (Abingdon: Routledge, 2014), p. 76.
5 Nye, Joseph S. *Soft Power: The Means to Success in World Politics.* (New York: Public Affairs, 2004), p. 5.
6 Gates, Robert. 'Remarks of Secretary of Defense Robert M. Gates.' *U.S. Naval War College Review* 63, No. 4 (2010): p. 14.

1 Defining naval diplomacy

What is diplomacy?

If contemporary naval diplomacy is little understood, it is perhaps because it is a subset of a broader topic which despite a long history and great study remains remarkably ill-defined. The common perception of diplomacy is one of formal state-to-state communication. That is certainly the meaning given in the 1961 Vienna Convention on Diplomatic Relations.[1] Martin Griffiths and Terry O'Callaghan echo many in the field of international relations when they state that diplomacy is 'the entire process through which states conduct their foreign relations';[2] but if that is the case, what exactly is meant by foreign relations? The same authors talk of diplomacy as 'the means for allies to co-operate and for adversaries to resolve conflicts without force', which does go some way to answering the question, but such an explanation rather limits the scope of what diplomacy is and what it has to offer. It is not simply codified discourse.

A broader view situates diplomacy at the very heart of international relations, and the theorists John Baylis, Steve Smith and Patricia Owens offer what at first reading appears to be a reasonable contemporary definition:

> In foreign policy it refers to the use of diplomacy as a policy instrument possibly in association with other instruments such as economic or military force to enable an international actor to achieve its policy objectives. Diplomacy in world politics refers to a communications process between international actors that seeks through negotiation to resolve conflict short of war. This process has been refined, institutionalized and professionalized over time.[3]

These writers are careful not to limit diplomacy to recognized states and they place it alongside 'other instruments' of policy though, interestingly, they still see it as separate and discrete. Yet, like Griffiths and O'Callaghan, they narrow the field again by connecting it directly to conflict resolution. International actors may indeed rely on diplomatic means to resolve conflict but that is just one part of the story. Similarly, the assertion that diplomacy operates 'short of war' surely needs to be challenged. Paul Sharp, a leading figure in the study of diplomatic theory, neatly counters this:

When force is resorted to, diplomacy need not necessarily come to an end. . . .
In the age of total war diplomacy continued, with even the attacks on Hiroshima and Nagasaki having their communicative components spelled out by
unofficial and third party contacts.[4]

Relating diplomacy to the exercise of power is one way to potentially clarify
its role and purpose. If Joseph Nye's description of power as 'the ability to influence the behaviour of others to get the outcomes one wants'[5] is accepted, then
perhaps a more accurate assessment would be to refer to diplomacy not in terms
of conflict resolution but as *a communications process that seeks to further the
interests of an international actor*, whatever those interests or whoever that actor
might be.

Of course, many observers acknowledge that diplomacy has grown to become
a 'profession'; perhaps it always was. By extrapolation, a *profession* requires
professionals, and these we call *diplomats*. Paul Sharp states that 'we can find
an uneasy consensus around the idea that diplomacy is whatever diplomats do,
but it quickly falls apart again around the question of who are the diplomats'.[6] He
investigates the notion of diplomacy and diplomats in the formal sense – that is,
as international actors on the world stage – and concludes that quite what diplomacy is remains a mystery. However, he does acknowledge that at a practical
level diplomacy consists merely of people doing the normal things of human
interaction such as bargaining, representing, lobbying and, of course, communicating that we find in all walks of life.[7] In this informal sense we are all diplomats,
though some of us may be better at it than others.

Niche diplomacy

Viewed this way, diplomacy can be exercised in a near-infinite number of ways,
adapted as required to best suit the circumstances of the case. Some actors, be they
individuals, organizations or states, by virtue of their particular strengths, weak-
nesses, interests and culture may favour one or more methods over another and
they can develop a methodology to serve their particular purpose.

Andrew Cooper coined the term 'niche diplomacy' in the mid-1990s and, at
state level, he discussed a range of 'middle powers' and how they differ in their
diplomatic approach to international relations. For example, he explained how
Canada tends to apply low-key institution-building policies while Argentina
forges economic ties with its neighbours to gain influence and Turkey emphasizes its strategic geographical position. Of non-state actors Cooper has more
to say:

a wide range of NGOs, especially those with an interest in issues such as
human rights and the environment, such as Amnesty International and Greenpeace, have worked to secure their own niches in international relations. . . .
Greenpeace has a greater influence on world policy than, say, the government
of Austria.[8]

Cooper's thesis is compelling. Diplomacy need not be limited to recognized states; international bodies such as the European Union and United Nations certainly participate in diplomacy, as do *de facto* administrations such as Hezbollah or Hamas or even the Taliban and ISIL/Daesh which, while not universally recognized as legitimate governments, have or do control territory and play a role on the world stage. Whether Greenpeace and Amnesty International fall into a similar category is debatable, but the fact that they have global strategies, operate across state boundaries and influence events is not.

For the purposes of this book, a simple definition is adopted. Diplomacy is assumed to be a communications instrument used in power relationships to further the interests of the international actors involved. Actors with particular relative strengths will seek to use them; it would be counter-intuitive to think otherwise. It is a logical deduction, therefore, that military force may be a niche which some actors will seek to exploit for diplomatic purposes.

The diplomatic use of military force

The supposed raison d'être of military forces, *war fighting*, is just one extreme manifestation of their utility. Joseph Nye describes a 'spectrum of behaviour' in international relations along which sit different types of power. Under 'hard power', within which he tends to place military action, comes coercion and inducement, while under 'soft power', which he defines as 'getting others to *want* the outcomes you want',[9] comes agenda setting and attraction. Initially a reader may assume that military forces are absent in the exercise of soft power. However, Nye is sufficiently astute to note that there is overlap.[10] Addressing the role military forces in particular, he states:

> The military can also play an important role in the creation of soft power. In addition to the aura of power that is generated by its hard power capabilities, the military has a broad range of officer exchanges, joint training and assistance programs with other countries in peacetime.[11]

Alongside Nye's 'spectrum of behaviour', and closely associated with the widely accepted concept of the 'spectrum of conflict',[12] there is a corresponding spectrum along which military force can be used to support political objectives. In operations other than war this spectrum includes such activities as coercion, deterrence, reassurance, humanitarian relief, stabilization and peace support. In the absence of war fighting, whether in total or more limited conflicts, it is the activities along this spectrum which generally provide effective day-to-day employment for the world's armed forces. The American scholar Robert Art captures the essence of this situation, particularly the 'hard' end, well:

> Military power can be wielded not only forcefully but also 'peacefully'. [. . .] To use military power forcefully is to wage war; to use it peacefully is to threaten war. Only when diplomacy has failed is war generally waged.

Mainly in the hope that war can be avoided are threats usually made. For any given state, war is the exception, not the rule, in its relations with other countries, because most of the time a given state is at peace, not war. Consequently, states use their military power more frequently in the peaceful than the forceful mode.[13]

Coercive diplomacy: deterrence, coercion and compellence

Notwithstanding Nye's soft power thesis, Art directly links the peaceful role of military power with the use of threat. From Sun Tzu through Machiavelli to the present day, much has been written on the utility of threatened force and it is important to distinguish between the positive and negative variants of this: coercion and deterrence. The difference is perhaps summed up best by Gordon Craig and Alexander George:

> Whereas deterrence represents an effort to dissuade an opponent from undertaking an action that he has not yet initiated, coercive diplomacy attempts to reverse actions which have already been undertaken by the adversary.[14]

Both coercion and deterrence are methods by which interests may be pursued without resort to all-out conflict. *British Defence Doctrine* has adopted very similar definitions for the terms and emphasizes their positive and negative connotations by connecting coercion with the word *persuade* and deterrence with the word *dissuade*.[15] However, some commentators use *coercion* as an umbrella term to cover both *deterrence* (the negative) and *compellence* (the positive) variants, and thus coercion and compellence can sometimes be read to mean the same thing.[16] Whether coercion is the opposite of deterrence or whether it describes both deterrence and compellence is debatable, but the academic pursuit of any difference between them inevitably results in a concentration on the ends rather than the ways and means of conflict resolution in an international relationship. At the military level, the threat or use of force may be enacted in exactly the same way, for example by the forward positioning of troops, whether it is meant to coerce/compel or deter.

The main body of contemporary academic literature on coercion, deterrence and compellence stems from the bipolar world of the last century. Deterrence, particularly nuclear deterrence, most often comes to the fore. An influential work of the period is *Deterrence and Strategy* by the French soldier-scholar Andre Beaufre. Beaufre discusses the 'laws of deterrence' and defines the concept quite simply: 'The object of deterrence is to prevent an enemy power taking the decision to use armed force'.[17] The effect Beaufre describes must be psychological, requiring the recipient of the 'threat' to calculate risk, determine that the likelihood of escalation is so high and the impact so unacceptable that the decision to use armed force is never taken. Given the nuclear backdrop at the time of his writing, it is unsurprising that Beaufre talks of 'fear' being engendered through deterrence.[18] Deterrence theory dominated politico-military strategy and major power diplomacy for almost half a century through successive arms races, the presumption of mutually assured destruction (MAD) and arms limitations talks.[19] The theory is important and well documented, but for the purposes of this book deterrence will be considered alongside coercion/compellence and the term *coercive diplomacy* will be used to cover all.

Sir Lawrence Freedman has written that 'the study of coercion in international relations remains dominated by work undertaken in the United States in the Cold War period and distorted through the preoccupation with deterrence'.[20] If coercion and deterrence are actually near-identical in means, then that criticism of distortion could be a debatable point. However, Freedman does offer his own definition of coercion as 'the deliberate and purposeful use of overt threat to influence another's strategic choice'.[21] Freedman's definition is significant because like Beaufre's deterrence it identifies coercion as a cognitive tool. As such it need not necessarily threaten 'war' as Robert Art suggests; rather, it is about influencing another's choice. Logically, coercion need not even be the 'overt' act that Freedman contends; subtlety in international relations can be a powerful alternative methodology. Furthermore, a threat does not need to be kept below the threshold of force; limited physical action leaving the recipient with the understanding that there could be 'more to come' can be a very effective strategy.

The work which laid the foundation of the Cold War study of coercive diplomacy was Thomas Schelling's 1966 book *Arms and Influence*.[22] A political economist inspired by game theory, Schelling laid down five theoretical conditions if a coercive strategy was to succeed. He said the conflict must be zero-sum; the threat made must be potent and convince the adversary that non-compliance would be too costly; the threat must be credible (i.e. through a convincing combination of will and capability); the coercer must assure the adversary that non-compliance will not simply result in more demands; and, importantly, the adversary must have time to comply.[23]

Schelling's conceptual theory was further developed by Alexander George who has been called 'the foremost analyst of coercive diplomacy'.[24] According to George, the practical difficulty with the abstract theory of coercive diplomacy that Schelling espoused is that it

> assumes pure rationality on the part of the opponent – an ability to receive all relevant information, evaluate it correctly, make proper judgments as to the credibility and potency of the threat, and see that it is in his interest to accede to the demand made on him.[25]

Such a rational actor does not exist in reality, of course, which makes predicting the outcome of coercive diplomacy a most inaccurate science. Conversely, some actors on the world stage who have been portrayed as irrational tyrants and dictators appear to play the coercive diplomacy 'game' quite well; North Korea's ruling family springs to mind.

George used the term 'complex interdependence' to describe the modern globalized world,[26] and it is this myriad of linkages and relationships in concert with fickle human behaviour which precludes any degree of certainty in advance of an action. George, along with Gordon Craig, attempted to build on Schelling's factors by identifying particular conditions required for the success of coercive diplomacy. To them the coercing power must create in the opponent's mind a sense of urgency for compliance with a demand, plus a belief that the coercer is more highly motivated to achieve his or her stated demand than the coerced is to oppose it. Finally, there must be a fear of unacceptable escalation if the demand is not accepted.[27] Additionally, in his book *The Limits of Coercive Diplomacy*, written in conjunction with William Simons, George gives 14 factors to be considered when judging likely success: the global strategic environment; the type of provocation; the image of war; whether the action is unilateral or part of a coalition; the isolation of the adversary; the clarity of objective; the strength of motivation; the asymmetry of motivation; a sense of urgency; strong leadership; domestic support; international support; any fear of escalation; and the clarity of terms offered.[28]

That there are 14 factors is indicative of the complexity involved. By analyzing these factors it can be seen that few are beyond the control of at least one of the actors involved, either the *coercer* or *coerced*, and that the initiative generally lies with the actor making the demand. According to realist tradition, relative strength is the paramount consideration in an inter-state relationship and, in military terms, this can be quite accurately determined. Art again:

> It is more desirable to be militarily powerful than militarily weak. Militarily strong states have greater clout in world politics than militarily weak ones. Militarily strong states are less subject to the influence of other states than militarily weak ones. Militarily powerful states can better offer protection to other states, or more seriously threaten them, in order to influence their behaviour than can militarily weak ones.[29]

The message is clear. At the 'hard' end of the spectrum strong military forces can be used as a means of influence to further the interests of an actor on the world stage.

Preventive diplomacy: the military contribution

But what of the 'soft' end? Therein lies the phenomenon known as 'defence diplomacy'. In essence, preventive defence diplomacy professes to further national interests not through threat or the limited use of force but through outreach, international engagement and conflict prevention. It is achieved by the exchange of attachés and other military personnel, by partnerships and coalitions, and by education and training. George Robertson, the British Secretary of State for Defence at the time of the Strategic Defence Review of 1998 neatly, if somewhat flippantly, summed up the task: 'Defence diplomacy is about the middle aged drinking together instead of the young fighting each other'.[30]

Such diplomacy, however, is not merely social exchange. It requires resource and planning, strategy and policy. It involves building relationships with an eye to the future, building capacity in allies and friends and building on the influence wrought through other instruments of policy. However, it can also be preventive, assuring security for the user by attempting to shape the future behaviour of the recipient. Martin Griffiths and Terry O'Callaghan have stated that the main focus of this type of discourse, preventive diplomacy, is to identify and respond to brewing conflicts in order to prevent the outbreak of violence. They go on to say that it may take many forms 'such as verbal diplomatic protests and denunciations, imposing sanctions, active monitoring and verification of agreements, peacekeeping, providing good offices and other forms of third party mediation'.[31] However, defence diplomacy is also about prevention at the very earliest stages; it is about making friends, not just dealing with enemies. For a militarily powerful state with a military employed predominantly in the 'peaceful' role, defence diplomacy has the potential to overtake more formal diplomacy and become the principal form of international relations in some areas. Joseph Nye makes this point well: 'Indeed, some observers worry that America's five military regional commanders sometimes have more resources and better access in their regions that the American ambassadors in those countries'.[32] This form of *informal* diplomacy is, of course, nothing new,[33] but its *formal* adoption into policy as a means to achieve ends is certainly a product of post-Cold War thinking. Defence diplomacy can be seen as an attempt to synergize preventive diplomacy and military capability into a more powerful and potent weapon to achieve national security.

The particular advantage of naval forces in diplomacy

Robert Art correctly identifies that in general military forces are used more frequently in the peaceful mode than the forceful, but he offers no quality judgement as to their value as political instruments. The same is not true of naval strategists who tend to be quick to point out the particular advantage of naval forces in diplomacy; to some it is the prime example of their utility. In the classic Cold War text *The Sea in Modern Strategy*, for example, L. W. Martin stated:

> The essential quality of a military navy is obviously its ultimate capacity to engage and fight an enemy. Yet, for the greater portion of its existence, a navy is not engaged in combat. During this time of peace, however, a navy by no means fails to exert an influence upon international affairs. This effectiveness short of war is difficult to characterize but is nevertheless pervasive and may well comprise the most significant benefit a nation derives from its naval instruments.[34]

Conventional wisdom ascribes a number of enduring 'attributes' to naval forces which help to explain their relative lead over land and air forces as diplomatic instruments. These attributes are reflected strongly and consistently in the academic literature,[35] and expressed in similar ways in the naval doctrine of numerous maritime states.[36] They include such factors as flexibility of use, presence without commitment and independence, all of which afford political leverage to the employing power. Air forces may have the advantage of speed of reaction within a given radius, assuming the availability of bases, but navalists argue that they lack persistence. Land forces can provide a 'human face', but their time-consuming and burdensome deployment inevitably carries significant political risk on both the domestic and international stage. Naval forces, however, can poise indefinitely, do not necessarily require access, basing or overflight rights, can be either overt or 'over the horizon' and can arrive with a fanfare and depart in silence or vice versa. The high seas, the global commons, provide a manoeuvre space that has traditionally been thought unavailable in other physical environments. They offer respective governments a range of options across the full spectrum of activity and are arguably the easiest and best *military* means of 'soft' influence through port visits, bilateral exercises and humanitarian assistance.

Remarkably however, these enduring attributes of navies have gone largely unchallenged in the mainstream academic literature for several decades and their relevance to the post-Cold War global order is therefore worthy of consideration – a point returned to in Chapter 7. However, to set the scene here, the conventional wisdom attributing certain enduring characteristics to naval forces will be accepted, particularly for the period 1991–2015.

In short, the maritime domain offers international actors rich pickings for their communicative endeavours. Maritime or naval diplomacy is therefore a niche that many choose to exploit. It follows that a reasonable definition, and the one that this book adopts, is that naval diplomacy is a subset of general diplomacy and a means of communication by maritime actors, both state and non-state, in pursuit of their interests.

Notes

1 United Nations. 'The Vienna Contention on Diplomatic Relations 1961.' http://untreaty.un.org/ilc/texts/instruments/english/conventions/9_1_1961.pdf (accessed 6 March 2011).
2 Griffiths, Martin & O'Callaghan, Terry (Eds.). *International Relations: The Key Concepts*. (Abingdon: Routledge, 2002), pp. 79–81.
3 Baylis, John, Smith, Steve & Owens, Patricia. *Globalization of World Politics, 4th Ed.* (Oxford: Oxford University Press, 2008), p. 579.
4 Sharp, Paul. *Diplomatic Theory of International Relations*. (Cambridge: Cambridge University Press, 2009), p. 186.
5 Nye, Joseph S. *Soft Power: The Means to Success in World Politics*. (New York: Public Affairs, 2004), p. 2.
6 Sharp, *Diplomatic Theory*, p. 75.
7 Ibid., pp. 1–3.
8 Cooper, Andrew F. *Niche Diplomacy: Middle Powers after the Cold War*. (Basingstoke: Macmillan, 1997).
9 Nye, *Soft Power*, p. 5.
10 Ibid., pp. 7–8.
11 Ibid., p. 116.
12 The spectrum of conflict is a widely accepted term, used throughout Western doctrine, meaning a full range of military activity from humanitarian assistance and peace support to counter insurgency and major combat operations in war. See, for example, Daniel Moran, 'The View from Afloat.' In Wirtz, James & Larsen, Jeffrey (Eds.). *Naval Peacekeeping and Humanitarian Operations: Stability from the Sea*. (Abingdon: Routledge, 2009), p. 14.

13 Art, Robert. 'The Fungibility of Force.' In Art, Robert & Waltz, Kenneth (Eds.). *The Use of Force: Military Power and International Politics, 6th Ed.* (Oxford: Rowman & Littlefield, 2004), pp. 3–4.
14 Craig, Gordon A. & George, Alexander L. *Force and Statecraft: Diplomatic Problems of Our Time, 3rd Ed.* (Oxford: Oxford University Press, 1995), p. 196.
15 United Kingdom. Ministry of Defence. *British Defence Doctrine.* (London: MOD, 1996), G.3/G.5.
16 Schelling, Thomas C. *Arms and Influence* (2008 Edition). (New Haven: Yale University Press, 2008), pp. 70–71. First published New Haven: Yale University Press, 1966. Also, Till, Geoffrey. *Seapower: A Guide for the Twenty-First Century, 2nd Ed.* (Abingdon: Routledge, 2009), pp. 265–275.
17 Beaufre, Andre. *Deterrence and Strategy.* (London: Faber & Faber, 1965), p. 24.
18 Ibid., p. 25.
19 Brown, Neville. *The Geography of Human Conflict.* (Eastbourne: Sussex Academic Press, 2009), pp. 207–219.
20 Freedman, Lawrence (Ed.). *Strategic Coercion: Concepts and Cases.* (Oxford: Oxford University Press, 1998), p. 1.
21 Ibid., p. 3.
22 Jakobson, Peter Viggo. 'The Strategy of Coercive Diplomacy: Refining Existing Theory to Post-Cold War Realities.' In Freedman, Lawrence (Ed.). *Strategic Coercion: Concepts and Cases.* (Oxford: Oxford University Press, 1998), pp. 64–65.
23 Schelling, *Arms and Influence*, pp. 3–5.
24 Jakobson, 'The Strategy of Coercive Diplomacy', p. 63.
25 George, Alexander L. 'The Coercive Diplomacy.' In Art, Robert & Waltz, Kenneth (Eds.). *The Use of Force: Military Power and International Politics, 6th Ed.* (Oxford: Rowman & Littlefield, 2004), p. 70.
26 Craig & George, *Force and Statecraft*, p. 290. The term 'interdependence' has become common in the past decade; the UK's first National Security Strategy, for example, adopts it in its title. United Kingdom. Cabinet Office. *The National Security Strategy of the United Kingdom: Security in an Interdependent World.* (London: The Stationery Office, 2008).
27 Craig & George, *Force and Statecraft*, p. 197.
28 Jakobson, 'The Strategy of Coercive Diplomacy', p. 68.
29 Art, 'The Fungibility of Force', p. 7.
30 Quote attributed to George Robertson, quoted in: Powell, R. L. *The Maritime Contribution to Defence Diplomacy.* Master's Thesis. Joint Services Command and Staff College, Bracknell, 2000. The thesis was written as a response to the SDR of 1998 and the introduction of Defence Diplomacy as a UK Military Task.
31 Griffiths & O'Callaghan, *International Relations*, pp. 255–257.
32 Nye, *Soft Power*, p. 116.
33 Brent, R. P. *Defence Diplomacy: Sound Bite or Sustainable Mission?* Master's Thesis. Joint Services Command and Staff College, Bracknell, 1999, p. 20.
34 Martin, L. W. *The Sea in Modern Strategy.* (New York: Praeger, 1968), p. 133.
35 For example, in Till, *Seapower*, pp. 33–34; Ken Booth, *Navies and Foreign Policy.* (London: Croom Helm, 1977), pp. 33–35.
36 UK doctrine, for example, lists access, mobility, versatility, sustained reach, resilience, lift capacity, poise, resilience and leverage as attributes: United Kingdom. Development, Concepts and Doctrine Centre. *British Maritime Doctrine, 4th Ed.* JDP 0–10. (Shrivenham: DCDC, 2011), pp. 2–1 to 2–6. For other examples see: Australia. Royal Australian Navy. *Australian Maritime Doctrine 2010.* (Canberra: Sea Power Centre, 2010); United States. Department of the Navy. *A Cooperative Strategy for 21st Century Seapower.* (Washington, DC: DoN, 2007); Canada. National Defence Headquarters. *Leadmark: The Navy's Strategy for 2020.* (Ottawa: NDHQ, 2001); India. Ministry of Defence. *Freedom to use the Seas: India's Maritime Military Strategy.* (New Delhi: Integrated Headquarters Ministry of Defence (Navy), 2007).

2 Theory through time

Naval diplomacy through the eyes of navalists

The classic naval texts of and about sea power are essentially Western and Atlanticist in nature, reflecting the concentration of maritime supremacy first in Europe and then in North America. Nonetheless, they offer generic principles which are applicable globally. The most influential naval writer, the American Alfred Thayer Mahan, whose works both endured and 'travelled well' to many and varied corners of the globe, focused his thesis in *The Influence of Sea Power upon History* primarily on navies at war. Looking particularly at the navies of England, France and Holland in the age of sail, his work did not specifically mention naval diplomacy. However, peppered throughout are examples and comments on the utility of threat and limited force offered by navies. In fact, he did acknowledge the importance of navies in peacetime, observing that the requirement for naval strategy differs from a land-centric military strategy in that it is as necessary in peace as it is in war.[1]

Detailed examination of Mahan's work for reference to naval diplomacy reveals two broad themes. In the 21st-century language of hard and soft power, Mahan could be said to view navies both as instruments of coercive diplomacy and as agents of national reputation or status. For instance, in the early sections of his major work Mahan talks of ancient Rome during the time of the Carthaginian wars, discussing how the Roman Fleet was positioned to 'check' Macedonia, an ally of Hannibal, and was so successful that 'not a soldier of the phalanx ever set foot in Italy'.[2] The principle employed by this threatening naval force was one of prevention and deterrence that would be familiar to many of today's practitioners of sea power.

In a collection of articles published at the turn of the 20th century, Mahan applied his own historical thesis to the events of the day. The Boxer Rebellion against Western imperialism in China, for example, threatened free trade and risked 'the interest of the commercial nations and of maritime powers'.[3] Without resorting to total war force was used extensively and an eight-nation alliance mounted naval policing and stabilization expeditions along the Chinese coast and inland into the major river systems, particularly the Yangtze, to quash the uprising.[4] Of course, one 'positive' aspect of this form of naval diplomacy, alliance and coalition building, which was seen on the coasts and waterways of China did not last. The eight nations involved were pitted against each other in the First World War less than a decade and a half later.

Nonetheless, Mahan did espouse the political benefits of the 'prestige' that a government might gain from having a powerful navy capable of worldwide, expeditionary operations. This, of course, was at a time when navies were the most powerful military forces in the world. He was a favourite of President Theodore Roosevelt, himself a navalist, and undoubtedly influenced the decision to sail the Great White Fleet in 1907.[5] Mahan's 'prestige', or the power of 'attraction' in the more recent words of Joseph Nye, is all about image and perception, not necessarily truth.

For Mahan, if naval 'prestige' was to be perceived to be of political utility to government it needed not only to be widely recognized but also carefully targeted by timely geographical presence. Though outlining his thesis in the context of the colonial powers of 17th-century and 18th-century Europe there is unambiguous read across to other ages, including our own. His point is that national security in peacetime can be aided by a 'decided preponderance at sea'.[6]

Like Mahan, Sir Julian Corbett's focus was predominantly on war, but it is equally possible to identify strands of thought related to naval diplomacy in his works too. He was certainly cognizant of the diplomatic role of naval power: 'the first function of the fleet is to support or disrupt diplomatic effort'.[7] However, Corbett's concept of 'war' was quite broad and he paraphrased Clausewitz in his description of the spectrum of operations on land, drawing parallels to the maritime environment:

> So he [Clausewitz] concludes there may be wars of all degrees of importance and energy from a war of extermination down to the use of an army of observation. So also in the naval sphere there may be a life and death struggle for maritime supremacy or hostilities which never rise beyond a blockade.[8]

There is no doubt that Corbett's theories on both naval and commercial blockade, and on the strategies of fleet-in-being and demonstration can be applied at different points on the spectrum of naval operations, and hence be used as an integral part of a diplomatic mission.

A near contemporary and 'disciple' of Corbett was the British admiral and theorist Sir Herbert Richmond. 'Sea power, in its full expression', he wrote, 'is a form of national strength capable of giving weight to national policy'.[9] Like his antecedents, Richmond's focus on war dominated his work, but his thoughts on the peacetime utility of naval force can be found in the pages of his publications. He attributed the expansion of the British Empire to naval power and saw it as a means to achieve national greatness and, ultimately, peace:

> All the greater naval nations assure the world that a great navy is the surest guarantee of peace; that it gives security against war, and is therefore a highly beneficial institution.[10]

Unlike Mahan and Corbett, Richmond also alerted his readers to other, non-military, naval roles such as humanitarian relief, non-combatant evacuation and peace enforcement, albeit under different terms.[11] Each of these fit well into the broad continuum of naval diplomacy. What is clear is that he thought, and wrote, and taught about the relationship between force and diplomacy and the ways that navies could be used as 'instruments of statecraft'.

It is evident that the writers of the classic naval texts understood the utility of naval forces in non-war situations, even if they did not always shine the torch of their attention on it. Terminology may have changed, but 'flying the flag' and 'prestige', 'gunboat diplomacy' and 'demonstration' equate to soft and hard power, defence and coercive diplomacy, respectively. However, writing at the end of the 19th century and beginning of the 20th century neither Mahan nor Corbett nor Richmond could possibly place their work in the context of a pre-Cold War world. As far as they were concerned they were recording for posterity the enduring principles of maritime strategy. With the benefit of hindsight later historians added a different perspective but the views of these writers have generally stood the test of time. Sir Herbert Richmond may have seen the gathering storm of World War II, but he could not have imagined that its aftermath would be so dominated by a different political rivalry, yet his thoughts are equally applicable now as they were then and as they were when he first captured them.

Multi-polarity in global affairs was often not as anarchic as might at first be assumed; it was generally accompanied by one dominant power. From the 18th century until at least the early 20th that dominant power was Great Britain, and the Royal Navy effectively enjoyed command of the sea. Robert Keohane coined the term 'hegemonic stability theory' to describe the situation in which a wider peace is the result of the diplomacy, coercion and persuasion of the leading power;[12] during the period of Britain's dominance this was commonly referred to as the Pax Britannica.

The role that the naval forces of a hegemonic power could play in maintaining the world order was widely accepted:

> throughout much of the nineteenth century, foreign expectations and fears about British power allowed Britain to get grudging unofficial recognition of the Pax Britannica, the doctrine of the Royal Navy keeping the peace of the sea for all to benefit.[13]

Some writers have labelled the British use of sea power during the Pax Britannica as 'altruistic',[14] but this rather misses the point. Britain maintained her leading position in the world through economic strength supported by military, and predominantly naval, might. The use of British sea power during the period was very much directed in the national interest and thus as an instrument of state power; it was all the more effective for rarely having to resort to force. It communicated strength.

Detailed analysis of the instances of naval diplomacy in the two world wars of the 20th century is beyond the scope of this book, but it is worth mentioning one case which has become a classic of its type. The *Altmark* incident took place in early 1940 when British naval forces under Captain Vian in HMS *Cossack* intercepted a German auxiliary, the *Altmark*, transporting British prisoners of war through Norwegian territorial waters. The case is interesting because of the complexities of the tripartite situation. Britain and Germany were at war, but at the time Norway remained neutral. Britain did not want to antagonize a neutral state, especially one of such strategic importance, but had limited time to liberate the prisoners if they were not to be lost for the remainder of the war. Germany likewise professed to observe Norwegian neutrality yet were in breach of it by transporting prisoners of war through its territorial waters. The eventual outcome, after protests from Norway and the presence of Norwegian warships, was that *Cossack* used limited force against *Altmark* and the prisoners were recovered. The norms of naval diplomacy were well expressed in the orders to Vian from the First Lord of the Admiralty, Winston Churchill: 'Suggest to Norwegian destroyer that honour is served by submitting to superior force'.[15]

Churchill's words, quoted in James Cable's seminal work *Gunboat Diplomacy*, are significant. The act of naval diplomacy was not the limited force used between the British and German protagonists but the leverage exerted on the Norwegians to ensure non-interference, and it was the result of a clear power relationship. Churchill, it could be surmised, would have been very comfortable with Cable's assertion that 'gunboat diplomacy is traditionally a weapon employed by the strong against the weak'.[16]

Connecting the ideas of pre-Cold War naval theorists, it is possible to build a generic 'classical' model of naval diplomacy. Grouping the whole under Mahan's banner of 'navies in peacetime' offers a convenient starting point, though 'peace-time' should probably be defined by what it is not (traditional war fighting) rather than what it is (the range of actions up to and including the use of 'limited' force). The use of the term 'navies in peacetime' would be almost certainly be recogniz-able and acceptable to Mahan, Corbett, Richmond and others as a simple alterna-tive to either 'limited war' or 'statecraft'. Beneath this banner can be found three major constituents of classical naval diplomacy.

Mahan's 'check' can be directly equated with Corbett's 'demonstration' and Richmond's 'guarantor of peace'. Each of these terms or phrases suggests a situ-ation in which a naval force, whether concentrated together to achieve a par-ticular result or dispersed more widely to provide latent effect, supports grand strategy by preventing total war. Similarly the military strategic benefits brought by a 'fleet-in-being', that existential force which limits an adversary's freedom of action and decision-making, can be considered in the same way. Taken together the first constituent part of classical naval diplomacy is deterrence; one reason why a government might choose to maintain a navy is to deter aggression.

Mahan talked of 'prestige' and 'flying the flag' while Richmond promoted the importance of navies in displaying 'national greatness'. At the time that the clas-sical writers shaped their theories, warships were the most complex pieces of machinery on earth and truly effective navies were a tool only available to those who could afford the expense. Like the ventures into space or the nuclear weap-ons 'club' to follow, active participants in a naval 'race' were signalling their

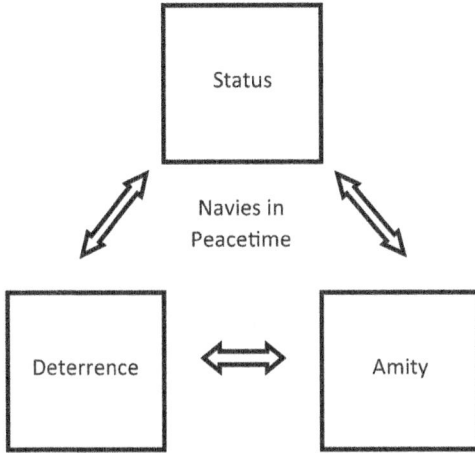

Figure 2.1 Interdependent classical naval diplomacy

economic strength and national prowess for the world to see. The second reason for a government to invest in a powerful navy, therefore, was to claim status or rank amongst competitor states.

Support to allies, the building of relationships, coalitions, partnerships and the spread of goodwill are also significant factors in the established employment of navies in peacetime. Mahan wrote at length about 'co-operation', emphasizing state-to-state benefits. Less well known but equally valid are the non-military roles described by Richmond which turn navies into agents of intervention able influence perception and thereby affect a government's wider national interests. The third constituent of naval diplomacy is the naval force's ability to deliver harmony and friendship amongst states; this can be termed 'amity'.

The three pillars of deterrence, status and amity, need not be mutually exclusive. In fact they can be seen operating almost as a virtuous circle. By building alliances, aggression can be deterred. By being perceived as strong in battle, friendships, whether real or of convenience, can be won. By balancing popularity and fear a certain status can be achieved. By occupying high rank in the pecking order of states, the more aggression is deterred and the more partnerships are attracted. It might be more appropriate, therefore, to acknowledge this interdependency and display the classical model differently. However it is displayed, the pre-Cold War naval thinkers willingly admitted that there is a place for naval power in international relations when not at war.

Into the Cold War

When the multipolar system gave way to the bipolar, two superpower world of the Cold War, the political climate placed more stringent limits on the use of force between the major blocs as the strategic focus turned to nuclear deterrence. However, Sir James Cable bucked the trend and turned his attention onto a little-studied aspect of naval strategy. Cable was instrumental in moving the understanding of naval diplomacy forward but, essentially, he was a Cold War writer. Although the period of his analysis, reported over three editions of his major book, ran from the end of the First World War to the early 1990s, it was inevitably viewed through a prism of binary state-to-state relations. Coercive by definition, his gunboat diplomacy was always 'done' by one side to another. It is telling that Cable chronicled each of the incidents through the seven decades of his study in terms of an 'assailant' and a 'victim'. Yet, as the *Altmark* case demonstrates, the reality can be far more complex. Binary it was not.

However, it must be borne in mind that the scrutiny given to naval diplomacy during the Cold War was set in the context of a global politico-military atmosphere of strategic deterrence. Emphasis was invariably placed on the coercive element of sea power, not the 'mere flag waving' at the softer end of the spectrum that Cable would go on to dismiss, and the attention tended to be limited to the state actors involved. In the words of Cable, 'gunboat diplomacy is something that governments do to foreigners'.[17]

The robust language used by Cable, who was a professional diplomat, is an enduring characteristic of his work. He believed that coercion was implicit in most aspects of international relations and that if a government was willing to 'reward friends and to punish enemies its wishes will at least receive careful consideration'.[18]

The realist tradition also provided a framework for Cable's explanation of coercion at sea. To him, gunboat diplomacy could be categorized into four modes which he discussed in descending order of effectiveness. *Definitive force* was explained as the act or threat of force which possessed a definitive purpose apparent to both sides. The intent of the employing force must be recognized as being limited and must be considered tolerable, if not exactly palatable, by the recipient. A tolerable result, he explained, would be one which in the eyes of the 'victim' is more desirable than resort to war.[19]

Cable offered the *Altmark* incident as one example of definitive force; for another he discussed the USS *Pueblo* incident of 1968.[20] *Pueblo* was a surveillance vessel operating off the coast of North Korea. She was approached and eventually fired on by North Korean warships and, being unarmed, gave way and was escorted into port. The ship's company was held captive for 11 months before being released. The use of force by North Korea was limited and definitive in that it had a readily identifiable goal of 'humiliating' the United States and putting an end to 'spying' on its coasts. Against the backdrop of the war in Vietnam, the assailant's calculation that the outcome was preferable to further escalation and therefore tolerable in the eyes of the United States was proved correct.[21] The *Pueblo* incident will be returned to in Chapter 8.

Purposeful force, according to Cable, is less direct and less reliable than *definitive*.[22] He explained it as limited naval force applied to change the policy or character of a foreign government. In itself the force does not *do* anything, it acts to induce the recipient to take a decision that would not otherwise have been taken.[23] One example he used for purposeful force was that of the actions of the superpowers in the Mediterranean during the Arab-Israeli October War of 1973. Israel was a 'client' state of the United States while Egypt and Syria looked to the Soviet Union for support. Following a Soviet threat to intervene on the Arab side, the US Sixth Fleet was reinforced and concentrated to the south of Crete on high alert. The Soviets responded with a series of provocative anti-carrier exercises which included the training of weapons on the American ships but, ultimately, they did not resort to combative intervention and the war ended.[24]

Catalytic force was described by Cable as when limited naval power 'lends a hand' to act as a catalyst in a situation the direction of which has yet to be determined.[25] Cable is rather ambiguous about the use of catalytic force and labels few of the incidents in his chronological appendix as such. In essence, he explained it as an act undertaken when there is an underlying feeling that 'something is going to happen'.[26] Less effective than either *definitive* or *purposeful* force, it is more likely to result in failure. The bombardment of targets in Beirut by USS *New Jersey* in 1983 when peacekeeping forces were under threat ashore is cited as an example,[27] though this, and other cases, could be just as easily be placed in one or other of Cable's categories.

The final mode of Cable's gunboat diplomacy, where warships are employed to emphasize attitudes or to make a point, is *expressive force* which Cable dismissed as 'the last and least of the uses of limited naval force' with vague and uncertain results.[28] Cable explained how the *purposeful* can descend into the *expressive*, such as in the Beira patrol of the 1960s when the British attempted to prevent the import of oil to Rhodesia,[29] or it can be discrete and stand-alone.

The first edition of *Gunboat Diplomacy* was published in 1971 and was met with positive praise which was still alive 35 years later. One writer offered the opinion that Cable's work 'sharpened to a point the theory and experience of "effectiveness short of war" and reminded navies of what they had been *doing* rather than what they had been *training for*'.[30]

Cable's work on naval diplomacy is certainly seminal and the extent to which it influenced others in the study of the diplomacy at sea is perhaps best summed up in the words written in his obituary in the *Daily Telegraph* in 2001: 'Post-Cold War naval thinking, especially in Britain and America, is replete with implicit and explicit references to Cable's ideas about the political influence of naval force'.[31] Indeed, a review of the current doctrinal publications of maritime powers shows this claim to be accurate.[32] The American maritime vision paper, *A Co-operative Strategy for 21st Century Seapower*, does not contain a direct reference to Cable but it does discuss the concepts of deterrence at sea and forward presence with which he would have been very familiar. When the US Center for Naval Analyses (CNA) published a historiography of 'capstone' documents and books which shaped the development of strategic thought, it expressly listed Cable's work as important in both the development of naval missions and as an influence on policy in the 1970s.[33]

Cable's influence can also be traced in academia, from the Cold War period when his ideas were first published through to the present day. He is referenced in Edward Luttwak's *The Political Uses of Sea Power* written in 1974,[34] in the 1995 book *Navies and Global Defence*,[35] and he can be found in the more recent (2010) generalist textbook *Strategy in the Contemporary World*,[36] amongst many other acknowledgements. That Cable's work can be traced through such wide and varied publications with direct influence on naval tactics, operations and strategy is of signal importance. His ideas manifestly set the standard, and though it carries some shortcomings it regularly provides the starting point for consideration of naval diplomacy. Later theorists may not have adopted all of Cable's concepts, in particular his classification of the various 'modes', but they have generally been consistent with his approach to gunboat diplomacy as an action taken by one state actor against another.

By his own admission, Cable's model of naval diplomacy is hierarchical. The categories of political influence which he identified (Definitive, Purposeful, Catalytic and Expressive) are discussed in a descending order of efficacy, from the 'fait accompli' of *definitive* force[37] to the 'last and least' of *expressive*.[38] Displaying this hierarchy diagrammatically would result in a simple tiering based on effectiveness. Cable, however, does acknowledge that an action or incident of naval or gunboat diplomacy may fall into two or more categories,[39] and that changing circumstances may mean that an action initially designed to fit one category could migrate to another. This could open an accusation of weakness in Cable's theoretical approach; however, it could also reflect reality and the versatility (planned or otherwise) of naval forces as instruments of statecraft. The tiers in the diagram are therefore not discrete but show the possibility of movement up and down through the various modes.

Finally, while Cable's model would not span the full continuum of international relations and is situated very much at the coercive, *harder* end of the spectrum of behaviour, dismissing as it does the more benign applications of naval influence in preventive diplomacy, such as friendly port visits, the categories can be positioned relative to each other on an axis from 'soft' to 'hard' power. From this it may be deduced that, in modern parlance, Cable's model suggests that the application of hard naval power is more effective than soft.

If it is accepted that naval diplomacy is a subset of general diplomacy and that diplomacy is a means of communication between international actors, then Cable's criteria for assessing the efficacy of action fits neatly into Schelling's and George's conceptual theories on coercive strategies discussed in Chapter 1. Accordingly, Cable's model bases its judgement of success against the original objective of the instigating party.[40] As a rational actor the 'assailant' chooses to influence behaviour using naval force and the 'victim' responds in either the predicted manner or, if the calculation is wrong, does not. Cable's views on the greater effectiveness of actions with clearly defined objectives are therefore a logical progression of his argument. Vague or even long-term incrementally approached objectives are, almost by definition, more difficult to measure and therefore more likely to be viewed as failures, or at least not clear successes. As a result of this perspective, the measurement of success or failure of an action on third parties, allies, the international community

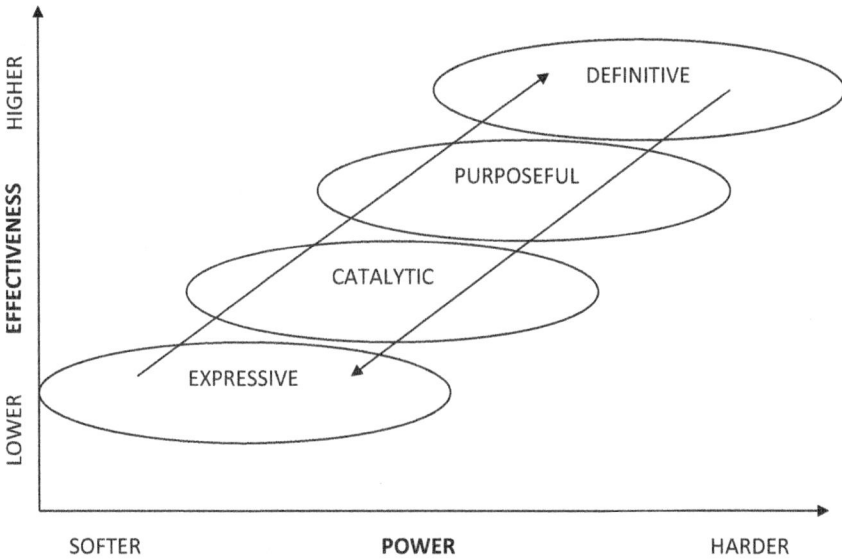

Figure 2.2 Cable's four mode model

or domestic audiences does not feature in Cable's work. As has been argued earlier, his approach is binary.

To illustrate the point it is worth considering one of Cable's own examples. Though of course conceding that the end result was 'war and defeat', *Gunboat Diplomacy*'s chronological appendix judges the original Argentinian seizure of the Falkland Islands in 1982 as a success of limited naval force.[41] The action is deemed *definitive*, Argentina is judged the 'assailant' and Britain is categorized as the 'victim'. Considered against an original objective assumed to be sovereignty of the islands held in Argentinian rather than British hands, the immediate result was clearly successful. However, this in itself then poses the question of timescale on measures of effectiveness: is the result to be judged without delay, or after a month, a year, or following a 'permanent' change of situation? What is permanent in international relations?

Cable is a useful starting point for the study of naval diplomacy in the Cold War, but even then he insufficiently captured the complexities and possibilities of coercive naval force; that he largely ignored the application of naval 'soft power' also limits the appeal of his model for planners and practitioners in the 21st century.

East versus West

In the years following publication of the first edition of *Gunboat Diplomacy* scholars from East and West responded with works of their own on the topic. The most influential writings were those of Turner, Luttwak, Booth and Gorshkov, which together shape what might be called the 'Cold War' model of naval diplomacy.

In an influential article in 1974, Vice Admiral Stansfield Turner USN explained what he saw as the US Navy's four missions – strategic deterrence, sea control, projection of power ashore and naval presence – which he claimed were the products of an evolutionary process.[42] Though a reader might question Turner's historical analysis (he asserted that 'the first and only mission of the earliest navies was Sea Control', and that 'warning and coercion . . . [and] demonstrations of goodwill effectively began in the nineteenth century'[43]), the codification of naval presence as a core role was a seminal moment in the development of theory. However, that role was akin to 'gunboat diplomacy',[44] and consisted of either deterrent or coercive elements, which could be accomplished by either *preventive* (a show of strength in peacetime) or *reactive* (responding to a crisis) deployments. The targets were to be the Soviet Union or its allies or unaligned third states.[45] The potential for naval forces to contribute to alliance or capacity building, assistance or co-operation was not mentioned by Turner.

Many commentators cite Turner's 1974 article when considering the development of naval diplomacy,[46] but few discuss the real genesis of his ideas. In 1970, on assuming the appointment of US Chief of Naval Operations Admiral Elmo Zumwalt initiated *Project 60*, a plan of action for his tenure which aimed to put the US Navy at the highest feasible combat readiness in the face of the Soviet threat.[47] It was in *Project 60* (admittedly drafted by Turner) that the naval mission of 'overseas presence in peacetime' was first revealed and its rationale was directly linked to the 'emergence of a strong, worldwide deployed Soviet Navy'.[48]

> Today the Soviet naval presence in the Mediterranean is as great as ours; 10 years ago it was negligible. We devote fewer than 800 ship days a year to limited parts of the Indian Ocean; the Soviets' reach over that area has gone from zero ship days to 2400 in the past 3 years.[49]

And:

> All of a nation's maritime capabilities bear on its influence around the world and its ability to establish a peacetime presence at a point of choice. We need not look hard to see how the Soviets have translated their naval presence into diplomatic leverage. Their strength in the Arab world today is not entirely attributable to the build up of their Mediterranean fleet, but it was surely an important factor. The Soviets have, in a sense, successfully turned NATO's southern flank.[50]

Crucially, however, the espousal of naval presence was not simply as a counter to a perceived threat. *Project 60* was also set against the realities of 1970s financial constraints, an unpopular war in Vietnam and a desire for allies to shoulder more of the burden. For the latter the paper pointed out that 'the commitment of even our closest friends will depend on their assessment of our naval power, compared with the Soviets'.[51] American naval diplomacy of the 1970s, then, was to varying degrees a reaction to an adversary, a means to encourage allies and an attempt to keep budgets under control. We may draw many similarities to today.

Stansfield Turner provided a diagram to show how the four 'interdependent naval missions' were configured (see Figure 2.3). Strategic deterrence was clearly the bedrock of his vision and as would be expected of the dominant theory of the time was based on the concept of nuclear deterrence and, in particular, on the ability to maintain an 'assured second strike' capability.[52] This deterrence evidently had a strong communicative base and could itself be placed under the naval diplomatic umbrella as defined earlier. However, it is the naval presence mission, which Turner defined as 'the use of naval forces short of war to achieve political objectives',[53] which demands the greatest analysis.

Turner framed his approach to naval presence on three levels. First, he offered the opinion that its use would be to achieve one of two broad 'objectives': it could 'deter actions inimical to the interests of the United States or its allies' or it could 'encourage actions that are in the interests of the United States or its allies'.[54] The latter objective could equally be termed coercion or compellence.

Second, Turner explained the 'tactics' by which these objectives might be accomplished. 'Preventive deployments' were those peacetime global dispositions which would be relevant to, and presumably targeted at, the areas in which 'problems might arise'. They should not involve forces which were 'markedly inferior to some other naval force in the neighborhood', and they should be able to

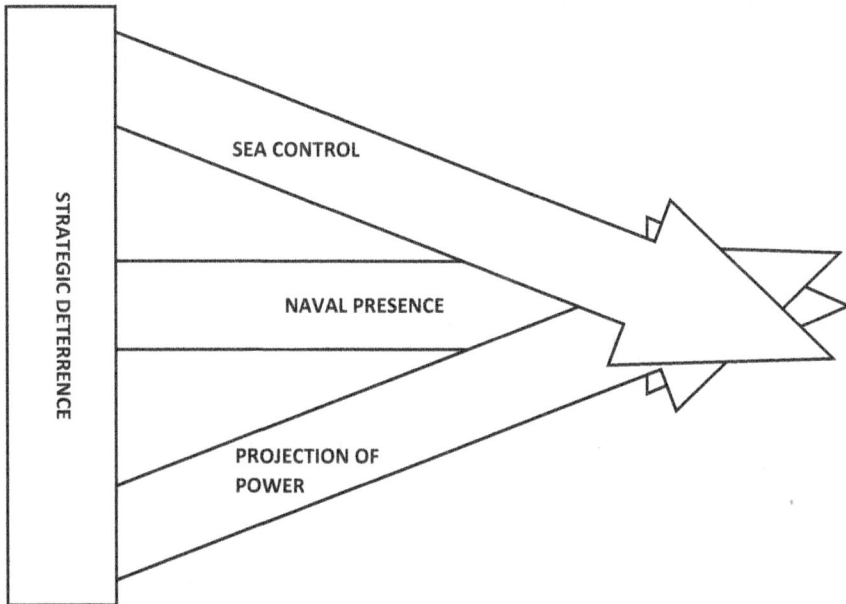

Figure 2.3 Turner's independent naval missions[55]

be reinforced if necessary.[56] Turner did not explicitly provide examples of where preventive deployments might be targeted but, given his work's origins in *Project 60*, it could be deduced that the Mediterranean and Indian Ocean would be priority regions. 'Reactive deployments' were described by Turner as those made in response to a crisis and which would need to possess 'an immediately credible threat and be prepared to have its bluff called'.[57] Preventive and reactive deployment can be directly aligned with Luttwak's latent and active suasion discussed below. Of note, they do not specifically include deployments designed to build amity or friendship amongst states.

Third, Turner outlined five basic 'actions' by and through which a naval presence force could achieve its aim: amphibious assault, air attack, bombardment, blockade and exposure through reconnaissance.[58] This *objective-tactic-action* approach can be criticized for not including the fleet-in-being concept, protection of trade, humanitarian assistance and disaster relief and for not acknowledging the potential of submarines.[59] However, it did break new ground by providing the first framework to describe what naval diplomacy *might* do, rather than what had *been* done in the past (that is, through historical analysis).

Turner's naval presence mission may be represented diagrammatically in the format below:

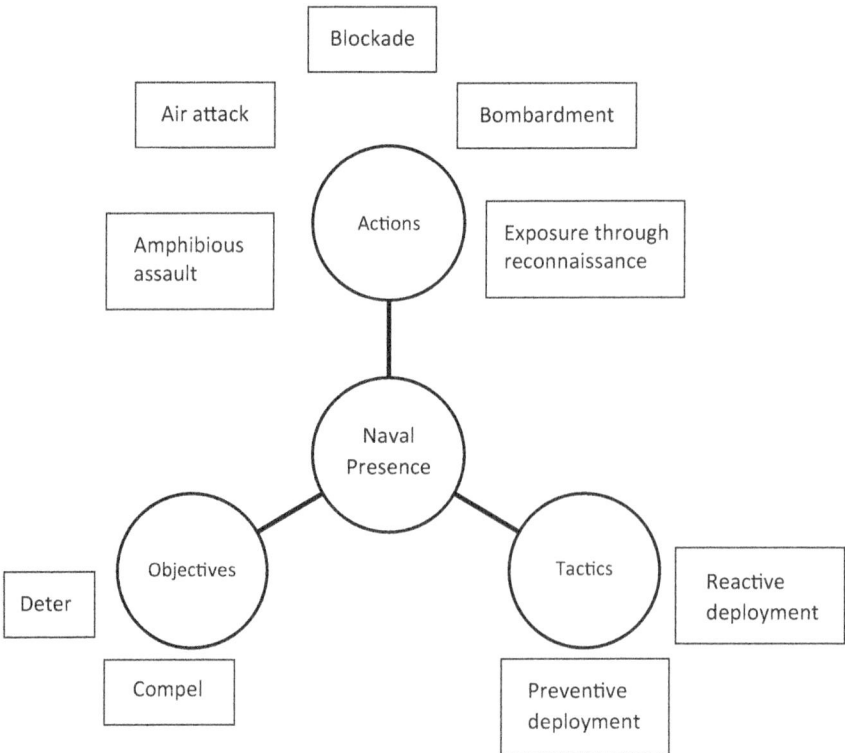

Figure 2.4 Turner's naval presence mission

Edward Luttwak, an American military strategist, published *The Political Uses of Sea Power* in 1974. The book, though short, ranges widely and debates the use of armed forces in general before settling on naval power. Rather than be constrained by concepts such as coercion and deterrence, Luttwak coined the term 'suasion' to frame his arguments. Suasion, he wrote, is a 'conveniently neutral term [. . .] whose meaning suggests the indirectness of any political application of naval force'.[60]

However, the 'political application of naval force' need not be 'indirect' as Luttwak states,[61] but his point is accepted; 'naval suasion' is a more subtle phrase than 'gunboat diplomacy', implying a degree of non-forceful influence rather than physical action. In this respect it is perhaps more sophisticated than Turner's hard power description of the naval presence mission.

Acknowledging the imprecision of the term when applied to sea power, Luttwak explained that suasion pertains to 'other's reactions, and not the actions, or intent, of the deploying party', a notable departure from Cable's and Turner's approach. The assumption of rationality in the cognitive decision-making process of all parties, articulated well in Alexander George's works on coercive diplomacy, is also acknowledged: 'Because suasion can only operate through the filters of others' perceptions, the exercise of suasion is inherently unpredictable in its results'.[62]

Under the umbrella of naval suasion Luttwak placed a spectrum of operations from routine deployments to deliberate action. At what might be called the 'softer' end, where he situated routine deployments, navies could deliver local, conventional deterrent or supportive functions. Luttwak labelled this end of the spectrum 'latent suasion' and it correlates well with Cable's *expressive* force; later commentators might also subsume it into wider preventive and 'defence diplomacy'. Deliberate action, the 'active' side of Luttwak's spectrum corresponding to *definitive* or *purposeful* force in Cable's terminology, was further broken down into the positive and negative elements of coercive diplomacy.

Like his contemporaries' Luttwak's work was very much a product of the Cold War, quite obviously influenced by Cable and Schelling (both are acknowledged) but it is less politically impartial than either of the earlier writers. Luttwak discussed differences in perceptions of military strength between the Western and Eastern blocs and US 'self-denigration', he criticized declining American influence in the Middle East, and he identified increasing multi-polarity during 1970s détente.[63] This is a conclusion which seems prescient if somewhat premature when read four decades later.

The reader of *The Political Uses of Sea Power* is assisted in understanding the concept by Luttwak's own diagrammatic representation:

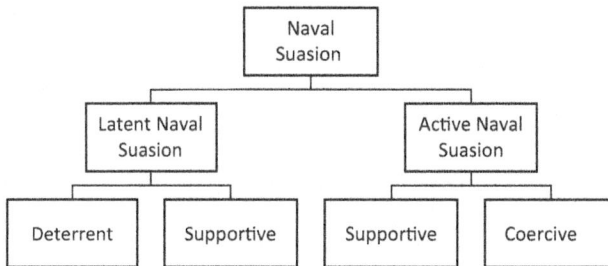

Figure 2.5 Luttwak's typology of naval suasion[64]

As can be seen, Luttwak divided naval suasion into two broad fields, active and latent. The former, he contended, existed when the deliberate exercise of naval suasion was intended to elicit a given reaction from a specified party.[65] This action-reaction relationship between parties, mechanistic but not as prescriptive as Cable's 'assailant' and 'victim' model, has the benefit of acknowledging the existence of wider stakeholders.

The second category, latent suasion, is more interesting, constituting as it does 'the undirected, and hence possibly unintended, reactions and consequences evoked by naval deployments maintained on a routine basis'.[66] It is also a reasonable approximation of the effects desired of Turner's preventive deployment tactic. Viewed even more simplistically, active suasion is the deployment of naval forces with a specific outcome in mind, whereas latent suasion is defined by both the expected and unexpected outcomes gained from routine, day-to-day activity.

Another potential limitation of Luttwak's model is that it discusses the political application of naval force in a qualitative manner and does not adequately capture the quantitative nature of practical sea power. On initial reading the categories and subsets of naval suasion appear to be given equal weighting. Luttwak does address this in a passing reference, stating that latent suasion is 'the most general (in terms of intensity) and geographically the most widespread form of deterrence' but he does not weigh supportive suasion against coercive, nor the basics of latent against active.[67] The Luttwak model, despite his attempts in the final chapter of *The Political Uses of Sea Power* to relate his thoughts to naval tactics, is essentially a theoretical construct, as opposed to a discussion of practical experiences.

Ken Booth's *Navies and Foreign Policy*, published in 1977, drew on Luttwak's ideas, which he acknowledged as 'useful' but went further in the development of the topic.[68]

Booth became the architect of the best-known 20th-century theoretical construct for the use of navies; his trinity of functions found its way into the official doctrine of navies, particularly large navies, worldwide.[69] In its most straightforward form the trinity explains how navies make use of the sea in military, policing and diplomatic roles:

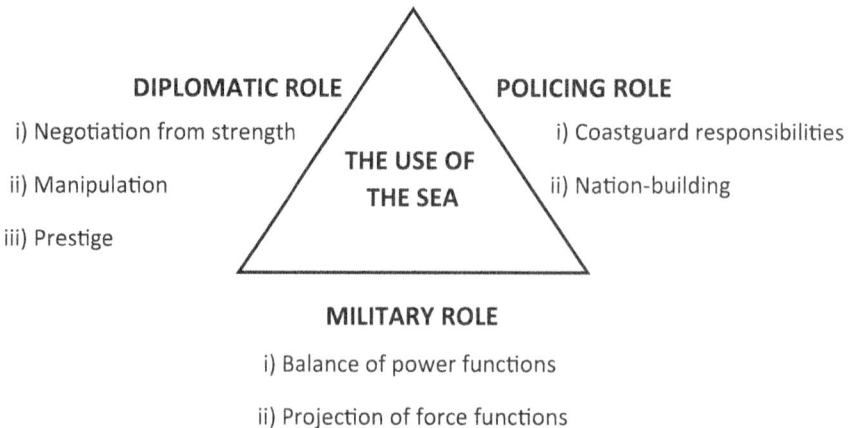

DIPLOMATIC ROLE

i) Negotiation from strength

ii) Manipulation

iii) Prestige

THE USE OF THE SEA

POLICING ROLE

i) Coastguard responsibilities

ii) Nation-building

MILITARY ROLE

i) Balance of power functions

ii) Projection of force functions

Figure 2.6 Booth's functions of navies[70]

The military and policing functions are not discussed at length here, but it is worthy of note that there is a degree of overlap between the categories. Booth's military role, for instance, can be divided into both peacetime and wartime activities including those under the heading of a 'balance of power' function, which Booth considered to be geopolitical or diplomatic tasks. Likewise, his policing role includes a 'nation-building' function which, though Booth chose to restrict 'mainly' to territorial waters, can stretch onto the high seas and be used to further national interest.[71] This aspect of sea power was particularly important to Booth as he claimed that for 'over one-third of the world's navies, coastguard and nation-building responsibilities represent the extent of their functions (and ambitions)'.[72] In essence, Booth was acknowledging a different type of naval power, one which grew bottom-up from the smaller navies, as opposed to the more common top-down perspectives of other writers who concentrated almost entirely on the most powerful navies.

However, concentrating on Booth's diplomatic role it can be seen that the author considered naval diplomacy to have three basic elements. The first, negotiation from strength, was the 'political demonstration of naval force' which required 'presence', including an ability to operate in the air and to project military power ashore, as well as mastering the traditional naval environment, the sea.[73] Booth's negotiation from strength entailed a number of supplementary objectives such as the reassurance of allies, the improvement of bargaining positions and the ability to affect the course of diplomatic negotiations.[74] It fits well with Luttwak's 'supportive' function which spanned both active and latent suasion and can also be considered an element in each of the three categories of the 'classical' model of naval diplomacy discussed earlier.

Manipulation, the second of Booth's diplomatic elements, is an extension of the influence tactics of the first. Booth himself acknowledged the difficulties in making a 'clear distinction between the exercise of naval power and the exercise of naval influence' because of the 'subtlety of the stages through which a warship can be transformed from a platform for a dance-band and cavorting local dignitaries, to a haven of refuge for nationals in distress, to a gun-platform for shore bombardment'.[75] However, this 'subtlety' can be navigated. Whereas Booth's concept of power and negotiation from strength tends towards the 'status' and 'amity' pillars of classical thought, manipulation is more concerned with coercion. It is the demonstration of naval power, the management of bargaining positions within an alliance and the gaining of access to new countries.[76]

The third element of Booth's diplomatic role is prestige. While prestige may initially be considered a concept less prominent in the modern era than it was in the days of imperialism, Booth is convincing of its relevance and devotes a whole chapter of *Navies and Foreign Policy* to its discussion, describing it crudely as 'the sex appeal of politics'.[77] Importantly in the context of naval diplomacy, Booth considered prestige as a factor both on the world stage, in common with the classical model derived from Mahan, Corbett and Richmond, and also domestically, as a means of garnering support from the general public and for 'oiling the wheels of intra-governmental bargaining'.[78] However, the management of self-image can have 'pitfalls' as Booth points out: sex appeal can create 'false expectations', and returning to the pejorative, 'one man's goodwill visit may well be another man's gunboat diplomacy'.[79] Nonetheless, Booth did identify a 'prestige race' taking place during the Cold War and stated that 'prestige may be sufficient justification for expenditure of resources'.[80] Effectively, he claimed that the seeking of prestige could be a rational strategy. Again, one might consider parallels in the 21st century.

Booth's points were not lost on the architect of the Soviet Navy, Admiral Sergei Gorshkov. Gorshkov suggested that Soviet naval growth after 1945 was managed in direct response to American naval advances and not simply designed for the furtherance of Soviet foreign policy.[81] However, he did use his knowledge of Western maritime strategy to introduce a forward presence mission to a fleet which had traditionally concentrated on coastal defensive tactics. He intuitively understood that the Navy could be extremely useful in operations other than war:

> Demonstrative actions by the navy in many cases have made it possible to achieve political ends without resorting to armed struggle. . . . The navy has always been an instrument of the policy of states, an important aid to diplomacy in peacetime.[82]

However, unlike Cable and Turner, Gorshkov's notion of naval diplomacy was not entirely adversary centred. In addition to its coercive potential he saw a role of sea power as being a means of 'holding in check' allies in order to manage or maintain power relationships,[83] a concept clearly reminiscent of Mahan's work. He was particularly intrigued by the UK-US relationship and thought it 'interesting' that the United States achieved its position of relative maritime pre-eminence in the 20th century through close partnership with Britain, a position which Germany had failed to reach through confrontation.[84]

Equally, Gorshkov was interested in amity and robustly promoted an 'ambassadorial' role for the Soviet Navy,[85] particularly for spreading influence in the Third World and amongst existing 'client' states and non-aligned countries. And, mirroring pre-Cold War naval thinkers, he associated maritime strength with national prestige.[86]

What is clear from Gorshkov's work is that it was written primarily for a domestic Russian audience. Indeed, in one critique a writer noted that three major objectives were apparent: Gorshkov was attempting to justify the importance of a navy to great power status, he was enlisting Communist Party support for the Navy and he was explaining his theory to Soviet sailors.[87] However, what is also apparent is that his vision was largely reactive and followed developments in the West. He saw NATO as 'an alliance of maritime states, with powerful naval forces occupying advantageous strategic positions in the World Ocean',[88] and he used strong rhetoric to illustrate the threat he perceived. The true intention of Western sea power in peacetime, he wrote, was 'gun diplomacy'.[89]

Gorshkov used the term 'local wars of imperialism' to describe his interpretations of Western strategy and offered the opinion that naval forces were the most suitable instruments of state military power because of their mobility, persistence, independence and ability to be deployed or withdrawn at will.[90] The attributes are clearly recognizable and though Gorshkov used them in his analysis of NATO strategy they are universal and equally applicable to his own forces. 'Local wars of imperialism' was obviously a politically charged term but the sense was familiar; the meaning can be directly equated to the 'limited wars' or 'limited use of naval power' of Cable's *Gunboat Diplomacy*.

At the end of the 1970s Bradford Dismukes and James McConnell of the US Center for Naval Analyses published a study titled *Soviet Naval Diplomacy*. Though Gorshkov had clearly been influenced by NATO practices, there was predictably little open source material emanating from the East for Western researchers to examine. 'While researchers have produced a number of papers and monographs on various aspects of the Soviet Union's use of its navy in a political role', Dismukes and McConnell stated, 'no comprehensive discussion of Soviet naval diplomacy is available'.[91] They attempted to remedy the situation, plotting trends in 'showing the flag', coercive diplomacy and superpower confrontation. On the whole, they stated, the Soviet naval diplomacy of the period was successful and played a greater relative role in overall strategy than its American equivalent did.[92] Gorshkov had watched, learned and improved upon what he saw.

Combing the thoughts from East and West, a simple construct for a Cold War model can be drawn with three pillars of naval diplomacy (Figure 2.7).

However, this model is too rudimentary to accurately reflect the complexities of the height of the Cold War and should be developed further. If the three categories are assumed to be naval capabilities as opposed to specific naval missions, that is the ability to coerce, to influence and to maintain alliances, and they are assumed to be inter-related, then the model can be displayed differently. In the context of the bipolar competition for dominance at the time, the central outcome of the combined capabilities can be judged to be prestige or status.

Though few governments of the modern age would consciously admit to national greatness being a goal it is irrational to dismiss it outright. Booth's discussion of prestige is convincing because it is based in credible, accepted theory and it deserves a place in the generic Cold War model. With hindsight, a 'prestige race' between East and West in the Cold War is plain to see.[93] An alternative model could then be as shown in Figure 2.8.

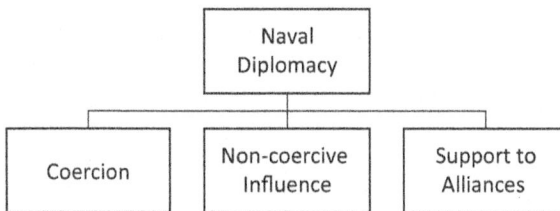

Figure 2.7 Naval diplomacy in the Cold War: an initial model

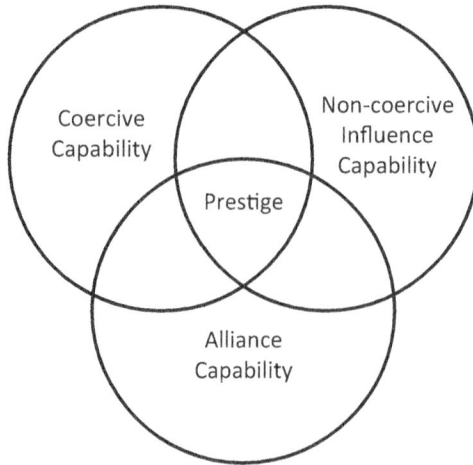

Figure 2.8 Prestige-focused naval diplomacy in the Cold War

Post-modernism in naval diplomacy

The immediate post-Cold War period from 1991 to 2015 was one of transformation and uncertainty in geopolitics. The collapse of the Warsaw Pact and the disso-
lution of the Soviet Union were the main catalysts for change but there were other
key milestones in social, political, economic and cultural spheres. The inexorable
rise of China and India, the financial crisis in Western capitalism, the embracing
of democratic peace theory and then the subsequent backlash of nationalist move-
ments, populism, insurgency and faith-spawned terrorism all played their part, as
did the ever-increasing commercial interactions, linkages and interdependencies
known as globalization.

If Cold War naval diplomacy was understood by practitioners and commentators to be a means to maintain bipolar balance through coercion, reassurance and
image management, then its immediate post-Cold War expression was not quite
so definitive. It was a period of change and for a time in the 1990s one of the
major blocs, the former Soviet Union, all but ceased naval activity on grounds
of affordability while the other sailed the world's oceans unopposed.[94] As the
remaining established navies continued to conduct 'business as usual' their professional leadership and academia debated their place in the new world order. The
immediate post-Cold War quarter century was no longer just about gunboat diplomacy, but also about promoting ties and co-operation between like-minded actors.

The argument for naval diplomacy and forward presence appeared compelling in the age of liberal intervention but it was too often limited by offerings
which focused on the naval forces of the West. Like other aspects of international relations it suffered from the problem of Western or Euro-centricity.[95] In
the early days of the aftermath of the Cold War virtually no attention was given to

the navies of the rising powers, a shortfall that has since begun to be addressed, though not yet fully. The navies and coastguards of small, not yet ascendant powers remain largely ignored.

In 2007 the Indian Navy deployed a squadron of warships to Singapore, Yokosuka, Qingdao, Vladivostok, Manila and Ho Chi Minh City. The deployment was a departure from previous Indian operating norms which, Geoffrey Till stated, bore 'more than a passing resemblance to the famous cruise of Theodore Roosevelt's Great White Fleet before the First World War'. The deployment delivered little in terms of specific exercises but was conducted 'for general purposes of greatness'. Specifically, there was undoubted rivalry between India and China in the region and the deployment was the clear staking of a claim of regional primacy by the Indians.[96]

Whether the Indian deployment was in reality any different to the naval activity of the superpowers during the Cold War and a return to an older *modus operandi* is uncertain. What is evident is that naval diplomacy was alive and well at the turn of the 21st century and not just by the global hegemon. When questioning the contemporary significance of naval diplomacy, many commentators came to the same conclusion: that it can achieve tangible results.[97]

China achieved such a 'tangible result' in 2008 when it dispatched two destroyers and a support ship to the Gulf of Aden for counter-piracy operations. The deployment, though small by Western standards, demonstrated China's ability to operate credibly and self-sustain over a prolonged period which had previously been assumed to be beyond its capability. Those People's Liberation Army (Navy) Naval Expeditionary Task Force deployments to the Middle East have continued.

The period of globalization and rapid geopolitical transformation from a bipolar through unipolar to multipolar world saw a significant change in the number and type of maritime actors. One proponent of naval power noted the change at state level and reported an increase in the number of navies by

> about two-thirds . . . in the past 50 years. The count is somewhat imprecise because many states maintain forces with maritime functions such as policing, customs enforcement, and a broad array of coast guard operations that are not organized as navies.[98]

On their varying utility as instruments of power, he added that offshore presence may no longer be 'visible' but that it was certainly still 'tangible':

> A coastal state might not be able to see ships cruising off its coasts, but it will 'feel' them. A widely dispersed presence mission by an ocean-going navy can serve as a warning to adversaries, an indication of support to allies, and a demonstration of resolve that cannot be ignored by neutrals.[99]

Non-state actors engaging in communicative action at sea to elicit responses from other parties have already been mentioned. Michele Flournoy and Shawn Brimley drew attention to what they termed 'the contested commons' in a 2009

US Naval Institute *Proceedings* article, highlighting Hezbollah's and al-Qaeda's maritime tactics and stating that 'there is a consensus that rising states and non-state powers, combined with continued globalization, will put great pressure on the international system as a whole'.[100] The 'international system' is made up of vested interests concerned with the maintenance of the status quo. Another *Proceedings* writer, Michael Quigley, turned attention back to those vested interests in the same issue:

> In May 2008 the Navy re-established the U.S. Fourth Fleet which had been dormant for nearly sixty years, thereby raising the profile of naval operations in the Caribbean and Latin America. [. . . This] high profile way to assert U.S. naval authority and underscore the strategic, diplomatic and political importance of Latin America. [. . .] The signal is being sent not only to Venezuela's Hugo Chavez but also to other leaders in the region who are hostile to the US.[101]

The explicit reference to a 'signal being sent' reaffirms the role of naval diplomacy as a means of communication.

According to Geoffrey Till, the 'post-modern' world in which we now live requires post-modern navies, which he defines as those belonging to states moulded for the information economy rather than the industrial and who embrace a cooperative world system of openness and mutual dependence.[102] Till argues that in a world very different to the bipolar system of the Cold War, post-modern navies would by necessity require different strategies and he presents them with four key missions: sea control, expeditionary operations, good order at sea and the maintenance of a maritime consensus. The first two, he claims, are adaptations of traditional roles; the latter two are new.[103]

A logical deduction from Till's reinterpretation of the maritime military environment is that naval diplomacy should receive a similar re-evaluation. Very much in keeping with Western strategic thought in the immediate post-Cold War period, Till's naval diplomacy effectively meant and required forward presence. Presence, he stated, is more than merely a navy in existence or a fleet-in-being, it is a strategy of having vessels forward deployed 'and handy for whatever may turn up in areas of concern'.[104] This fundamental requirement of Till's model may also be its main weakness. If it is to be based on anything more than the pure luck of being in the right place at the right time, presence in the way that he defines it requires quantity and is therefore effectively limited to larger navies able to field a high number of platforms if it is to be exercised on a global or even multi-regional scale.

From presence, with its implications for force composition, readiness and deployment routines, came three 'components' of naval diplomacy. When Till published an early version of his sea power theory in the *Journal of Strategic Studies* in 1994, the components he identified were coercion, alliance or coalition building and international maritime assistance;[105] collectively, they were not dissimilar to the 'Cold War' model. A decade later, however, he had changed his position and the 'international maritime assistance' component had been removed, its place being taken by 'picture building'.[106]

Till's work has made him one of the key figures of early 21st-century naval thought. One writer remarked in 2008 that he was 'prescient with regard to the USN's new pre-occupation with building maritime security networks, leaving one to ponder the influence of Till's work within the USN hierarchy'.[107] That observation was penned as part of a critique of Admiral Mike Mullen's concept, the '1,000-ship navy'.

Mullen, who went on to become the US chairman of the joint chiefs, was chief of naval operations when he launched the idea of the 1,000-ship navy in a speech at the US Naval War College in 2005. In the speech Mullen told his audience that changes in the world meant that there was a need for 'a new image of sea power' for which he drew a picture of a partnership, not just between navies, but with 'the DEA, or the FBI, or the Customs and Border Control agencies of any number of other nations, not just our own'.[108] Mullen was effectively calling for collaboration among maritime stakeholders to better combat the uncertainties of the age.

The importance of the global war on terrorism in the forging of Mullen's concept is plain to see in an article published just two months after his speech was delivered. Writing in the USNI *Proceedings* journal, John Morgan and Charles Martoglio, two USN flag officers and Mullen acolytes, reminded readers of the challenges faced after the al-Qaeda attacks of 11 September 2001 and called for a 'combination of national, international and private-industry cooperation' at sea.[109] The article was not coincidental. It applauded Mullen's speech and clearly aimed to take the debate to the next level. In it can be found the roots of a 'Mullen model' for naval diplomacy and the authors identify two objectives within the 'overarching goal of the 1000-ship navy': they are 'increasing maritime domain awareness' and 'posturing assets to respond to crises or emergencies'.[110] The first, which they describe as gaining the 'knowledge of anything at sea that affects a nation's security, safety, economics or its environment', can be equated with Till's 'picture building'.[111] The second, posturing, may just as accurately be termed forward naval presence.

The Mullen model may use familiar concepts but it places them in an unfamiliar configuration. Where Till places 'presence' at the pinnacle of his hierarchy of naval diplomacy with coalition building as a supporting pillar, Morgan and Martoglio (for Mullen) reverse the arrangement. The model also places greatest emphasis on the softer end of the power spectrum in an attempt to attract support from less 'aggressive' stakeholders and ignores the harder effects of coercion and war fighting. Paradoxically, this was opposite to the position of the US Navy 30 years earlier as articulated by Stansfield Turner.

The concepts of hard, soft and smart power devised by Joseph Nye after the Cold War have been subject to continued debate. Some commentators have equated 'soft' with non-military power and 'hard' with military alone, making the two effectively mutually exclusive. However, the original meaning of soft power has 'been distorted, misused and – in extreme cases – abused'.[112] Clearly this was not Joseph Nye's intention, and since the initial publication of his ideas in 2004

H										S
A	→								←	O
R	Command	Coerce	Threat	Pay	Sanction	Frame	Persuade	Attract	Co-opt	F
D										T

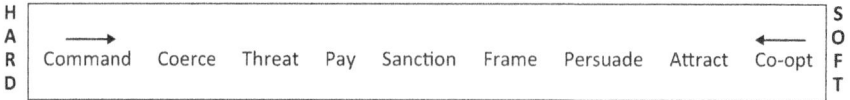

Figure 2.9 Nye's spectrum of power behaviours

he has unambiguously stated that not only can military resources contribute to soft power they are most effective when used under a smart power construct.[113]

Nye portrayed power as the ability to realize 'behavioural outcomes' in others and identified three means by which any desired end could be reached: it could be through coercion, reward or attraction.[114] From these three basic modes he derived a spectrum of behaviours which stretched from the 'tangibles' of hard power, such as money and force, to the 'intangibles' of ideas, values and culture which constitute soft power.[115]

By examining Nye's spectrum the contribution of militaries can begin to be understood. They are obviously vital at the hard end where their war-fighting capabilities are brought to bear, but they offer more. Nye explained that even under an objectionable dictatorship military prowess and 'myths of invincibility' might 'attract others to join the bandwagon'.[116] In other words, hard power can be attractive. Of note, Nye used a naval example to make his point that a single element of power need not be limited in application to a single point on the spectrum:

> Naval forces can be used to win battles (hard power) or win hearts and minds (soft power) depending on what the target and what the issues are.[117]

Nye's ideas have certainly resonated within the defence and security community and the role of the military in soft and smart power has received significant attention since the concepts were published, among both politicians and practitioners.

Nye identified four 'modalities' of military power in *The Future of Power* but only one, fighting, fits into the realm of pure hard power. The other three, coercive diplomacy, the protection afforded by alliances, and the assistance offered by aid and training tend towards the 'soft'.[118] Again, to illustrate his point, Nye used naval examples. He described the deployment of ships as a 'classic example of coercive diplomacy', he highlighted the dispatch of a US warship to the Baltic during a major Russian exercise in 2009 as a case of support and assistance to a nervous ally (Latvia), and he applauded the publication of the US *Co-operative Strategy for Twenty-First Century Sea Power* for its forthright message of international partnering and mutual trust.[119] In short, the smart power concept which Nye produced calls for substantial military and naval involvement.

More recently Christian Le Mière took another step towards updating the concept of naval diplomacy with his book *Maritime Diplomacy in the 21st Century*. In it he acknowledged the rather limited 'gunboat' or coercive methods beloved by previous writers and then introduced two additional classifications of his subject: *cooperative* and *persuasive* maritime diplomacy.[120] The first, as the name suggests, requires willing participants on all sides and covers such missions and tasks as joint exercises and operations, goodwill visits and even humanitarian assistance and disaster relief. The second, *persuasive*, is something rather more nebulous, covering presence and prestige but falling short of out-and-out threatening behaviour. Together coercion, co-operation and persuasion make the whole, and the whole, Le Mière says, is the use of maritime assets in the management of international relations.[121]

Maritime Diplomacy is an important contribution to the debate on sea power in operations other than war, but it too relies on the assumption of state-centrism and two party 'action-reaction' relationships that held back previous theories. Indeed, Le Mière leans heavily on game theory to illustrate his points, where player A and player B do things to achieve the best outcome for themselves. The reality, as the author tries to point out, is much more complex with a potential stakeholder mix of military, paramilitary, commercial and NGO actors on the stage.[122]

Le Mière aids the reader by showing certain 'properties' as pentagons in a series of diagrams referring to specific incidents in his analysis. The efficacy of the properties can be plotted against a subjective scale. Figure 2.10 shows a non-specific example of an event assessed as highly pre-emptive, broadly symmetrical, non-kinetic, and possibly vague but sustainable.

The 'properties' diagram could be a valuable tool for post-event analysis. There are clearly subjective assessments to be made about Le Mière's choice of property (he does not include context, legitimacy or cost, for example) but the diagram

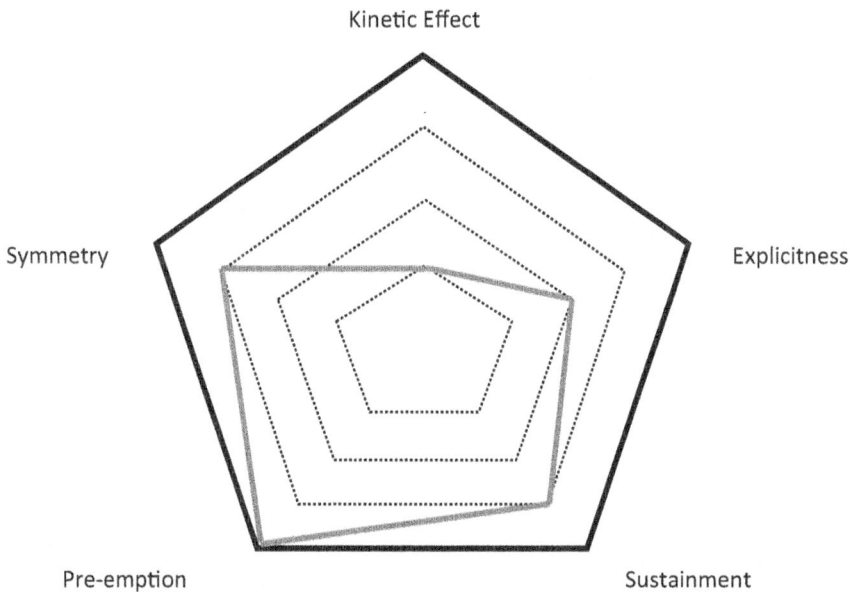

Figure 2.10 Le Mière's properties of maritime diplomacy visualised[123]

could be adapted for the particular requirements of the analyst or circumstances of the case and it would be particularly useful for comparative studies. However, the principal shortcoming of the tool is its inability to display degrees of success or failure – highly kinetic, explicit, sustainable, pre-emptive, and symmetrical applications of maritime diplomacy are arguably no more likely to succeed in their instigator's aim than those which display the opposite qualities. It is therefore of less use for planning or prediction of outcome.

When comparing the 'post-modern' naval literature a question is raised of whether the Till model really applies to those states still reliant on industrial economies and not yet fully embracing of globalization or whether Le Mière's model would provide a better fit. The logical assumption would be that the post-Cold War world is undergoing a period of transition and that 'modern' (as opposed to 'post-modern') navies should adhere to the older Cold War model as the best approximation of their circumstance. The result could be a hybrid maritime military environment in which modern and post-modern navies co-exist and in which they operate in both paradigms simultaneously. The alternative would be to adopt on a global scale Mullen's concept of the '1,000-ship navy', the global maritime partnership, and thereby gain presence of numbers not as a single force but as a networked partnership of like-minded states and non-state actors. Till and Mullen, therefore, might offer mutually supportive world views.

The conclusion from this discussion is that a post-Cold War model of naval diplomacy can be determined by applying the post-modern interests of building maritime situational awareness, building coalitions and alliances and engendering attraction to the sliding scale of Nye's smart power concept. It is shown graphically in Figure 2.11.

Comparative analysis of the various 'models' of naval diplomacy helps to identify a number of enduring themes which can be divided into two categories: *construct*, that is how the model is framed within the context of international relations; and *content*, or the outcomes and effects desired by the proponent's strategy. With the exception of those provided directly by Luttwak, Booth, Nye and Le Mière,[124] it must be pointed out that the models of naval diplomacy described in this chapter are not the pure product of the writers or era to which they are

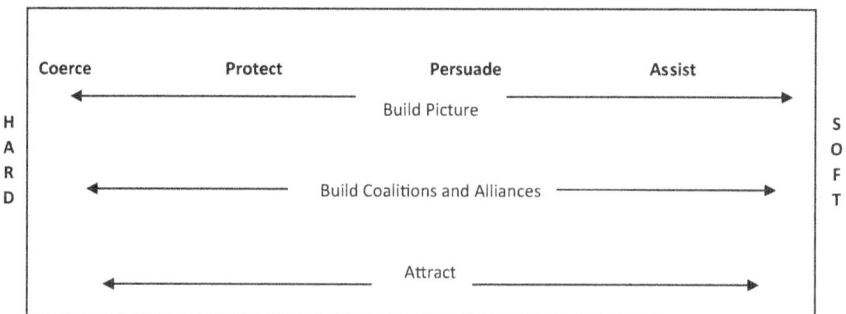

Figure 2.11 Post-modern model of naval diplomacy

accredited. Any discussion of construct, therefore, is a secondary argument. However, if that point is accepted then it can be seen that each of the models is based on four underpinning principles.

First, each is based in the *realist* theoretical tradition of international relations and is focused on power relationships. Second, each model is essentially *state centric*. Third, each model is based on a mechanistic methodology in which one 'side' does something and the 'other side' reacts. Fourth, and following on from the previous three principles, the realist, state-centric, binary models of naval diplomacy are all outcome based and thus demand that decisions be made.

These four principles form the bedrock of the existing models of naval diplomacy, but they are not discrete. Shown diagrammatically they would not constitute four equally sized pillars on which outcome-based naval diplomacy sits. Rather, they are best viewed as inter-related and hierarchical and, perhaps, as akin to a Russian nesting doll. Existing models of naval diplomacy have:

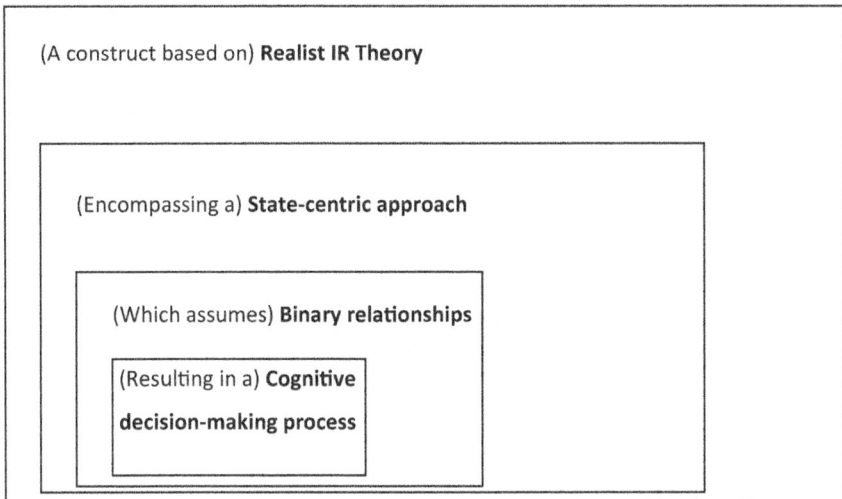

(A construct based on) **Realist IR Theory**

(Encompassing a) **State-centric approach**

(Which assumes) **Binary relationships**

(Resulting in a) **Cognitive decision-making process**

Figure 2.12 The basic principles underpinning existing models of naval diplomacy

If a common *construct* of naval diplomacy can be determined, then so too can a shared set of *content*, which shifts in emphasis from era to era. Though the words and terminology used differ from writer to writer, a careful interpretation of their works can find threads of similar meaning throughout the body of naval and strategic thought over the past century and a half. As might be expected, the development of ideas has been iterative and evolutionary.

Through the use of the models eight major traits of naval diplomacy can be identified: coercion, deterrence, picture building, prestige, co-operation, reassurance, attraction and assistance. Taking the writers and models in broadly chronological order, it can be demonstrated that the traits most indicative of hard power, such as coercion and deterrence, are commonly cited, whereas it is the later writers who place the greatest emphasis on the soft power effects of assistance and attraction. The following chapters will explore this mix in an attempt to determine if reality reflects theory.

Notes

1   Mahan, Alfred, T. Influence of Sea Power *Upon History*. (Mineola, NY: Dover, 1987), p. 22. First published Boston: Little, Brown and Co., 1890.
2   Ibid., p. 16.
3   Mahan, Alfred T. *Retrospect and Prospect: Studies in International Relations Naval and Political*. (Boston: Little, Brown and Co., 1903), pp. 32–33.
4   The eight-nation alliance comprised Great Britain, Russia, the United States, France, Germany, Austria-Hungary, Italy and Japan. See Dugdale-Pointon, T.D.P. 'The Boxer Rebellion, 1900.' 19 September 2004. www.historyofwar.org/articles/wars_boxer. html (accessed 3 February 2011).
5   For an account of the Great White Fleet and Mahan's influence see, for example, Wimmel, Kenneth. *Theodore Roosevelt and the Great White Fleet: American Sea Power Come of Age*. (Washington, DC: Brassey's, 1998); Hendrix, Henry, J. *Theodore Roosevelt's Naval Diplomacy: The US Navy and the Birth of the American Century*. (Annapolis: Naval Institute Press, 2009).
6   Mahan, *Influence of Sea Power*, p. 82.
7   Corbett, quoted in Till, Geoffrey. *Seapower: A Guide for the Twenty-First Century, 2nd Ed*. (Abingdon: Routledge, 2009), p. 253.
8   Ibid.
9   Richmond, Sir H. W. *Sea Power in the Modern World*. (London: Bell & Sons, 1934), p. 17.
10   Ibid., p. 189.
11   Ibid., pp. 193–194.
12   Keohane, Robert. *After Hegemony: Co-Operation and Discord in the World Political Economy*. (Princeton: Princeton University Press, 1984), pp. 32–39.
13   Black, Jeremy. *Naval Power: A History of Warfare and the Sea from 1500*. (Basingstoke: Macmillan, 2009), p. 118.
14   Hore, Peter. *The Habit of Victory: The Story of the Royal Navy 1545–1945*. (London: Pan Books, 2006), p. 243.
15   Cable, James. *Gunboat Diplomacy 1919–1991: Political Applications of Limited Naval Force, 3rd Ed*. (Basingstoke: Macmillan, 1994), p. 19. The prisoners were British sailors picked up after their ships had been sunk in the South Atlantic by the German battleship *Graf Spee*. They were being transported to Germany through Norwegian waters.
16   Ibid., p. 25.
17   Ibid., p. 7.
18   Cable, James, *Diplomacy at Sea*. (Basingstoke: Macmillan, 1985), p. 3.
19   Cable, *Gunboat Diplomacy*, pp. 20–21.
20   The USS *Pueblo* incident is discussed at greater length in Chapter 6.
21   Cable, *Gunboat Diplomacy*, pp. 25–29.
22   Ibid., p. 33.
23   Ibid.
24   Ibid., pp. 42–46, 200.
25   Ibid., p. 47.
26   Ibid., p. 46.
27   Ibid., p. 208.
28   Ibid., p. 62.

29 Ibid., p. 63.
30 Hill, Richard. 'Naval Thinking in the Nuclear Age.' In Till, Geoffrey (Ed.). *The Development of British Naval Thinking*. (London: Routledge, 2006), p. 167.
31 *Daily Telegraph*. 'Sir James Cable.' Obituaries, 13 October 2001. www.telegraph. co.uk/news/obituaries/1359279/Sir-James-Cable.html (accessed 11 February 2012).
32 United Kingdom. Development, Concepts and Doctrine Centre. *British Maritime Doctrine, 4th Ed.* JDP 0–10. (Shrivenham: DCDC, 2011); Australia. Royal Australian Navy. *Australian Maritime Doctrine 2010*. (Canberra: Sea Power Centre, 2010), p. 210; Canada. National Defence Headquarters. *Leadmark: The Navy's Strategy for 2020*. (Ottawa: NDHQ, 2001), pp. 36–39.
33 United States. Center for Naval Analyses. Swartz, P. M. & Duggan, K. *U.S. Navy Capstone Strategies & Concepts (1970–2009)*. D0019819.A1. (Arlington, VA: CNA, 2009), pp. 224, 148.
34 Luttwak, Edward. *The Political Uses of Sea Power*. (Baltimore: Johns Hopkins University Press, 1974), pp. 3, 19.
35 Neilson, Keith & Errington, Elizabeth J. (Eds.). *Navies and Global Defence: Theories and Strategy*. (Westport: Praeger, 1995), p. 221.
36 A text box discussing 'gunboat diplomacy' does not reference Cable by name, but does describe familiar themes and advises Geoffrey Till for further reading which, in turn, does reference Cable. See Moran, Daniel. 'Geography and Strategy.' In Baylis, John, Wirtz, James & Gray, Colin (Eds.). *Strategy in the Contemporary World, 3rd Ed.* (Oxford: Oxford University Press, 2010), p. 132.
37 Cable, *Gunboat Diplomacy, 3rd Ed.*, p. 22. This presumption is supported by Robert Mandel's study of 133 incidents of gunboat diplomacy ranging from 1946 to 1978. Mandel's evidence suggests that the most effective gunboat diplomacy involves a definitive, deterrent display of force undertaken by an assailant who has engaged in war in the victim's region and who is militarily prepared and politically stable compared to the victim. See: Mandel, Robert. 'The Effectiveness of Gunboat Diplomacy.' *International Studies Quarterly* 30, No. 1 (1986): p. 59.
38 Cable, *Gunboat Diplomacy, 3rd Ed.*, p. 62.
39 A number of the examples in Cable's chronological appendix are categorized in more than one mode, See, for example, Cable, *Gunboat Diplomacy, 3rd Ed.*, pp. 70, 197.
40 Cable, *Gunboat Diplomacy, 3rd Ed.*, p. 158.
41 Ibid., p. 207.
42 Turner, Stansfield. 'Missions of the U.S. Navy.' *U.S. Naval War College Review* 26, No. 5 (1974): p. 3.
43 Ibid., p. 4.
44 Turner uses the term 'gunboat diplomacy' some three years after publication of Cable's work but does not reference him – or any other writer – in his article.
45 Turner, 'Missions of the U.S. Navy', pp. 14–15.
46 See, for example: Till, *Seapower*, p. 222; Speller, Ian. *Understanding Naval Warfare*. (Abingdon: Routledge, 2014), pp. 81–82; Le Mière, Christian, *Maritime Diplomacy in the 21st Century: Drivers and Challenges*. (Abingdon: Routledge, 2014), p. 21.
47 Zumwalt, Elmo, *Memorandum for All Flag Officers (And Marine General Officers)*. Op-00 Memo 00334–70. (Project 60, 16 September 1970). Reproduced in Hattendorf, John (Ed.). *U.S. Naval Strategy in the 1970s*. Newport Paper 30. (Newport, Rhode Island: Naval War College Press, 2006), pp. 3–30.
48 Ibid., p. 4.
49 Ibid., p. 6.
50 Ibid., p. 14.
51 Ibid., p. 29.
52 Turner, 'Missions of the U.S. Navy', p. 5.
53 Ibid., p. 2.
54 Ibid.

55 Ibid., p. 14.
56 Ibid.
57 Ibid.
58 Ibid.
59 Center for Naval Analyses, *U.S. Navy Capstone Strategies & Concepts (1970–2009)*, p. 27.
60 Luttwak, *The Political Uses of Sea Power*, p. 3.
61 Those instances of naval diplomacy which Cable categorized as 'definitive', for instance, might be considered 'direct.'
62 Luttwak, *The Political Uses of Sea Power*, p. 6.
63 Ibid., pp. 44–47, 63–68.
64 Ibid., p. 7. Table reprinted with permission of Johns Hopkins University Press.
65 Ibid., p. 11.
66 Ibid.
67 Ibid., p. 13.
68 Ken, Booth, *Navies and Foreign Policy*. (London: Croom Helm, 1977), p. 45.
69 Booth's trinity can be traced in British, American, Canadian, Australian and New Zealand naval doctrine, amongst others. For a useful précis of Western doctrinal development see: Australia. Jackson, Aaron P. *Keystone Doctrine Development in Five Commonwealth Countries: A Comparative Perspective*. Papers in Australian Maritime Affairs No. 33. (Canberra: Sea Power Centre, 2010).
70 Booth, Navies and Foreign Policy, p. 16.
71 Booth cites the UK/Icelandic 'Cod Wars' as an example of a small navy (Iceland) using a nation-building technique to press a point on the international stage. Ibid., p. 18.
72 Ibid.
73 Ibid., p. 19.
74 Ibid., pp. 18–19.
75 Ibid., p. 27.
76 Ibid., pp. 19–20.
77 Ibid., p. 50.
78 Booth, *Navies and Foreign Policy*, p. 74.
79 Ibid., pp. 50, 80.
80 Ibid., p. 52.
81 Gorshkov, Sergeï Georgievich. *The Sea Power of the State*. (Annapolis, MD: Naval Institute Press) pp. 178–212.
82 Quoted in Till, *Seapower*, p. 254.
83 Ibid., p. 2.
84 Ibid., p. 249.
85 Ibid., pp. 251–252.
86 Gorshkov, *The Sea Power of the State*, p. 59.
87 Hibbits, John. 'Admiral Gorshkov's Writings: Twenty Years of Naval Thought.' In Murphy, Paul (Ed.). *Naval Power in Soviet Policy*. (Washington, DC: US Air Force, 1978), p. 2.
88 Gorshkov, *The Sea Power of the State*, p. 159.
89 Ibid., p. 6.
90 Ibid., p. 235.
91 Dismukes, Bradford & McConnell, James (Eds.). *Soviet Naval Diplomacy*. (New York: Pergamon Press, 1979), p. xiv.
92 Ibid., p. 3.
93 Booth discusses what he considered the various sources of prestige through the ages, concluding that in the 1970s the military element was of greatest significance. (See Booth, *Navies and Foreign Policy*, pp. 55–56.) Following the end of the Cold War, however, other factors, such as economic strength, may be considered to have overtaken the military when determining relative status between states.

94 Hattendorf, John (Ed.). *U.S. Naval Strategy in the 1990s*. Newport Paper 27. (Newport, Rhode Island: Naval War College Press, 2007), p. 1.
95 Sharp, *Diplomatic Theory*, p. 149.
96 Till, *Seapower, 2nd Ed.*, p. 343.
97 Murfett, Malcolm. 'Gunboat Diplomacy: Outmoded or Back in Vogue?', pp. 85–86. In A. Dorman, M.L.R. Smith & M.Uttley (Eds.). *The Changing Face of Maritime Power*. (London: Macmillan, 1999), pp. 81–93.
98 Barnett, Roger. *Navy Strategic Culture: Why the Navy Thinks Differently*. (Annapolis: Naval Institute Press, 2009), p. 33.
99 Ibid.
100 Flournoy, Michele & Brimley, Shawn. 'The Contested Commons.' *U.S. Naval Institute Proceedings* 137, No. 7 (2009): p. 20.
101 Quigley, Michael J. 'Ships of State.' *USNI Proceedings* 137, No. 7 (2009): p. 57.
102 Till, *Seapower, 2nd Ed.*, p. 1.
103 Ibid., p. 3.
104 Ibid., p. 258.
105 Till, Geoffrey. 'Seapower Theory and Practice.' *Journal of Strategic Studies* 17, No. 1 (1994): p. 180.
106 Till, *Seapower, 2nd Ed.*, p. 257.
107 Australia. Chris Rahman. *The Global Maritime Partnership Initiative: Implications for the Royal Australian Navy*. Papers in Australian Maritime Affairs No. 24. (Canberra: Sea Power Centre, 2008), p. 59. However, Professor Till refutes the claim of 'influence' over the USN hierarchy, stating that the two parties arrived at the same conclusions independently (Till, Geoffrey. Discussion with author, 25 June 2012).
108 Mullen, Mike. 'Speech Delivered to U.S. Naval War College 31 August 2005.' www. navy.mil/navydata/cno/speeches/mullen050831.txt (accessed 25 June 2012).
109 Morgan, John G. & Martoglio, Charles W. 'The 1000 Ship Navy: Global Maritime Network.' *USNI Proceedings* 131, No. 11 (2005): p. 15.
110 Ibid., p. 16.
111 Ibid.
112 Kazuo, Ogoura. 'The Limits of Soft Power.' *Japan Echo* 33, No. 5 (2006): p. 48.
113 Nye, Joseph, S. *The Future of Power*. (New York: PublicAffairs) p. 86. Smart power refers to the strategies which combine hard and soft power. Ibid., p. 10.
114 Ibid.
115 Ibid., p. 21.
116 Ibid., p. 86.
117 Ibid., p. 21.
118 Ibid., pp. 41–42.
119 Ibid., pp. 45–47.
120 Le Mière, *Maritime Diplomacy*, pp. 7–15.
121 Ibid., p. 66.
122 For a more detailed analysis of *Maritime Diplomacy in the 21st Century* see: Rowlands, Kevin. 'Book Review of *Maritime Diplomacy in the 21st Century*.' *RUSI Journal* 159, No. 5 (2014): pp. 98–99.
123 Ibid., p. 61.
124 The model accredited to Nye is a reproduction of his 'spectrum of behaviours' diagram; the original was not specifically about naval diplomacy. See Nye, *The Future of Power*, p. 21.

3 Surveying the historical record

This chapter presents an insight into hundreds of examples of naval diplomacy which took place in the 20-year period from 1991 to 2010. It is not intended to be a comprehensive compendium; such a complete history would be impossible to compile. But it does capture evidence of some 528 incidents, catalogued in the Appendix, in which the use of sea power for political purposes occurred. In many ways it is an extension of the chronological survey that Sir James Cable included in the three editions of his *Gunboat Diplomacy*. Cable constructed his model of naval diplomacy based on an analysis of an average of five incidents per year over seven decades. The analysis here is based on an average of 25 incidents annually over the first two decades after the end of the Cold War. There is no claim that this book is more thorough than Cable's, merely that Cable was more discriminating in his choice of examples and certainly quicker to dismiss non-conforming incidents when shaping his own opinions and arguments. As was made clear in Chapter 2, Cable concentrated on the coercive element of naval diplomacy and largely ignored the day-to-day, year-to-year ambassadorial roles which are vital naval business and are included here.

When considering a large evidence base it is important to understand the criteria used for inclusion. The criteria used in this book are straightforward but inherently subjective. Put simply, examples of incidents which met the definition presented in Chapter 1, that naval diplomacy is a communications process seeking to further the interests of an international actor with maritime capabilities, were included. Those that did not meet the definition were discarded. Further, this book does not include examples of naval action during war, except that which involved neutral or third parties, but it does include the action which may have taken place between belligerents prior to the start or after the end of a major conflict. For example, the coercive coalition posturing before the Gulf War of 1991 and the long period of containment of Iraq from 1991 until 2003 are included, but the use of force by navies during the actual liberation of Kuwait or the toppling of Saddam Hussein is not.

Similarly, examples of multinational acquisition (by which is meant collaborative acquisition by two or more sovereign states) which could potentially reflect a political discourse between the actors involved are generally not included, though this does represent a topic worthy of further research – much can be read into the interdependence of relationships in the global economy. Conversely, examples of 'gifting' of naval assets, such as Australia's award of patrol vessels to Fiji in July 1992 following the normalization of relations after the latter's coup of 1987, are included. These represent clear attempts to build amity between actors rather than to seek immediate commercial profit.

In addition, some examples of significant changes to the global naval picture have been included, such as the launch of the first vessel of the newly formed fleet of an independent Croatia in May 1992 and China's purchase of a previously owned aircraft carrier in 1998. These moments in time were matters of great prestige for the actors involved and became a means of communicating their 'message' to the international community in a way that the 'routine' procurement activities of the long-established leading navies are not.

It is also important to understand the source or provenance of the evidence that is included. Primary sources were used wherever possible with examples of naval activity fitting the definition being taken from the official publications of eight major maritime states – the United States, the United Kingdom, Canada, Australia, Russia, China, India and Japan. These eight would be classified as major or medium global and regional force projection navies under a widely used typology.[1] If those countries deemed an example of their navy's employment worthy of mention in operations databases, white papers and reports to their respective legislatures, then they are included here. These countries were chosen because their records are openly published and accessible, they are geographically dispersed, and they field naval forces at differing though substantial scales. It is entirely probable that by extending the review to include other states' official publications more examples would be uncovered, particularly the activities of the smaller coastal navies and coastguards which may be classified as purely adjacent force projection, offshore and inshore territorial defence, constabulary and 'token' under the same typology.[2]

Secondary sources including books, academic journal articles, specialist and generalist open media reporting and online resources were also data-mined to corroborate the 'official' version of an incident and to provide additional examples not revealed elsewhere. *Jane's Defence Weekly* and *Jane's Navy International* were particularly rich resources. A health warning: the evidence presented here is not the definitive word on every example of naval diplomacy during the immediate post-Cold War period. Instead, it seeks patterns, and patterns are discernible in the incidents included.

It is worth highlighting that even these broad selection criteria may have resulted in many otherwise pertinent examples of naval diplomacy being overlooked. For example, the 'routine' day-to-day business of the major global navies such as port visits and low-level bilateral exercises may not be deemed worthy of reporting even by the navy involved, whereas any departure from the norm by a small, traditionally coastal navy is, such as a long out of area blue-water deployment. Similarly, picture building or intelligence collection, that intrinsic and valuable part of any general diplomatic activity, would more often than not be conducted clandestinely and so may only be reported when discovered. Therefore, while an initial glance at the examples could lead to the conclusion that they are skewed in favour of the activity of the major established navies, under-reporting by them may mean that in reality the reverse is the case.

Some of the incidents took place at a specific point in time, with a very clear and distinct start and end date. However, it must also be borne in mind that in common with other forms of international diplomacy and communication much naval activity is enduring. The US Navy's basing of forces in Japan or the Royal Navy's persistent presence mission in the Persian Gulf from 1979 onwards are obvious examples. There are many more. It is perhaps inevitable in a work of this kind to find a structural bias towards reporting the contingent at the expense of the enduring.

When referring to the Appendix, it should be noted that the description given for each example consists of a very short summary which aims to distil at times complex scenarios into a sentence or two. To aid brevity, it has been assumed that the reader will have some general knowledge of world events, such as the fragmentation of the Soviet 'empire', the rise of the BRICS[3] and the first and second Gulf Wars. The description of the incident used in the Appendix is, in the majority of cases, a précis of the source material and therefore does not redress any potential misrepresentation or bias in the original account; it is for the reader to determine whether the report is entirely accurate. However, each incident is accompanied by a reference which, generally, will give a fuller account; many are cross-referenced and contrasting interpretations seen. Importantly, for the purposes of this book, the fact that an incident did occur, that at least some of the participants can be identified and that it can be classified according to previously determined criteria is sufficient justification for inclusion and a basis for analysis. Some of the examples which represent the key events and themes of the period are expanded upon greater detail as case studies later.

The actors named in each example tend to be the principal active participant(s) and principal target audiences. They are not listed in any order of importance and they are not classified as 'assailant' or 'victim' as they are in Cable's work. Often, the term 'Int[ernational] Community' is used to highlight occasions when an incident of naval diplomacy is judged to have been conscious and obvious messaging to the world at large, rather than to just a single polity. An example is that of France in February 2003, when the FS *Charles de Gaulle* carrier task group sailed for the eastern Mediterranean after the French government had declared its opposition to military intervention in Iraq; the move signalled to both sides of the conflict that France could mobilize if necessary, and to the world in general that France was an independent player on the stage.[4] Occasionally the terms 'Dom[estic] Community' or 'Regional Community' are used when the messaging is deemed to be more geographically focused and less 'scatter gun'; examples of this type include the Royal Australian Navy's outreach to its country's remote aboriginal communities in March 1993,[5] or French peace support exercises with eastern and southern African countries in February 2002.[6]

The column titled 'Cable Classification' is an attempt to categorize the examples according to the criteria which James Cable used in *Gunboat Diplomacy*.

The letter used indicates whether an incident would have been deemed *definitive, purposeful, catalytic* or *expressive*. Cable's third volume, which took his survey to the end of 1991, included only two entries for that year: a US non-combatant evacuation operation from Somalia in January and a British 'reassurance' mission to Grenada in July; both are included in this summary and both show the same classification that Cable gave. The 'Cable Classifications' of the remaining incidents are supposition but they are consistent with his approach; for instance, non-combatant evacuation operations are judged to be *purposeful* and major representational deployments and visits are *expressive*.

A few other examples, such as those in the Tamil Tiger/Sri Lankan government conflict which ran throughout much of the period, or naval agreements or public announcements on maritime matters, such the signing of a Maritime Consultative Agreement by the United States and China in January 1998, are marked '–'. This indicates that they do not sit naturally into any of Cable's categories; they are included in this survey because they fit the definition of naval diplomacy used in this book.

In the final column, 'Composite Classification', the incidents are categorized according to those major traits of naval diplomacy identified in Chapter 2: coercion, deterrence, co-operation, prestige, reassurance, picture building, attraction and assistance. The majority of incidents have a 'composite classification' of two or more traits. Categorizing naval diplomacy according to a single effect or outcome is evidently easier said than done.

Finally, to determine whether the immediate post-Cold War era really was different to the Cold War itself, two 'control' periods have also been analyzed to provide a suitable benchmark. These control years (from 1960 to 1964 and from 1980 to 1984) were selected because they represent respectively the culmination of the *first* Cold War around the time of the Cuban Missile Crisis, and the period of heightened tensions during the Reagan-Brezhnev *second* Cold War following the end of detente.[7] Many of the entries are in Cable's own work and thus provide an additional cross-check for consistency in classification, and they are also separated by time. When set against the main body of evidence, they offer periods for analysis at roughly 20-year intervals and are therefore useful for identifying trends. The criteria used for the inclusion of incidents in all sections are identical.

The actors

It is perhaps unsurprising that during the Cold War approximately 40 per cent of reported incidents of naval diplomacy involved the major players of either the Eastern or Western blocs interacting with third parties.[8] This analysis is supported by the 1960–64 and 1980–84 control periods detailed in the Appendix. It might be presumed therefore that following the end of the bipolar order other maritime actors would feel less constrained and consequently increase their influence activity at and from the sea. In fact, this was one of the hypotheses proposed in the introduction. However, the evidence base shows that in the immediate post-Cold War era the reverse was true. The overwhelming majority of incidents at that time involved NATO members. In effect, the early 1990s saw a naval scene absolutely dominated by the West, with the United States and her allies sailing unchallenged in the Mediterranean and Middle East, attempting to forge new relationships with former adversaries and exercising with previously non-aligned states. Interestingly, NATO members' dominance of naval diplomatic action did not diminish as the Cold War receded into 'history'. By 2010 they were still players in approximately 40 per cent of all reported incidents.

In contrast, the former Warsaw Pact countries disappeared from the seas virtually overnight. Russia, the possessor of the dominant Warsaw Pact navy during the Cold War, attempted several times to reassert her position as a major maritime power including numerous submarine forays into Swedish waters and surface ship deployments to the Mediterranean and North Atlantic. But these were isolated occasions, at least until around 2008 when Russian resurgence at sea really did begin. However, it is interesting to note that the former Soviet Union did make use of its navy in August 1991 during the attempted coup to oust President Gorbachev; ships blockaded the port of Tallinn, and part of the Pacific Fleet poised in port in Vietnam.[9] Navies, evidently, can play a part in influencing internal affairs as well as international crises.

Just as important, the evidence shows clearly that incidents of naval diplomacy are seldom limited to just two parties. In a significant number of cases three or more actors are involved, and often there is also a plain intent to send a message to domestic audiences, regional neighbours or the international community. One useful example took place in November 1994 between the United States, Thailand, North Korea and China. The United States wished to pre-position its ships in Thai territorial waters as a deterrent to North Korean posturing against the South, but Thailand refused permission for the move because it did not want to offend North Korea's only ally, China.[10] The example shows the complexity of international relations and the corresponding intricacy of naval diplomacy. Any attempt to describe the incident in bilateral terms between the United States and North Korea, the United States and Thailand, the United States and China or even China and North Korea would be unsophisticated and erroneous.

The first Gulf War of 1991 was an important milestone for naval diplomacy. Not only did it see the first major post-Cold War use of military force, it also afforded an opportunity for previously undemonstrative actors to begin to make their mark. Germany and Japan both deployed vessels in the aftermath of the conflict and the Middle East became a focal point for naval grandstanding. Countries with a maritime agenda wanted to be there and be seen to be there. Kuwait, a country not normally considered a leading naval actor, took centre stage in this activity for a number of years after its conflict with Iraq. The United States and United Kingdom exercised independently with Kuwait in early 1992 and even Russia, a state whose prestige (as the USSR) had suffered in the Islamic world as a result of its occupation of Afghanistan in the 1980s, conducted a naval exercise with Kuwait in December 1993.[11]

If Kuwait was a participant in naval diplomacy by virtue of its unwanted circumstances, other states were participants through calculation. Ghadaffi-era Libya, for instance, may be judged to have been 'rewarded' with naval visits for its less confrontational posture as the new century grew. Indian warships visited Libyan ports in June 2006 and were followed by a visit by a US coastguard vessel in June 2009. It was the first American military visit to the country since President Ghadaffi seized power in a coup in 1969. After the fall of Ghadaffi and the ensuing turmoil, visits were not quite so forthcoming.

After the initial domination of the West in the early to mid-1990s, the new rising powers began to increase their presence at sea. India, for example, announced plans for more exercises with the established blue-water navies in March 1992 and by August 2008 was showing signs of considerable maritime maturity by contributing to the multinational counter-piracy mission off the Horn of Africa. Similar development can be tracked in relation to China and to a lesser extent and South Africa. This will be explored further in the next chapter.

Though state actors dominate the examples, it is apparent that not all participants are countries. Insurgent or terrorist organizations and pressure groups all appear; examples include Hezbollah's use of force against Israel in July 2006, Israel's use of force against the Gaza Freedom Flotilla in May 2010, Greenpeace's campaigning in the North Sea and High North and the complex situation developing between various parties in the Niger Delta region from the mid-2000s onwards. It is clear that naval diplomacy remains an activity primarily but not exclusively carried out by states.

History and geography

Historical legacy undoubtedly plays a part in determining the dynamics of many incidents. Portugal's interaction with Guinea-Bissau in July 1998, when the foreign ministers of Portugal and Angola met Guinea-Bissau rebels on board the warship *Vasco da Gama* in an attempt to broker peace, is one example.[12] Another is the UK's involvement in the civil war in Sierra Leone in 2000. Both could be seen as manifestations of former colonial 'responsibility'. More often, though, geography is the principal driver. There are many more regional than global navies and the evidence shows that in numerical terms the vast majority of interactions are by neighbouring actors in their adjacent seas. There are numerous examples throughout the period of Asian states interacting in and around the South China Sea, but there are others in less 'visible' parts of the world. There was significant and ongoing engagement between Argentina and Chile, for example, which ran from 1998 until 2007. Interestingly, this contrasts sharply with the reported activity during the Cold War. At that time the major Western and Eastern navies tended to interact with third parties at greater range. Of the 105 incidents investigated in the control period, only 47 (45 per cent) could be described as regional, and there was no discernible difference between the periods 1960–64 and 1980–84.

Enmity or amity?

Naval diplomacy is not synonymous with gunboat diplomacy, as even a cursory review of the type of platform used will show. It was explained in Chapter 2 that

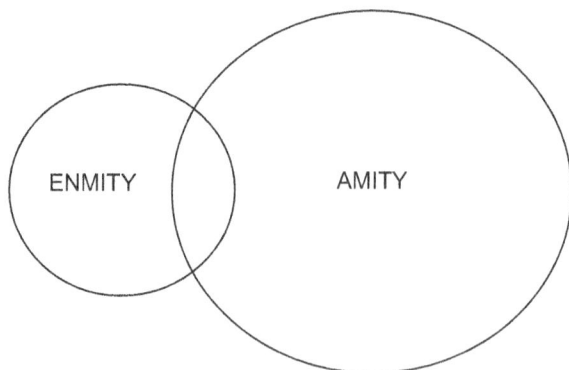

Figure 3.1 The 'negative'/'positive' balance in naval diplomacy

writers and theorists of the past tended to focus their work on the use of naval and military forces to influence adversaries, either through coercion or deterrence or both. Historically, relatively little attention was paid to the soft power of navies, particularly their utility in forging friendships. Quantitatively, the evidence shows that only a quarter of the reported incidents in the post-Cold War period could be described as indicative of any form of enmity between the parties involved. Conversely, some 90 per cent have some degree of amity in their purpose.[13] (The sum is more than 100 per cent because the two are not mutually exclusive and purposes are rarely binary.) Activities which may be deemed to be aimed at an actual or potential adversary can also involve an element of reassurance or support to allies or domestic populations. It is striking that when analyzed in greater detail the 'negative' effect of *deterrence* is invariably paired with the more 'positive' effect of *reassurance*. In complex relationships signals of enmity and amity can be and are made concurrently. For example, Australian port visits to Indonesia in 1991 were in part aimed to balance contemporary actions being taken by the RAN to limit illegal fishing by Indonesian vessels.[14] Overlapping or multiple outcomes from naval diplomacy are not exceptional; they are the norm.

However, when the Cold War control periods are analyzed a very different picture emerges. The incidents then are almost evenly split between amity and enmity. Of course, this could be attributed to the existence of established blocs and proxies during the Cold War or to any one of a number of other factors, not least the tendency to under-report 'good news'.[15]

Degrees of engagement

As actors seek to extend their influence they do so by a variety of means. There is quantitative evidence to support the view that there are varying degrees of engagement within naval diplomacy and that the state of a relationship can often be assessed by the type of engagement practiced. In short, engagement can be weighted. At the lowest end of the scale are goodwill visits, which can be means of ongoing 'relationship maintenance' for established allies, symbolic first forays into amity for those with a more adversarial association or even rewards for 'good behaviour'. When navies begin to exercise together they usually engage in non-war-fighting training such as search and rescue. Complexity and interoperability in exercises progressively increase until the very closest of allies are capable of fully integrated operations in difficult and dangerous scenarios. Clearly, the former are more commonly found than the latter. Figure 3.2 shows a diagrammatic representation of various levels of engagement identified in the Appendix with supporting examples.

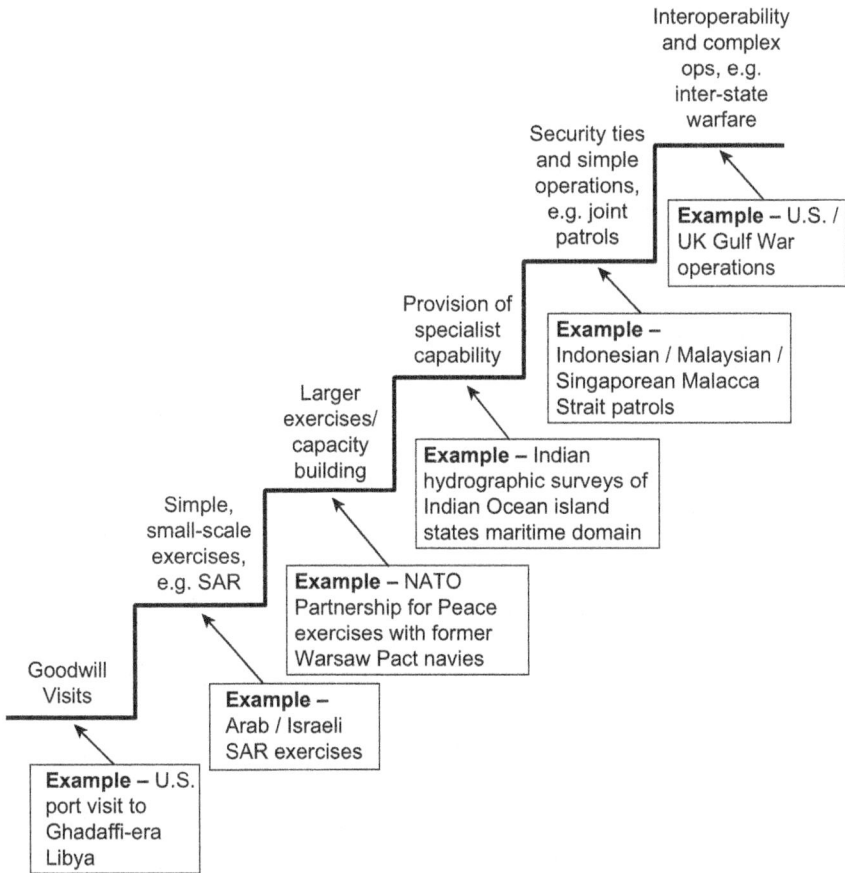

Figure 3.2 Degrees of engagement in 'soft' naval diplomacy[16]

Disengagement

One aspect of naval diplomacy which does not directly fit either Cable or any other known form of classification but that is readily apparent from the evidence of real world activity is the communicative impact of *not* doing something. Cancelled port visits, such as Australia's suspension of its navy's visits to French Pacific territories in January 1995 in protest at France's nuclear testing programme, can send as powerful a diplomatic message as an inaugural visit after a long period of animosity. Likewise, the cancellation of planned exercises such as the annual US-South Korean *Team Spirit*, deferred for several years in a row in the 1990s as an incentive to North Korea to halt its nuclear development programme, can be used to make or reinforce a position. As in other aspects of life, disengagement can be a potent communicative tool.

However, disengagement can also result in unintended consequences. In December 1992, for example, the United States redeployed an aircraft carrier from the Persian Gulf to Somalia for Operation *Restore Hope*, and Iraq exploited its absence to escalate pressure on visiting UN weapons inspectors and to violate the southern no-fly zone which the carrier had helped to enforce.[17] A similar exploitation of a gap was seen in October 1994 when, during another USN aircraft carrier absence, Iraq moved 80,000 troops towards its border with Kuwait. The situation was only reversed when a substantial Western coalition naval presence was resumed.[18] The lesson to be learned is that when a path is chosen, particularly when it involves enduring presence, it is not always easy to reverse course.

Symbolism and tokenism

As might be expected from historic precedent, the post-Cold War world saw a continued symbolic role for naval forces. Warships were used as backdrops for political announcements and as independent sovereign territory when the situation dictated. For example, Romania's declaration of its intention to join the Partnership for Peace (PfP) was made during the USS *Tortuga*'s visit to the country in August 1994.[19] Similarly, HMNZS *Te Kaha* was employed as a venue for inter-party peace talks in the Solomon Islands in August 2000.[20] However, some states resorted to deploying naval forces in a manner more akin to campaigning pressure groups than to military forces. One such example was New Zealand's dispatch of HMNZS *Tui* to the Mururoa Atoll in September 1995, where it demonstrated against French nuclear testing alongside a civilian 'protest flotilla'.[21] This is perhaps an example of the blurring of lines between traditional state and non-state roles in global politics.

Symbolism can take other forms and Iran's contribution to counter-piracy operations off the Horn of Africa in 2009 was an attempt by that country to present itself as a responsible member of the international community.[22] The stakes were low and the message was simple. The Seychelles' contribution to the same task at the same time was similarly a matter of prestige for a small state acting on the issue of the day, not an act of military or economic necessity.[23]

There have been occasions in naval diplomacy which can best be described as examples of tokenism. When Russia decided not to join the Partnership for Peace in February 1994, it softened its position by immediately sending a warship to conduct a search and rescue exercise, that most basic of building blocks, with NATO forces.[24] As has been previously argued, the ease and rapidity with which naval forces can be visibly (or invisibly) put to work to give demonstrable support to their government's position is a particular strength in international relations.

Continuity or change? Taking *Gunboat Diplomacy* into the 21st century

It has already been stated that the survey in this book's Appendix includes more examples than Sir James Cable chose to catalogue in his work. It must be assumed, therefore, that if he had lived to produce a fourth volume of his *Gunboat Diplomacy* then many, perhaps the majority, of the examples cited here would not have been used. Nonetheless, the bulk do fit into one or more of his categories and a very significant proportion are deemed *expressive*, the 'last and least' mode of limited naval force which Cable so readily dismissed.[25]

However, given the numerical differences and the non-availability of equivalent source material from each period a direct comparative analysis is not possible, but an indirect approach can be adopted. If *expressive* examples of naval diplomacy are omitted from both this analysis and from Cable's chronological index, a remarkable truth can be observed. While acknowledging Cable's warning about the use of his data for numerical purposes, a simple statistical review shows that there is little discernible difference in the relative ratios of *definitive, purposeful* and *catalytic* incidents in the pre-Cold War, Cold War and post-Cold War eras. In each period just over half of non-*expressive* incidents are deemed *purposeful*, approximately a quarter are *definitive* and less than a fifth are *catalytic*. In Cable's terms, the desired outcomes of naval diplomacy do not change significantly over time. Figure 3.3 shows the approximate ratios (pre-Cold War incidents are taken from Cable's work; Cold War incidents are Cable's plus the author's own survey; post-Cold War data is from the author's survey alone).

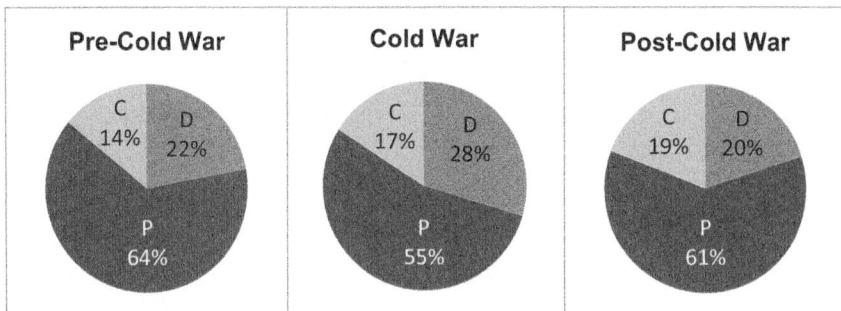

Pre-Cold War	Cold War	Post-Cold War
C 14%	C 17%	C 19%
D 22%	D 28%	D 20%
P 64%	P 55%	P 61%

Figure 3.3 Ratios of types of gunboat diplomacy according to Cable's classification

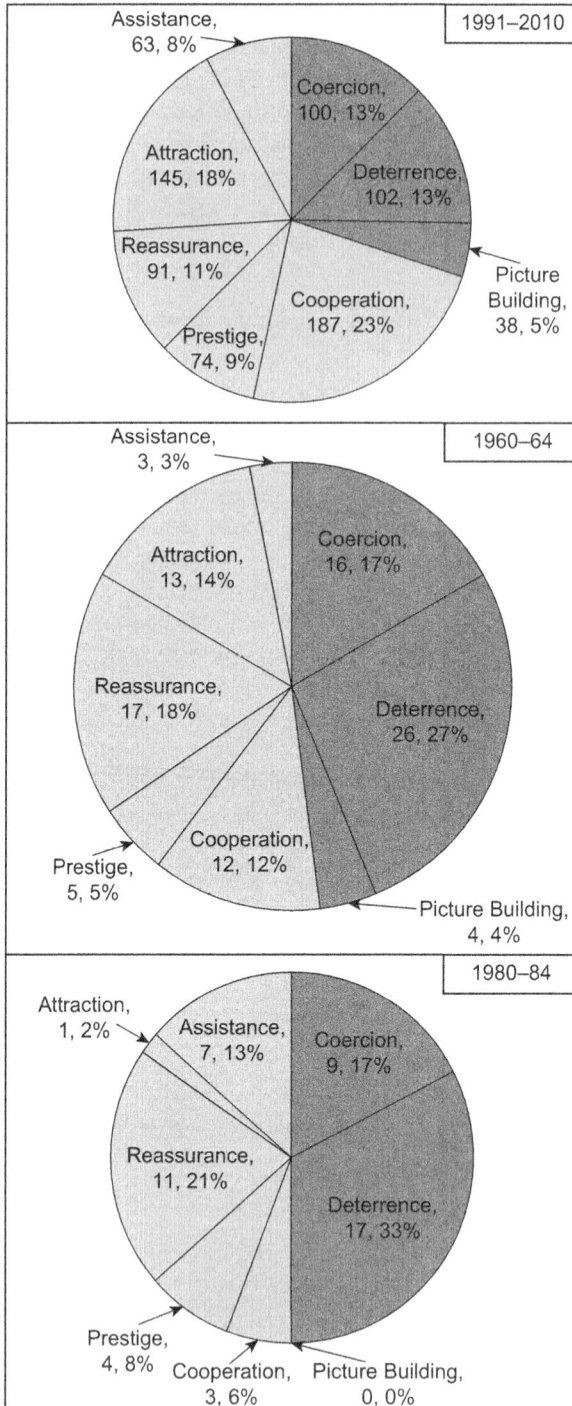

Figure 3.4 Ratios of survey results using composite classifications (1991–2010 and control periods)

However, in non-Cable terms a different trend can be seen. It has already been stated that the engagements involving 'amity' became more prevalent than those involving 'enmity' after the Cold War, as Figure 3.4 shows. By comparing classifications between the primary survey (i.e. 1991–2010) and the control periods (1960–64 and 1980–84), the relative incidence of each form of engagement can be seen.

The occurrence of *assistance* operations, be they navies providing disaster relief after the Indian Ocean tsunami of December 2004, gifting patrol vessels or providing hydrographic surveys in areas beyond the capabilities of the sovereign state, has certainly increased over time. The ability to 'lend a hand' in times of need has become a matter of importance on the world stage, and altruism a sign of international responsibility, to an extent not seen during the Cold War. Similarly, *co-operation* in the form of bilateral or multilateral exercising has quantitatively increased. Interestingly, as coercion and deterrence have reduced in relative terms, reassurance (often the other side of the same coin) has not. Again, it is an indication of the increasing recognition of the value of naval diplomacy in positive massaging, and not merely the negative.

The survey provides a useful but inevitably incomplete overview of naval diplomacy since the end of the Cold War. The themes which can be drawn from it suggest both continuity and change and are certainly worthy of further qualitative analysis. It shows that naval diplomacy is primarily but not exclusively carried out by states and that the appetite of non-state actors to become involved in international communication on the global seas might be increasing. It shows that sea power is numerically used more for purposes of amity than for enmity, though at the 'harder' end of the spectrum of operations there is little difference in the desired outcomes either before, during or after the Cold War. Cable's model, therefore, is as applicable now as it was at the height of the superpower standoff when he devised it. At the 'softer' end of the scale there are degrees of engagement which, when considered objectively, can be used to judge the health of any particular international relationship. However, the impact of disengagement, or actively not doing something, should not be underestimated. Navies are, and have always been, used for symbolic purposes and that symbolism perhaps approached a new zenith in the post-Cold War era with an international doctrine of humanitarianism and friendly co-operation.

The next chapter will build on these themes and example to investigate further the macro-trends and micro-actions of naval diplomacy since the end of the Cold War.

Notes

1 Grove, Eric, *The Future of Sea Power*. (London: Routledge, 1990), pp. 236–240.
2 Ibid.
3 Brazil, Russia, India, China and South Africa.
4 *Jane's Defence Weekly* [*JDW*] 39, No. 6 (2003): p. 4.
5 Australia. Royal Australian Navy. *Database of Royal Australian Navy Operations, 1990–2005*. Working Paper No. 18. (Canberra: Sea Power Centre, 2005).

6 *JDW* 37, No. 10 (2002): p. 16.
7 Booth Ken, 'Cold War States of Mind.' In Booth, Ken. *Statecraft and Security: The Cold War and Beyond.* (Cambridge: Cambridge University Press, 1998), pp. 30–31.
8 Of the 193 incidents documented by Sir James Cable from 1946 onwards, 76 could be described as being 'by' a NATO or Warsaw Pact state against a lesser developed state. See Cable, James. *Gunboat Diplomacy 1919–1991: Political Applications of Limited Naval Force, 3rd Ed.* (Basingstoke: Macmillan, 1994), pp. 159–213.
9 *JDW* 16, No. 8 (1991): p. 297; *JDW* 16, No. 12 (1991): p. 500.
10 *JDW* 22, No. 19 (1994): p. 11.
11 Hughes, Geraint. *From the Jebel to the Palace: British Military Involvement in the Persian Gulf, 1957–2011.* Corbett Paper 10. (Shrivenham: The Corbett Centre for Maritime Policy Studies, King's College London, 2012), p. 6; *JDW* 20, No. 25 (1993): p. 9.
12 *JDW* 30, No. 1 (1998): p. 6.
13 Of the 528 incidents catalogued, only 135 (25 per cent) were categorized as coercion, deterrence or picture building/intelligence collection. Four hundred seventy (90 per cent) were categorized as co-operation, prestige, reassurance, attraction or assistance.
14 Australia. RAN. *Operations Database.*
15 Of the 105 incidents in 1960–64 and 1980–84, 60 can be deemed to have some degree of enmity and 57 some degree of amity in their purpose.
16 Figure 3.2 is the work of the author, but is adapted from a format used to describe US-Chinese maritime co-operation: see Collins, Gabriel. 'China's Dependence on the Global Maritime Commons.' In Erickson, Andrew, Goldstein, Lyle & Li, Nan (Eds.). China, the United States and 21st Century Sea Power: Defining a Maritime Security Partnership. (Annapolis: Naval Institute Press, 2010), p. 33.
17 United States. Center for Naval Analyses. Siegel, Adam. *To Deter, Compel, and Reassure in International Crises: The Role of U.S. Naval Forces.* CRM 94–193. (Alexandria, VA: CNA, 1995), p. 28.
18 Ibid., p. 3; UK, *RN Operations 1970–2013.*
19 *JDW* 22, No. 8 (1994): p. 4.
20 *JDW* 34, No. 8 (2000): p. 18.
21 *JDW* 24, No. 9 (1995): p. 4.
22 *JDW* 46, No. 22 (2009): p. 18.
23 *JDW* 46, No. 19 (2009): p. 19.
24 *JDW* 21, No. 7 (1994): p. 8.
25 Of a total of 528 examples, 285 (54 per cent) are classified as *expressive*.

4   The post-Cold War context

Situating naval diplomacy in the post-Cold War era is a complex business. As has already been discussed, the fall of communism and the end of a half century of superpower standoff left the world an uncertain place. Nevertheless, for the purposes of this book the Cold War is assumed to have ended in or around 1991 and brought in its aftermath a sea change in societal, economic, political and military norms, readily identifiable from those which went immediately before and which had the potential to influence the theory and practice of naval diplomacy.

To make sense of the new global order it would be judicious to attempt to identify the macro trends which characterize it. Many writers and commentators have tried to describe post-1991 global trends and there can be found a significant degree of concurrence. Some, for instance, pointed to an era defined by the globalization of capitalism, US hegemony, Russian reform, the rise of China, European integration and the rise of radical Islam.[1] Others identified a very similar set of trends, albeit by other names: German reunification, the break-up of the USSR and the subsequent 'wars of succession', the Yugoslav break-up, US predominance, a willingness to engage in humanitarian intervention and a changing balance in the developing world.[2] The themes are simultaneously and intuitively both recognizable and right.

The themes may be recognizable and right, but in list form they can appear disparate and unrelated. Some writers have sought to find an even broader overview by which to simplify the period. One view, for instance, divided the first 20 years of the post-Cold War world into three 'distinct periods': the rapidly changing and unpredictable security environment of the 1990s; the global war on terror after the al-Qaeda attack on the United States on 11 September 2001; and then the re-emergence of great power rivalry.[3] The attack on the World Trade Centre towers in New York can be determined to the minute, but precisely where and when the last 'period' began is unclear. The renowned Cold War historian John Gaddis simplified matters even further, seeing just two stimuli at work after 1991, the dual forces of integration and fragmentation.[4] However, that argument, written before the rubble of the Berlin Wall had been cleared away, was perhaps made a little prematurely.

All of these themes offer potential frameworks within which to investigate naval diplomacy. In the following three chapters an amalgam is used through which to view the topic. It begins with fragmentation and the uncertain security situation after the collapse of communism, looks in turn at the resultant nationalism and opportunism which followed, coinciding with the assumption of, and then challenge to, US hegemony and finishes with the return of great power rivalry. Throughout, the role of non-state actors, the diffusion of influence to regional powers and, arguably, increasing constraints on the use of force by and between states are considered. Though the themes chosen may logically appear to be chronological and exhibit a causal relationship, in reality that is not always the case. It quickly becomes apparent that throughout much of the 20 years after 1991, the trends and themes identified co-existed and the edges blurred.

The examples chosen to explore these themes are illustrative, not exhaustive. However, they do display a range of actors and methods which are characteristic of the post-Cold War period and the macro-trend which they represent. The majority of the examples, particularly those used to highlight fragmentation, nationalism and American hegemony may be considered discrete and many others could have been selected in their place. Those used to describe the naval diplomacy wielded to support the rise of the Asia-Pacific powers in Chapter 6 are more thematic in nature. Nonetheless, the whole picture is one of a quarter century period in which naval diplomacy has been far from absent in global affairs.

Fragmentation and the uncertain security situation

The decline of communism and the rapidly changing map of central and eastern Europe led to a particularly uncertain security situation in the early 1990s. The victors were quick to reap the supposed 'peace dividend', the savings to be made against military expenditures which had become almost prohibitively expensive in the final years of the Cold War. As one commentator later put it, 'the reduction in East-West tension also resulted in a great decrease in inter-state conflicts. . . . Defense budgets in many parts of the world radically decreased'.[5] However, as the same commentator went on to say, it would be 'unwise' to argue that the world was at peace, as it began to see the emergence, or re-emergence, of many serious armed conflicts in areas that had been 'relatively quiescent' during the Cold War.[6] From a Western perspective a great number of dangers such as 'regional rivalry, terrorism, transnational crime, nationalism and ethnic and religious conflicts' rose to prominence in the 1990s, 'replacing the Soviet Union as the main concern'.[7]

Some have described the post-Cold War world not as a series of geopolitical 'happenings' but in terms of societal or conceptual changes. It is certainly the case that, amongst a number of post-1991 trends, there was the emergence of the 'comprehensive' or 'whole of government' approach to foreign and defence policies which called for closer and better aligned civil-military partnerships.[8] This approach is reminiscent of Joseph Nye's 'smart power' ideas and may explain a commonly held perception that there was an increased acceptance of the use of militaries in operations other than war from the 1990s onwards.

However, the change in emphasis in military employment may be more than a subtle improvement in joined-up government; it could be symptomatic of a re-evaluation of the whole role of military forces. Rob de Wijk, writing about coercion, captured the post-Cold War concept: 'Traditionally, states use force to protect territory and to conquer land. Today, liberal democracies use force mainly as a foreign policy instrument to influence the strategic choices of their opponent or target'.[9] Whether this view is applicable after the liberal democracy–led regime-changing campaigns in Iraq and Afghanistan is questionable. Christopher Coker went straight to the core of the issue; the West, he argued, had changed from being a 'threat community' to being a 'risk community' in its attitude to security.[10] Military forces, it would follow, would necessarily change from countering the threat posed by a potential 'enemy' to assisting in the management of generic 'risks' to national interests – not necessarily the same things.

Two examples of naval diplomacy typify this bout of fragmentation, the management of risks, and the subsequent vying for influence in the former Eastern bloc. Though the examples are a decade apart in time, both involved the West, both involved former communist states and both were closely scrutinized by a non-independent third party, namely Russia. Arguably, they represent prima facie attempts to exercise hard and soft power respectively.

The first example, the violent fragmentation of Yugoslavia, was not an obvious candidate for the application of sea power. In fact,

> there was little apparent role for maritime forces in an intra-state campaign taking place on land, in which neither side has a significant navy or a grave vulnerability to the interdiction of its maritime trade. In practice, however, the naval contribution was both substantial and significant.[11]

What became apparent in the crowded waters of the Adriatic Sea in the 1990s was an age-old truth: the purpose of a navy is not only to fight an opposing navy.[12]

Though the conflict in Yugoslavia and subsequently in the newly independent states of Serbia, Croatia, Bosnia-Herzegovina and Kosovo ultimately saw the employment of ground troops and a substantial application of air power, both from land and sea, in the maritime environment a steady trickle soon became of flood of actors appearing on the Balkan stage. The central issue in this example is perhaps the number, range and differing objectives of those actors.

As the situation deteriorated in the former Yugoslavia, the United Nations Security Council passed a series of increasingly aggressive resolutions to quell the turmoil,[13] including UNSCR 787 in November 1992 which authorized the enforcement of sanctions.[14] This resolution had the effect of giving Western action 'some degree of bite' but the sanctions were 'inevitably slow to have an effect, and that effect was modest'.[15] However modest that effect might be, the Western powers were keen to act and be seen to do so. Early in 1993 the North Atlantic Council offered to police the Adriatic using its Standing Naval Force Mediterranean (STANAVFORMED). It was, Fabian Hiscock asserted in *The Naval Review*, the first live operation ever conducted by NATO,[16] and as Eric Grove added, a 'notable first in international naval co-operation – support of UN resolutions'.[17] These claims, though appealing, are not strictly accurate.

A more authoritative 2013 analysis of naval support of UN resolutions identified seven to date, including two (Southern Rhodesia in 1965 [UNSCR 217] and Iraq in 1990 [UNSCR 665]) which pre-date Yugoslavia.[18] Nonetheless, after the quarter-century hiatus between the naval enforcement of sanctions of Southern Rhodesia and those authorizing action against Iraq, there was a flood of UN mandated maritime activity in Haiti (1993), Sierra Leone (1997), Lebanon (2006) and Libya (2011).[19]

However, according to NATO, in the three years that the naval operations took place in the Adriatic, 14 countries contributed forces.[20] France, outside the NATO military structure at the time, felt able to become involved through the auspices of the Western European Union (WEU), which also committed forces.[21] The British formed a national task group in January 1993 based around the aircraft carrier HMS *Ark Royal* under the command of Jeremy Blackham, and a Dutch frigate joined it in February.[22]

Notwithstanding the practical issue of sanction enforcement, it is clear that the Adriatic of the early to mid-1990s provided an opportunity for states to publicly demonstrate their willingness to participate in coalition and alliance action in order to help shape the changing world order. There was, in effect, a scramble for a piece of the Adriatic. Additionally, the multinational response to support UN Resolutions was arguably a strengthening, if not practical legitimizing, of the role of international organizations in the post-Cold War world. In international relations terms, it spoke to the liberal agenda.

Blackham stated that his immediate priority was to 'familiarise ourselves with the geography, oceanography and pattern of activity in the Adriatic' and that his mission was to 'poise'. The same mission, he stated, 'similarly drove the thinking of the U.S. and French commanders' and are 'the most classic, most ancient, and in the future, probably most likely form of naval operations'.[23] However, that assessment is perhaps an oversimplification, as each of the contributing parties had their own objectives. From the start of the conflict until 1995 US policy had been based around its refusal to deploy ground troops,[24] and it consequently relied heavily on its aircraft carrier contribution to Operation *Deny Flight* against the Serbian air force to communicate its intent. Meanwhile, French warships were primarily supporting troops ashore, while standing NATO naval forces, from both the Mediterranean and later from the Atlantic, and the Western European Union, were conducting embargo operations.[25] By the time operations completed in 1996, over 74,000 ships had been challenged by navies maintaining a continuous vigil at sea, and although the Yugoslav Navy attempted to interfere and assist an oil tanker to break the embargo in 1994, the enforcement was deemed completely successful.[26]

Ships were also used as neutral meeting grounds for negotiations between the Yugoslav constituent states and parties. Dr David Owen, the co-chairman of the Standing Committee of the International Conference of the Former Yugoslavia from 1992 to 1995, was aware of the symbolism of holding a peace conference on board a third party warship and acknowledged that the 'union of the three republics' plan was 'finalized on HMS *Invincible*' in 1993.[27]

In his analysis of the Adriatic operations from a British perspective, Eric Grove highlighted the complexities of integrating into an 'environment with two other national carrier groups, American and French, two multinational forces, NATO and WEU, not to mention Italian and NATO command structures'.[28] Others similarly commented on the challenges of having 'as many as four aircraft carriers in the Adriatic at any one time'.[29]

The achievement of the 1990s naval diplomacy in the Adriatic was not just its obvious impact on its 'victim', the disintegrating Yugoslavia, but its realization of coalition building, its visible signals to the international community, and its reassurance to a myriad of domestic audiences that action was being taken in support of a popular humanitarian cause. According to the US special envoy Richard Holbrooke, it gave the US Navy a platform of success from which to lobby Congress.[30] It also sent a message to Russia that the West was still a force to be reckoned with at sea, despite the cuts made to defence spending since the end of the Cold War. That message, however, did have an adverse impact on relations between the two former superpowers.[31]

The second example of naval diplomacy from the fragmented, former Eastern bloc is an example of a situation in which naval diplomacy fails. In the Adriatic the contributing states may have had dissimilar aims, but they were at least aware of the environment in which they operated. That was not the case in the summer of 2006 when the United States led an initiative aimed at enhancing the interoperability and maritime capabilities of the Black Sea states. By the use of targeted naval diplomacy Washington hoped to further its own foreign policy objectives of securing the region from terrorism, promoting democracy and ensuring the free flow of goods. The United States was absolutely clear in its aim but it was not fully cognizant of the context. Since 1992 Russia, still the dominant power in the region, had viewed Yugoslavia as a distraction to its main naval aim, the resolution of the 'problem' of Ukraine and the future of its Black Sea Fleet.[32]

The US-led *Sea Breeze* series of exercises had begun in 1997 and was seen as an important vehicle for coalition building.[33] The 2006 exercise was to be held off the Crimean peninsula, co-hosted by Ukraine, and involved participating forces from 17 countries, all belonging to either NATO or the Partnership for Peace (PfP). For its part Ukraine saw *Sea Breeze* as an aid to its own longer-term objectives of NATO membership, progressing military modernization and increasing interoperability with other countries' forces.[34]

Though the exercise was actually a US-Ukrainian bilateral enterprise with a number of other invited states, it was seen by many, and particularly by Russia, as a *de facto* NATO endeavour and part of its attempt to expand to the east. At the end of May 2006 the US-flagged merchant ship *Advantage* arrived as planned at the Ukrainian port of Feodosiya with a number of military reservists and 500 tonnes of construction material for use in *Sea Breeze*. The Russian Duma, sending a clear warning to its neighbour, voted on 6 June by 435 to 0 for a resolution expressing 'serious concern' over Ukrainian plans to join the NATO Alliance. Pro-Russian demonstrators then began to 'picket' the American 'warship'.[35] The Russian vote had been timed to pre-empt a Ukrainian parliamentary motion to allow foreign troops into the country for the exercise.[36] Since an earlier Ukrainian election there had been a political impasse, with no party enjoying a clear majority, which made it difficult to achieve 'the constitutionally required parliamentary authorization of foreign troops on Ukrainian soil'.[37] However, it was subsequently and success-fully argued within Ukraine that because *Advantage* was not a 'warship' and that because its cargo was not ammunition, the port had every right to admit it without reference to parliament.[38] That point notwithstanding, the political turmoil and anti-NATO sentiment in the predominantly ethnically Russian Crimea was such that it could be exploited for political gain.[39] The definitive article on the incident, written by Deborah Sanders in 2007, stated that:

> The offloading of *Advantage* became a lightning rod for a widespread cam-paign against the government's proposed foreign policy in general. Resi-dents of Feodosiya blockaded the city's port, protesting what they saw as an attempt by NATO to establish a presence in the Black Sea. . . . The day after the arrival of *Advantage* the Feodosiya town council declared the town a 'NATO-free area'; a week later the Crimean parliament declared the penin-sula a 'NATO-free territory'.[40]
>
> Within two weeks the ship would be forced out of port, its equipment and cargo impounded by Ukrainian customs and the reservists forced to fly home, their mission unachieved.[41]

By early August when the Ukrainian parliament did vote to allow the foreign troops into the country to exercise, it was too late.[42] The external pressure from Moscow and the internal demands within the Crimea were so great that the Ukrai-nian government was forced to alter course. In a visit to Brussels in September 2006, Prime Minister Viktor Yanukovych stated that Ukraine was 'not ready' to join NATO.[43]

Sanders used the *Sea Breeze* incident as a case study through which to ques-tion the 'generally accepted' view of the diplomatic utility of naval power. Naval diplomacy, which she defined as the use of naval power in peacetime to secure influence, could be counterproductive.[44] In this case of an American attempt to influence Ukraine through simple naval exercising, it failed to produce the desired effects for either side and could, she argued, have caused unforeseen damage.[45] Sanders combined elements of the works of Ken Booth and Edward Luttwak when reaching her conclusion:

> The relationship between naval diplomacy and domestic factors is com-plex. It has been argued that success is in the eyes of the 'locals', that the psychological environment of a 'target' state affects its decision makers and 'internal opinion forming groups'. Naval diplomacy, then, must take account of a state's political, historical, economic and military worldview; domestic politics – the policy environment, the decision-making arena, and internal pressures – shape the parameters and likelihood of what can be achieved.[46]

Military personnel engaged in planning for and participating in future coalition building exercises will clearly need to understand the culture, history and sensitivities of host states as well as of their neighbors.[47]

The success of this example of naval (and wider) diplomacy, if there was any, belonged to Russia, a state which had been neither a direct participant nor a deliberate 'target' of the exercise planners. Moscow's own counter to American and NATO naval presence in the region was its encouragement for and joining of the Black Sea Force (BLACKSEAFOR) in 2001. In common with the aims of *Sea Breeze*, BLACKSEAFOR was established to enhance peace and stability among the region's six littoral states, which it did through biannual naval exercises under the banner of Operation *Black Sea Harmony*.[48] As *Sea Breeze 2006* was unravelling, a *Black Sea Harmony* exercise was underway.[49] Russia's annexation of the Crimea some eight years later is well known.

As the Appendix shows, within the uncertain security situation there are examples of non-state actors using the sea to challenge states. One such example involved the so-called Gaza Freedom Flotilla which achieved enormous publicity in 2010. As part of the ongoing Middle East peace process, Israel had unilaterally withdrawn from the Gaza Strip in 2005 but retained control of its borders. Hamas, a US State Department–designated foreign terrorist organization, subsequently won the Palestinian election and took control of the territory in 2007. Israel imposed a blockade of Gaza in response to Hamas's takeover and restricted the flow of goods.[50] Israel and the international community differed about the severity of the blockade's effects on the humanitarian situation on Palestinian residents of Gaza, but it was clear that the territory's economy and people were affected.[51]

On 22 May 2010, the MV *Mavi Marmara*, a former Istanbul passenger ferry owned by the Turkish Humanitarian Relief Foundation, rendezvoused with five other ships and the flotilla headed for Gaza in an attempt to break the blockade and deliver 10,000 tonnes of humanitarian aid. In addition to the material cargo, the ships carried about 700 activists from 38 countries. On 30 May, the ships refused Israel's offer to unload at the port of Ashdod so that their cargoes could be inspected before delivery.[52]

The next day, when the ships were in international waters between 80 and 100 miles from the Israeli coast, the Israeli Navy intercepted and boarded them. Some activists on board the *Mavi Marmara* resisted and a violent clash ensued; nine passengers were killed.[53] The ships were diverted to Ashdod, the remaining passengers were detained, the cargo was unloaded and eventually it was delivered to Gaza and distributed under the auspices of the UN.[54]

Though the subsequent UN investigation into the incident, chaired by former New Zealand Prime Minister Sir Geoffrey Palmer, determined that the blockade had been 'legitimate' and that the flotilla had acted 'recklessly'.[55] The result was near-universal condemnation of Israel's actions. Nicaragua broke off diplomatic relations, while Ecuador and South Africa recalled their ambassadors and many other governments summoned Israeli ambassadors and chargés d'affaires to register their protests. The European Union, Russia and China urged Israel to open the borders to Gaza.[56] The action of the 'Gaza Freedom Flotilla' had an impact on the international community out of all proportion to that which might have initially been expected by a relatively small-scale humanitarian delivery. It showed that diplomacy at sea is not the sole preserve of state navies.

Notes

1 Cox, Michael. 'From the Cold War to the War on Terror.' In Baylis, John & Smith, Steve (Eds.). *Globalization of World Politics, 3rd Ed.* (Oxford: Oxford University Press, 2005), pp. 139–153.
2 Young and Kent describe how the 'wars of succession' took various forms from ethnic tensions and border disputes to ideological conflict. They cite as examples the attempts to establish the Transdniester Republic in Moldova (1990–94), the civil war in Tajikistan (1992–97) and the ongoing troubles in the Caucasus: Ngorno Karabakh (1992–93, 1999), Abkhazi revolt against Georgia (1992–93) and Chechnya from 1994 onwards. See Young, John W. & Kent, John. *International Relations since 1945: A Global History.* (Oxford: Oxford University Press, 2004), p. 631.
3 Lundesgaard, Amund. *U.S. Navy Strategy and Force Structure after the Cold War.* IFS Insight 4/2011. (Oslo: Institutt For Forsvarsstudier [Norwegian Institute for Defence Studies], 2011), p. 5.
4 Gaddis, John L. 'Toward the Post-Cold War World.' *Foreign Affairs* 70, No. 2 (1991): p. 102.
5 Yilmaz, Muzaffer Ercan. 'The New World Order: An Outline of the Post-Cold War Era.' *Alternatives: Turkish Journal of International Relations* 7, No. 4 (2008): p. 44.
6 Ibid., p. 45.
7 Lundesgaard, *U.S. Navy Strategy and Force Structure after the Cold War*, p. 4.
8 Hofmann, Stephanie & Weisbrode, Kenneth. 'Will the Post-Cold War Era Ever End?' www.worldpolicy.org/blog/will-%E2%80%9Cpost-cold-war-period%E2%80%9D-ever-end (accessed 16 January 2013).
9 Wijk, Rob de. *The Art of Military Coercion.* (Amsterdam: Mets & Schilt, 2005), p. 11.
10 Coker, Christopher. *Rebooting the West.* Whitehall Paper 72. (London: Royal United Services Institute, 2009), p. 60.
11 Benbow, Tim. 'Maritime Power in the 1990–91 Gulf War and the Conflict in the Former Yugoslavia.' In Dorman, Andrew M., Smith, Mike Lawrence & Uttley, Matthew R. H. (Eds.). *The Changing Face of Maritime Power.* (Basingstoke: Macmillan, 1999), p. 117.
12 Ibid., p. 107.
13 Resolutions 713 in 1991, 757 in 1992, 787 in 1992 and 820 in 1993.
14 For a detailed chronology of events in the Former Yugoslavia see: Allcock, John, Milivojevic, Marko & Horton, John (Eds.). *Conflict in the Former Yugoslavia: An Encyclopaedia.* (Santa Barbara, CA: ABC-CLIO, 1998), pp. 351–388.
15 Benbow, 'Maritime Power in the 1990–91 Gulf War and the Conflict in the Former Yugoslavia', p. 114.
16 Hiscock, Fabian. 'Operation Sharp Guard.' *The Naval Review* 82, No. 3 (1994): p. 224.
17 Grove, Eric. 'Navies in Peacekeeping and Enforcement: The British Experience in the Adriatic Sea.' *International Peacekeeping* 1, No. 4 (1994): p. 468.
18 Fink, M. D. 'Maritime Embargo Operations: Naval Implementation of UN Sanctions at Sea under Articles 41 and 42 of the UN Charter.' *Netherlands International Law Review* 60, No. 1 (2013): p. 74. Of note, UNSCR 83, which authorized military assistance (including naval) to South Korea following the North's attack in 1950, was a response to aggression, not an enforcement of sanctions. See: United Nations. Security Council. *Resolution 83 (1950) of 27 June 1950.* S/RES/83 (1950). (New York: UN Security Council, 1950).

19 Fink, 'Maritime Embargo Operations', pp. 73–92.
20 The contributors were Belgium, Canada, Denmark, France, Germany, Greece, Italy, the Netherlands, Norway, Portugal, Spain, Turkey, the United Kingdom and the United States. See: NATO. 'NATO/WEU IFOR Final Fact Sheet.' 2 October 1996. www.nato. int/ifor/general/shrp-grd.htm (accessed 21 February 2013).
21 Hiscock, 'Operation Sharp Guard', p. 224.
22 Grove, 'Navies in Peacekeeping and Enforcement', pp. 462–463.
23 Blackham, Jeremy. 'Maritime Peacekeeping.' *RUSI Journal* 138, No. 4 (1993): p. 19.
24 Latawski, Paul & Smith, Martin. *The Kosovo Crisis and the Evolution of Post-Cold War European Security.* (Manchester: Manchester University Press, 2003), p. 161.
25 Grove, 'Navies in Peacekeeping and Enforcement', pp. 466–467.
26 NATO. 'NATO/WEU IFOR Final Fact Sheet.'
27 Owen, David. *Balkan Odyssey.* (London: Victor Gollancz, 1995), p. 190.
28 Grove, 'Navies in Peacekeeping and Enforcement', p. 463.
29 Sargent, Richard. 'Deliberate Force Combat Air Assessments.' In Owen, Robert C. (Ed.). *Deliberate Force: A Case Study in Effective Air Campaigning.* (Maxwell, AL: Air University Press, 2000), p. 349.
30 Holbrooke, Richard. *To End a War.* (New York: The Modern Library, 1998), p. 145.
31 Carpenter, Ted (Ed.). *NATO's Empty Victory: A Postmortem on the Balkan War.* (Washington, DC: Cato Institute, 2000), p. 86.
32 Edemskii, Andrei. 'Russian Perspectives.' In Danchev, Alex & Halverson, Thomas (Eds.). *International Perspectives on the Yugoslav Conflict.* (Basingstoke: Macmillan, 1996), p. 33.
33 Sanders, Deborah. 'US Naval Diplomacy in the Black Sea: Sending Mixed Messages.' *U.S. Naval War College Review* 60, No. 3 (2007): p. 62.
34 Ibid., p. 63.
35 BBC. 'Russia Warns Kiev over NATO Plans.' 7 June 2006. http://news.bbc.co.uk/1/hi/ world/europe/5054506.stm (accessed 19 February 2013).
36 Ibid.
37 Sanders, 'US Naval Diplomacy in the Black Sea', p. 65.
38 International Centre for Policy Studies. 'Sea Breeze 2006: The Campaign to Promote NATO Is Being Lost.' www.icps.com.ua/eng/comment/1994.html (accessed 19 February 2013).
39 Perepelytsia, Grigory. 'NATO and Ukraine: At the Crossroads.' *NATO Review* (2007). www.nato.imt/docu/review/2007/issue2/english/aert2.html (accessed 19 February 2013).
40 Sanders, 'US Naval Diplomacy in the Black Sea', p. 66.
41 Ibid., p. 65.
42 Ibid.
43 BBC. 'Ukraine "Not Ready" to Join NATO.' 14 September 2006. http://news.bbc. co.uk/1/hi/world/europe/5345406.stm (accessed 19 February 2013).
44 Sanders, 'US Naval Diplomacy in the Black Sea', p. 61.
45 Ibid., p. 62.
46 Ibid., p. 63.
47 Ibid., p. 69.
48 The Black Sea Force members are Russia, Ukraine, Turkey, Georgia, Bulgaria and Romania. See: Gorenburg, Dmitry. 'Ten Years of BlackSeaFor: A Partial Assessment.' http://russiamil.wordpress.com/tag/black-sea-harmony/ (accessed 19 February 2013).
49 Sanders, 'US Naval Diplomacy in the Black Sea', p. 68.
50 United States. Congressional Research Service. Migdalovitz, C. *Israel's Blockade of Gaza, the Mavi Marmara Incident, and Its Aftermath.* R41275. (Washington, DC: CRS, 2010), p. 1.
51 United Nations. Office for the Coordination of Humanitarian Affairs. Between the Fence and a Hard Place. 'OCHA Special Focus Report August 2010.' (New York:

OCHA, 2010). www.ochaopt.org/documents/ocha_opt_special_focus_2010_08_19_english.pdf (accessed 7 March 2013).

52 United States. CRS. *Israel's Blockade of Gaza*, pp. 2–3.

53 Israel. 'Report of the Public Commission to Examine the Maritime Incident of 31 May 2010.' (The Turkel Commission). www.turkel-committee.gov.il/files/wordocs/7896summary-eng.PDF (accessed 7 March 2013).

54 United States. CRS. *Israel's Blockade of Gaza*, pp. 2–3.

55 United Nations. 'Report of the Secretary General's Panel of Inquiry on the 31 May 2010 Flotilla Incident.' (The Palmer Commission). (New York: UN Security Council, 2011), p. 4. www.un.org/News/dh/infocus/middle_east/Gaza_Flotilla_Panel_Report.pdf (accessed 7 March 2013).

56 United States. CRS. *Israel's Blockade of Gaza*, p. 6.

5   Pax Americana and US hegemony at sea

Nationalism and opportunism

Though the island of Taiwan is ethnically Chinese, it has had an ambiguous relationship with the mainland for centuries. Incorporated into the Qing dynasty in the 17th century, it had subsequently been ruled in part or whole by the Dutch, Spanish and French. From 1895 until 1945 it was a Japanese colony and legally recognized as such by all of the major powers. Only at the end of the Second World War did the Nationalist government in Nanking gain sovereignty.[1] Within four years, however, the Chinese communists under Mao had wrested control of the mainland in a civil war and the Nationalist Kuomintang, under Generalissimo Chiang Kai-Shek, fled to the island and established the Republic of China (RoC) there. The RoC remained officially at war with the People's Republic of China (PRC) until 1991. 'Terminating that "war" at the same time as the Cold War ended should have given Taiwan greater security. It did just the opposite'.[2]

Trade grew rapidly between China and Taiwan after 1987 when the Taiwanese authorized travel to the mainland.[3] However, an increasing sense of economic optimism on the island gave sustenance to a growing movement for true Taiwanese independence.[4] To the PRC the developments on the island were unwelcome:

> From Beijing's perspective, Taiwan has developed into a hotbed of secessionist sentiment, guided by a confederacy of island born leaders determined to evolve a political culture, economic infrastructure, and foreign policy that defines a destiny for their island distinct from that of the mainland. . . . The Republic of China quickly shed its image as a reliquary of Nationalist 'bitterenders' dedicated to a *reconquista* of the mainland. . . . PRC leaders became incensed as Taipei picked apart the Beijing-constructed arms embargo to purchase modern frigates and aircraft from France and the United States.[5]

Taiwan had fewer than 30 diplomatic allies in the world at the end of the Cold War and it thus developed a 'calculated strategy' to keep itself at 'the forefront of international attention' and remind the world of its plight.[6] China-watchers believe that threatening gestures against Taiwan can be traced to the emergence of a new leadership in China as early as 1992, but it was not until 1995–96 that tensions came to a head.[7] Taiwan embarked on its own naval diplomacy aimed at building prestige and amity; in 1995 the Taiwanese president launched his country's fifth *Oliver Hazard Perry* class guided missile frigate and 'dispatched a "friendship fleet" to Singapore, to the delight of the Chinese community there'.[8] At around the same time there were moves in Taipei to achieve another diplomatic coup and get President Lee Teng-huito to visit America.

Since 1949 the United States had followed a 'one-China' policy, which from the 1970s onwards recognized only the Beijing government as the legitimate representatives of the whole Chinese people, and no Taiwanese leader since then had been granted permission to travel to the United States. The long-established political stance was subtly changed by President Clinton in 1995 when he decided to grant a visa to Lee, not in an official capacity but as a private citizen. The decision to grant the visa was greatly influenced by the Republican-controlled House of Representatives, which was susceptible to the Taiwan lobby.[9] After repeatedly declining his previous requests, the United States allowed President Lee to make an unofficial visit to his alma mater (Cornell University) in 1995, to which the PRC objected.[10] The subsequent crisis could, therefore, be said to have been precipitated by Lee's political and diplomatic posturing.[11]

Beijing's decision to respond to the Taiwan issue through military demonstration could have been a result of its assessment of Western military-diplomatic methodology. Douglas Porch, writing about the Taiwan Strait Crisis three years after the event, judged that 'on the basis of Chinese analysis of the Gulf War, advocates [. . .] preached that a display of the PLA's capabilities during a crisis would deter an enemy'.[12] The 'enemy' to whom he is referring was both the RoC and the United States. Chinese missile 'tests' were consequently conducted from July 1995 until March 1996. In August and October 1995 air and maritime exercises were held in the East China Sea involving the firing of anti-ship missiles, and in November an amphibious exercise took place around Dungshan Island, south of the strait and similar to Taiwan in geography, terrain and weather; it made a 'good rehearsal ground'.[13] The PRC's message to intimidate, coerce and deter was clear. The November exercises were well timed to coincide with approaching Taiwanese parliamentary elections; the tactics seemed to bear fruit as candidates favourable to reconciliation with China were returned.[14] 'For China coercion and deterrence in the Taiwan Strait are as much a matter of communication and diplomatic signaling as of putting to sea potent ships, aircraft and missiles'.[15] Deterring the United States from intervening in some future 'showdown' in the strait assumed top priority for Beijing.[16]

The United States, however, was not deterred, and China's budding attempt at naval diplomacy did not entirely succeed. On 19 December 1995, following continuing tensions, the United States responded by sending the USS *Nimitz* carrier battle group through the Taiwan Strait, the first carrier to make that passage since 1979.[17] The mission for the carrier group was not to fight, but to be a highly visible and symbolic demonstration of interest. James Holmes, writing in 2009, saw the US action as entirely consistent with the Schelling's conceptual theory of coercive diplomacy discussed in Chapter 1. Carriers were sent, he reasoned, to 'protect and deter'.[18]

Taiwanese presidential elections were scheduled to take place in March 1996 and Beijing, mindful of its earlier successes in the 1995 vote, employed a similar strategy of military coercion in order to 'intimidate' Taiwan and influence the results.[19] The PRC announced that it would hold further live firing exercises in the Taiwan Strait. The United States responded in kind and directed the USS *Independence* battle group towards Taiwan, shifted the USS *George Washington* from the Adriatic to the Persian Gulf to backfill and ordered the USS *Nimitz* battle group from the Gulf to Taiwan.[20]

There is some speculation over the true target audience for the US action. It has been suggested that President Clinton dispatched the two carrier groups to the Taiwan Strait to constrain Beijing and demonstrate US naval power, but also to circumvent intense pressure from the US Congress if he failed to act.[21] The deployment became the most significant naval display in the East China Sea since the 1950s.[22]

Douglas Porch argued that the

> conventional wisdom, especially in U.S. government and naval circles, may be wrong. It holds that the arrival of two carriers effectively deterred Beijing's intimidation of Taiwan. Unfortunately, a close analysis of the crisis yields little evidence to support this thesis.[23]

Porch's point is that although the deployment of the American ships may have given the Chinese leadership 'pause', it did not alter their plans at all. The missile firings continued.[24] However, President Lee turned the missile firings to his own advantage in his political campaign and denied Beijing the successes they had enjoyed in 1995. In the March 1996 election he won handsomely with a popular vote of 54 per cent.[25] A reassessment of Porch's assertion may in fact result in a different conclusion; the conventional wisdom may be partly right. Beijing may not have been deterred but US action did reassure nationalist Taiwanese and give them the courage to side with Lee in the knowledge that they were being backed by the world's superpower. In their eyes, it would have been Pax Americana in action.

The Taiwan Strait Crisis is fascinating because it shows naval diplomacy being used to counter naval diplomacy, with interlocking activities by three parties and multiple audiences. Who the ultimate victor was, however, is still not clear. Some commentators, for instance, argued that the crisis demonstrated that the PRC was far from possessing the combination of hard and soft power it needed to become a global leader.[26] On the other hand others, such as Porch, acknowledged that the subsequent PRC investment in anti-access/area denial missile technology could work to minimize any potential US participation in a future crisis, by effectively keeping its naval forces at bay. Missiles, he stated, 'remain the near term PLA trump card'.[27] However, it was clear that 'China's response to the United States was mostly symbolic and stopped short of blatant retaliation. Beijing remained clear headed enough not to jeopardize its overall interests by sidelining China-US relations'.[28] The PRC's rise to power will be discussed further later in Chapter 6.

One of the longest running political and military operations of the 1990s and early 2000s involved ground and air participants, but also included a significant naval diplomatic element. Following the first Gulf War of 1991, the Iraq 'problem' was, in effect, 'contained' until the second Gulf War of 2003. Containment, of course, had been the strategy applied by the West to hold communism in check for most of the Cold War.[29] Western naval forces had been present in the Arabian/ Persian Gulf before 1991 and remained so throughout the containment period and beyond. They were tasked with presence through routine patrols, reassurance of partner states through bilateral and multinational exercises and operations, interdiction of vessels attempting to breach the UN sanctions which had been applied against Iraq and clearance of the residual mine threat from both 1991 and, more likely, the earlier Iran-Iraq War of the 1980s.[30] A longstanding 'general' regional role for extra-regional forces, mainly Western, became more focused in the 1990s. In many ways the Gulf mirrored the Adriatic Sea in the same period. It was crowded with the warships of interested parties, their roles were various and their underlying rationale for being there wide-ranging. To classical naval strategists such as Corbett, the naval action in the Gulf would have looked remarkably familiar: it would undoubtedly have been described as a *blockade*. An Australian naval officer and commentator agreed; James Goldrick, writing about the containment strategy, stated that 'it stretched over 13 years and was one of the longest blockade operations in history'.[31]

Unlike in East Asia, where the United States had long attempted to deter regional conflict by applying a balance of power strategy against China, in the Middle East the global superpower approached matters in a different way. This apparent lack of coherence in the American approach to foreign policy and geopolitics at the time could be because the United States did not attempt to balance *power* in the Gulf, but rather it adopted a 'balance-of-threat' approach. That is, it positioned itself and its allies not against the most powerful state but rather against one it perceived as the greatest threat.[32] It was another indication of the United States' deepening role as guarantor of peace. Iraq's influence and power beyond military adventurism was limited in comparison to wealthier states like Saudi Arabia or culturally persuasive states such as Iran, but nonetheless it did become the main target of the West's naval diplomacy.

However, the containment strategy did not just apply to Iraq. The Clinton administration from 1993 onwards shifted to a policy of 'dual containment' of both Iraq and Iran.[33]

> Dual containment had several goals. First, it aimed not only to impede the ability of Iran and Iraq to threaten neighbors but also to undermine their ability to build conventional and unconventional military capabilities. This approach, unlike deterrence, would cripple their ability to be aggressive in the first place rather than deterring already capable states from being aggressive.[34]

Iraqi containment was more militarily aggressive than that targeted at Iran. There were substantial numbers of ground troops stationed in the region and air power was used extensively. When it came to Iran, the containment was more subtle in its military dimension. It would have been politically unacceptable to use land and air power in the same way and the particular advantages of sea power in this regard, discussed in Chapter 1, meant that the burden of responsibility to demonstrate political intent fell to naval forces.

According to James Goldrick, 18 countries contributed to the naval effort in the Gulf at some stage. Beyond the United States, the United Kingdom was the 'most consistent', usually providing a single destroyer or frigate, but due to other tasks it was not always on station.[35] Much of the action can be tracked through the entries for this period in the Appendix. The building of coalitions, which were such a factor in the wars of both 1991 and 2003, also became a distinguishing trait of the intervening period. Interestingly, the mine countermeasures effort in particular became home to those who were politically unwilling or unable to become involved in more direct forms of war fighting; in addition to the United States and United Kingdom, six countries contributed (Belgium, France, Germany, Italy, Japan and the Netherlands).[36] As well as being a visible signal of support to Gulf region states, this naval diplomacy was used to demonstrate commitment to the United States, the coalition leader, and European allies. The coalition-building element of the mission was important but there were also tangible, physical results to their efforts which could be used as demonstrable evidence of success to domestic audiences. For instance, hundreds of bottom, moored and floating mines were located and appropriately dealt with.[37]

Whenever Iraq failed to act in accordance with the desires of the international community, the rheostat of coercion was turned up. At these times, those less-willing contributing states maintained their lower level constabulary and diplomatic action, leaving the projection of harder military power to others. For instance, in December 1998 following the Iraqi refusal to allow access to UN authorized weapons inspectors, the United States and United Kingdom responded with Operation *Desert Fox*, an intense four-day bombing campaign against Iraq's security infrastructure. Some of the ordnance used was land based, but much came from missile-firing warships and submarines and from aircraft carriers at sea. It caused a series of uprisings within Iraq against the regime and, possibly, a coup attempt.[38]

Containment of Saddam Hussein's Iraq lasted for 13 years but the political mood changed in the early 2000s following the al-Qaeda attacks on the United States and the Western response, much of it from sea, in Afghanistan in late 2001. It became apparent that containment had run its course and that greater military action was likely. Even at that stage, however, naval diplomacy continued to play a role. William Langenheim, writing in late 2002, immediately before the US-led invasion of Iraq, discussed the ongoing coercive diplomacy in the Gulf as a means both to garner support for war and to provide an exit strategy for Iraq. It was about giving the 'enemy' a final chance.[39] The assumption that rational actors would undertake rational, cognitive decision-making was alive and well. Indeed, playing out such arguments in the specialist naval media could be seen as a political act in itself.

The use of the sea for political gain is not limited to states. Hezbollah, for example, 'scored a major strategic coup' in July 2006 when it attacked the Israeli corvette *Hanit* with anti-ship missiles.[40] The Israeli Navy had been operating in the eastern Mediterranean, engaging land targets in Lebanon and enforcing a blockade during its small 'war'.[41] Israel was, in effect, exercising continued sea control in its locality, which had gone unchallenged since the Arab-Israeli wars of 1967 and 1973. According to Israeli figures, the operation had been successful with its ships, spending some 8,000 hours at sea and firing their weapons over 2,500 times.[42] On 14 July 2006, however, Hezbollah fired two missiles from the shore; one hit and sank a Cambodian registered cargo ship 60 km offshore while the other hit *Hanit* and killed four sailors.[43] The attack was proof that 'insurgent groups . . . do use the sea'.[44] The attack did not alter the military power dynamics of the region but perceptions were changed. The lasting 'memory' of the 2006 naval campaign is not the myriad Israeli successes, but one Hezbollah action.

The ability of Hezbollah to launch such an attack came as a surprise both to Israel and to the international community. Martin Murphy explained why terrorism and insurgency are more likely to be experienced on land:

> The reason for the low incidence of maritime terrorism is that the risk-reward ratio rarely computes. The resources groups need to undertake acts of violence at sea tend to be specialized and therefore cost more than the resources needed to mount equivalent attacks on land. More important, the rewards terrorists look for, publicity in particular, are hard to achieve at sea.[45]

However, publicity can be achieved by the unusual. Within minutes of the *Hanit* attack Hezbollah had used its own TV station, *Al Manar*, to broadcast the news and reach some 200 million viewers; it also posted a film on YouTube.[46] It is also believed that Hezbollah had acquired the missiles (understood to be the Chinese C802) from Iran, its state sponsor, and that Iran was operating by proxy.[47] Extrapolating, the Hezbollah attack on Israel was an indirect or proxy Iranian attack on the United States.

Pax Americana and the resistance to US hegemony

The examples of naval diplomacy cited thus far involve at least in part the sea power of the United States. There is a privileged discourse in international relations which supports the premise that the end of the Cold War left the United States, at least for a period of time, as the sole superpower. It might therefore be expected that the US Navy would play a significant role in consolidating American this hegemony in the early 21st century.

> With the collapse of the communist regimes in Eastern Europe and disintegration of the Soviet Union, the bipolar international system dominating the

Cold War period disappeared, leaving its place to basically a unipolar system under the leadership of the United States, speaking especially from a military/ political point of view.[48]

A Congressional Research Service Report of 2009 explained that

> although U.S. forces have traditionally focused on fighting and winning wars, defence strategy is now evolving to look at conflict prevention, or 'Phase Zero', addressing threats at their inception through increased emphasis on theater security cooperation and capacity building of allies.[49]

As has already been discussed, navies, particularly leading navies, have always acted to further national and political interests by active and latent suasion and building partnerships. However, in the 1990s and 2000s, the US Navy re-evaluated its basic functions.[50] Among other concepts, it developed the idea of the Global Fleet Station which, while not revolutionary, did much to formalize a longstanding *informal* role.

Global Fleet Stations (GFS) were an attempt to put 'presence' missions on a more permanent footing. By continuously deploying to areas of interest, it was envisaged that the GFS could exert leverage to strengthen relationships and build capacity within the targeted countries and regions. In addition, they could also be used to indirectly counter the attempts by other 'forward-leaning' states, such as China, to garner influence of their own. They are a maritime, 21st-century manifestation of the 19th century's 'Great Game' or the late 20th century's Cold War by proxy. Often working in parts of the world not subject to general public or mainstream media attention, the GFS had little in the way of a domestic agenda within the United States and their political and diplomatic utility was therefore almost entirely concentrated on the area with which they were engaged. With its GFS, the United States was effectively reasserting its place as a naval superpower and putting naval diplomacy at the centre of its strategy.

The US Southern Command sponsored the first pilot GFS mission from April to September 2007, using the high-speed vessel (HSV 2) *Swift*. During the course of its deployment *Swift* visited seven Caribbean and Central American countries and its ship's company conducted almost 40,000 man-hours of 'subject matter expert' exchanges with partners in topics such as leadership, small boat operations, port security and small unit tactics.[51]

The pilot was deemed to be a success, with commentators writing such positive reviews as 'the GFS represents a great opportunity to build civil-military communication and coordination practices that can be leveraged in any theater in the event of war'.[52]

Buoyed by the initial experience of Southern Command, the newly formed Africa Command developed its own GFS and concentrated its efforts along the Atlantic coastline of West Africa. Commenting on the initiative, one writer stated that 'it is salutary that the U.S. Navy, rather than the Army, is taking the lead in a new strategic effort in Africa'.[53] Salutary it may be, but based on historical precedent, it should be no surprise.

The Africa Command GFS was named the Africa Partnership Station (APS) and consisted of a small and varied group of warships and completed its first six-month deployment in the Gulf of Guinea in 2008.[54] The APS was designed to assist the regional maritime community to develop better maritime governance and to serve as a base from which to deliver humanitarian assistance and disaster relief if required.[55]

> The African Partnership Station has already earned the confidence and enthusiastic participation of most littoral West African states, and it remains at once the most operationally effective and politically agreeable component of the military engagement of the United States with sub-Saharan Africa. In that light it may well prove Africa Command's most politically valuable strategic asset.[56]

How the APS went about its business, however, was not necessarily original. As with countless flag-flying or ambassadorial deployments before it, the ships of the APS relied on manipulating the basic building blocks of human nature: 'In addition to providing relief assistance during the visit, sailors from *Swift* will conduct a community relations project, meet with local officials, play soccer with the Cameroon Navy, and support a diplomatic reception aboard the ship'.[57] In 2013 the US Africa Command was still employing the APS in support of its primary naval mission, 'to improve the maritime security capability and capacity of African partners'.[58] There is much to be said about learning from the lessons of history, however trivial they might initially appear.

Three years later, however, the *Swift* became the central feature in very different circumstances. Transferred to the United Arab Emirates and used in support of the Saudi-led coalition's conflict in Yemen, *Swift* was attacked and badly damaged in the Bab-el-Mandeb Strait, allegedly by Houthi rebel fighters.[59] The ability of a non-state actor (albeit with *de facto* territorial control within failed state) to effectively close one of the world's strategic choke points became a matter of grave concern, particularly for the US Navy. It also came of no great surprise in the information war when a video of the attack on the *Swift* was posted on YouTube.

However, before the *Swift* incident the US Navy engaged in partnership ventures in other parts of the world. A former US naval and marine attaché to Vietnam described a visit to Danang in July 2007 by the Pacific Partnership, a humanitarian assistance mission conducted in several South East Asian ports by USS *Peleliu*, an amphibious assault ship, and its embarked medical, dental and engineering teams. Though it was not the first US ship visit since the end of the Vietnam War, it was characterized as a 'watershed in the development of the bilateral military relationship'.[60]

If the early post-Cold War era was a time of Pax Americana, it was not made so by the United States alone. Its closest allies and partners adopted much the same methodologies, either by design or dint of circumstance. Australia's experiences in East Timor are perhaps a good example. After the withdrawal of the colonial power, Portugal, East Timor's larger neighbour Indonesia overran the state in

1975. After the invasion the local population had an uncomfortable relationship with their new overlords and never accepted Indonesian sovereignty.[61] Violence periodically erupted and came to a head in 1999. In September of that year the United Nations created the International Force East Timor (INTERFRET) and it deployed under Australian leadership. The violent conflict was quelled and the operation ended on 23 February 2000 when INTERFRET handed over to the UN Transitional Administration East Timor.[62] Subsequently, Indonesia accepted East Timorese independence.

Like many peace missions, the ultimate success or failure of INTERFRET was determined on the ground, amongst the people. However, the commander of the operation, Major General P. J. Cosgrove, was in no doubt about the contribution that the coercive power of navies made:

> Another military blinding glimpse of the obvious . . . the persuasive, intimidating or deterrent nature of major warships was not to me as the combined joint force commander an incidental, nice to have 'add on' but an important indicator of national and international resolve and most reassuring to all of us who relied on the sea lifelines. It was a classic case of the 'presence' pillar of sea power.[63]

However, there are consequences of intervention and the East Timor experience was no exception. Challenges to US-led Western hegemony come in various forms and it has been suggested that the bombing of a Bali disco popular with Australian tourists in 2004 may have been a direct result of Australia's involvement four years earlier.[64]

A particular challenge to US and Western hegemony came from one notoriously opportunistic quarter, and one not reluctant to use its own military and naval forces for political advantage: North Korea. As the Taiwanese commentator To-hai Liou has written:

> There is a Chinese saying that weak countries have no diplomacy at all. Realists in the West, particularly neo-realists, also believe that international engagement is largely shaped by major powers. Minor and middle powers have no choice but to follow the rules of the game as constructed by major powers, but not without exception. North Korea's diplomacy in the post-cold war era is the best example of a minor power making a difference in world politics.[65]

To-hai Liou went on to explain that because of its extremely limited economic capacity, North Korea had no choice but to focus on strengthening its military capabilities in an attempt to negotiate from a position of relative strength.[66] Despite being mired in economic woes, North Korea has a track record of threatening its more powerful rivals with military action. It has 'deliberately and repeatedly' resorted to brinkmanship in order to benefit from the crises it creates. For example, during a 1993–94 crisis surrounding North Korea's attempts to develop a nuclear capability, it overtly threatened to wage all-out war with the South if the United States dared to initiate any military action against it. It is an approach with historical precedent on the Korean peninsula and is perhaps another example of Schelling's classic game theory being put to practical use. Its strategy could be considered successful because, in the end, Pyongyang obtained two light-water nuclear reactors from the United States along with an annual supply of 500,000 tonnes of heavy oil.[67] In these stark terms, brinkmanship worked.

North Korea's strategy often relies on playing one adversary off against another, particularly South Korea and the United States, and it has been regularly applied at sea. Its use of naval diplomacy is an interesting variation on what might be described as 'standard' practice. A notable example took place in September 1996 when a North Korean submarine was discovered in South Korean territorial waters. South Korea regarded the incursion as an attempted 'spying' mission while, at least publicly, the United States had to be convinced that it was anything more than a navigational error. Similar incursions by Soviet submarines had, of course, been relatively commonplace in European waters during the Cold War. Notwithstanding the fact that Washington acknowledged the necessity of a diplomatic apology from North Korea and Pyongyang's promise not to commit the same mistake again, the United States did not agree with Seoul's more aggressive approach of attempting to use to the incident as leverage against the construction of the North Korean nuclear reactors. North Korea's *mea culpa* effectively allowed it to be portrayed as the reasonable party, the victim of South Korea's disproportionate response. However, the Clinton administration did not want to see its previously agreed and hard-won framework damaged by South Korea's tough stance towards Pyongyang.[68] North Korea had, quite simply, applied a simple tactic of submarine naval diplomacy to stoke disagreement over response between its two major critics. At the time of writing (2018), US/North Korean tensions are once again high and threats are made on both sides.

A more aggressive application of submarine naval diplomacy by North Korea took place in March 2010. Considered by some in the South to be the severest military provocation since the Korean War armistice, the North attacked and sank the Southern warship *Cheonan*.[69] Previous conventional naval skirmishes between the two Koreas, such as an exchange of fire in the Yellow Sea off Daechung in November 2009 when warships from the North entered disputed territorial waters, had tended to end in greater military success for the South.[70] The North's solution to its comparable naval disadvantage was to turn to asymmetric tactics, particularly those which could carry a degree of plausible deniability.[71]

Accusations of responsibility for the sinking of *Cheonan* with the loss of 46 lives were rejected by Pyongyang, though there was little doubt amongst the international community that the North Korean regime was to blame. What is interesting about the *Cheonan* incident is why North Korea took the seemingly irrational action that it did, and the reaction to it by other parties. Mikyoung Kim, a South Korean academic working at the Hiroshima Peace Institute in Japan, wrote that neither Seoul nor Tokyo could provide a convincing motive for the attack.[72]

This underlines an unchanging truth about the efficacy of naval diplomacy: outcomes will be limited if the intended audience cannot understand the policy which forms its context. However, Kim did proffer the opinion that Pyongyang's behaviour could have its genesis in its exaggeration of external threats, which it used to consolidate its power with its domestic audience. Influence over the succession of leader and forcing the United States to the negotiating table in order to secure other benefits could also have been factors in its political calculations.[73] Such an exaggeration of threat in order to legitimize subsequent actions is classic 'securitization'. Should Pyongyang's actions indeed be the product of a securitization agenda, it is perhaps a new outlet for naval diplomacy.

Though the UN Security Council condemned the sinking, and the United States claimed that the incident had 'strengthened' its alliance with the South, North Korea achieved its aim. The East Asia region was 'rattled' by the unprovoked action.[74] However, there was no immediate decisive response from China, North Korea's only ally, to either condemn or restrain its behaviour.[75] In fact, one leading Chinese commentator went so far as to state that since the incident Beijing's assistance to and investment in North Korea had increased. From the viewpoint of the Chinese leadership, the survival of the Pyongyang regime worked to its advantage because it forced Washington, Seoul and Tokyo to co-operate on building regional security, rather than focus on Chinese military expansion as a source of regional instability in itself.[76] China's role in the aftermath of the *Cheonan* affair is not dissimilar to its stance after the *Pueblo* incident of four decades earlier. As an exercise in naval diplomacy the *Cheonan* incident might be regarded as achieving successful outcomes for its instigator, but also indirectly benefiting another, larger neighbour.

Notes

1 Copper, John F. *Taiwan: Nations State or Province?, 4th Ed.* (Boulder, CO: Westview Press, 2003), p. 186.
2 Ibid., p. 185.
3 Clough, Ralph. *Cooperation or Conflict in the Taiwan Strait.* (Oxford: Rowman & Littlefield, 1999), p. ix.
4 Porch, Douglas. 'The Taiwan Strait Crisis of 1996: Strategic Implications for the United States Navy.' *U.S. Naval War College Review* 52, No. 3 (1999): p. 16.
5 Ibid., p. 17.
6 Lijun, Sheng. *China's Dilemma: The Taiwan Issue.* (Singapore: Institute of South East Asian Studies, 2001), p. 2.
7 Porch, 'The Taiwan Strait Crisis of 1996', p. 16.
8 Ibid., p. 18.
9 Lijun, *China's Dilemma*, p. 25.
10 Clough, *Cooperation or Conflict in the Taiwan Strait*, p. 2.
11 Bush, Richard. *Untying the Knot: Making Peace in the Taiwan Strait.* (Washington, DC: Brookings, 2005).
12 Porch, 'The Taiwan Strait Crisis of 1996', p. 18.
13 Lijun, *China's Dilemma*, p. 28.
14 Porch, 'The Taiwan Strait Crisis of 1996', p. 19.

15 Holmes, James. 'Schelling Goes to Sea: Managing Perceptions in China's Contested Zone.' *Defence Studies* 9, No. 2 (2009): p. 189.
16 Ibid., p. 191.
17 Porch, 'The Taiwan Strait Crisis of 1996', p. 19.
18 Holmes, 'Schelling Goes to Sea', p. 190.
19 Ibid.
20 Porch, 'The Taiwan Strait Crisis of 1996', p. 20.
21 Copper, *Taiwan*, p. 206.
22 Porch, 'The Taiwan Strait Crisis of 1996', p. 15.
23 Ibid., pp. 15–16.
24 Ibid., p. 21.
25 Ibid., p. 22.
26 Lijun, *China's Dilemma*, p. 56.
27 Porch, 'The Taiwan Strait Crisis of 1996', p. 30.
28 Lijun, *China's Dilemma*, p. 68.
29 For the classic text on containment, see George Kennan's 'long telegram': Kennan, George. 'Telegram to George Marshall.' 22 February 1946. www.trumanlibrary.org/whistlestop/study_collections/coldwar/documents/pdf/6-6.pdf (accessed 15 February 2013).
30 Davis, Steven J., Murphy, Kevin M. & Topel, Robert. *War in Iraq versus Containment.* (Chicago: University of Chicago, 2006), p. 1.
31 Goldrick, James. 'Maritime Sanctions Enforcement against Iraq 1990–2003.' In Elleman, Bruce & Paine, S.C.M. (Eds.). *Naval Blockades and Seapower: Strategies and Counter-Strategies 1805–2005.* (London: Routledge, 2006), p. 201.
32 Yetiv, Steve A. *The Absence of Grand Strategy: The United States in the Persian Gulf, 1972–2005.* (Baltimore: Johns Hopkins University Press, 2008), p. 4. For 'balance of threat' see: Walt, Stephen M. 'Alliance Formation and the Balance of World Power.' *International Security* 9, No. 4 (1985): pp. 3–43.
33 Yetiv, *The Absence of Grand Strategy*, p. 91.
34 Ibid., p. 92.
35 Goldrick, 'Maritime Sanctions Enforcement against Iraq 1990–2003', p. 209.
36 Pokrant, Marvin. *Desert Storm at Sea.* (Westport, CT: Greenwood Press, 1999), p. 193.
37 Ibid., p. 196.
38 Langenheim, William S. 'Give Peace a Chance: First, Try Coercive Diplomacy.' *U.S. Naval War College Review* 55, No. 4 (2002): p. 65.
39 Ibid., p. 50.
40 Hilburn, Matt. 'Hezbollah's Surprise.' *Sea Power* 49, No. 9 (2006): p. 10.
41 Polmar, Norman. 'Hezbollah Attack: Lesson's for the LCS.' *USNI Proceedings* 132, No. 9 (2006): p. 88.
42 Cordesman, Anthony, Sullivan, George & Sullivan, William. *Lessons of the 2006 Israeli-Hezbollah War.* Significant Issues Series Vol 29, No. 4. (Washington, DC: Center for Strategic & International Studies, 2007), p. 133.
43 Ibid., p. 131.
44 Murphy, Martin. 'The Unwanted Challenge.' *USNI Proceedings* 134, No. 12 (2008): p. 46.
45 Ibid.
46 Caldwell, William, Murphy, Dennis & Menning, Anton. 'Learning to Leverage New Media: The Israeli Defence Forces in Recent Conflicts.' *Military Review* 89, No. 3 (2009): p. 4.
47 Hilburn, 'Hezbollah's Surprise', p. 10.
48 Yilmaz, Muzaffer Ercan. 'The New World Order: An Outline of the Post-Cold War Era.' *Alternatives: Turkish Journal of International Relations* 7, No. 4 (2008): p. 45.
49 United States. Congressional Research Service. Ploch, L. *Africa Command: U.S. Strategic Interests and the Role of the U.S. Military in Africa.* RL34003. (Washington, DC: CRS, 2010), p. 4.

50 In the first ten years after the end of the Cold War the US Navy subjected itself to almost continuous reassessment. Its outlook and vision was published in 'The Way Ahead' (1991), 'The Naval Policy Book' (1992), '. . . From the Sea' (1992), 'Naval Warfare' (1994), 'Forward . . . from the Sea' (1994), 'The Navy Operational Concept' (1997), 'Anytime, Anywhere' (1997), and 'Navy Strategic Planning Guidance' (2000). For a precis and critical evaluation of each see Hattendorf, *U.S. Naval Strategy in the 1990s.*

51 Sohn, Kathi A. 'The Global Fleet Station: A Powerful Tool for Preventing Conflicts.' *U.S. Naval War College Review* 62, No. 1 (2009): p. 50.

52 Ibid., p. 48.

53 Stevenson, Jonathan. 'The U.S. Navy into Africa.' *U.S. Naval War College Review* 62, No. 1 (2009): p. 61.

54 United States. Congressional Research Service. Ploch, *Africa Command: U.S. Strategic Interests and the Role of the U.S. Military in Africa*, p. 20.

55 Sohn, 'The Global Fleet Station', p. 45.

56 Stevenson, 'The U.S. Navy into Africa', p. 64.

57 Sohn, 'The Global Fleet Station', p. 51.

58 United States. Africa Command. *U.S. Naval Forces Africa.* www.africom.mil/about-the-command/subordinate-commands/navaf.htm (accessed 17 June 2013).

59 Al Jazeera. 'Yemen: Houthis Claim Attack on UAE Military Vessel.' 2 October 2016. www.aljazeera.com/news/2016/10/yemen-houthis-claim-attack-uae-military-vessel-161001212236896.html (accessed 21 February 2018).

60 Lucius, Robert E. 'Pacific Partnership Visits Vietnam.' *U.S. Naval War College Review* 60, No. 4 (2007): p. 125.

61 Australia. Alan Ryan. *From Desert Storm to East Timor: Australia, the Asia-Pacific and the New Age Coalition Operations.* Study Paper 37. (Duntroon, ACT: Land Warfare Studies Centre, 2000), p. 10.

62 Ibid., p. 135.

63 Stevens, *The Royal Australian Navy*, Vol 3, pp. 292–293.

64 Cotton, James. *East Timor, Australia and Regional Order.* (Abingdon: Routledge, 2004), p. 141.

65 Liou, To-hai. 'North Korea's Diplomatic Strategies in the Post-Cold War Era: Fishing in Troubled Waters.' *International Journal of Korean Unification Studies* 10, No. 2 (2001): p. 79.

66 Ibid., p. 82.

67 Ibid.

68 Ibid., p. 92.

69 Kim, Duk-Ki. 'The Republic of Korea's Counter-Asymmetric Strategy.' *U.S. Naval War College Review* 65, No. 1 (2012): p. 55.

70 Foster, Peter. 'North and South Korea Warships Exchange Fire.' *Daily Telegraph*, 10 November 2009.

71 Kim, 'The Republic of Korea's Counter-Asymmetric Strategy', p. 55.

72 Kim, Mikyoung. 'The Cheonan Incident and East Asian Community Debate: North Korea's Place in the Region.' *East Asia* 28, No. 4 (2011): p. 285.

73 Ibid.

74 Kim, 'The Cheonan Incident and East Asian Community Debate', p. 276.

75 Zhu, Feng. 'Flawed Mediation and a Compelling Mission: Chinese Diplomacy in the Six Party Talks to Denuclearise North Korea.' *East Asia* 28, No. 3 (2011): p. 203.

76 Ibid., pp. 195–196.

6 The return of great power rivalry

If the immediate post-Cold War period was a moment of superpower victory for the United States and its supporting allies, then the newly unipolar world view did not go unchallenged for long. The opportunist and nationalist agendas of some actors have already been discussed, but it was the relentless economic rise of the BRICS, and China and India in particular, which did most to bring about a new global multi-polarity. As the former prime minister of India, I. K. Gujral, wrote: 'we are [. . .] witnessing the emergence of multiple economic power centres that are beginning to assert themselves with different perceptions and different goals'.[1] Indeed, as another commentator suggested, 'from an economic/political point of view [. . .] the international system can be said to be multipolar, rather than unipolar'.[2]

This Indian and Chinese economic ascendency differed significantly from that of the late 20th-century powerhouses of Germany and Japan, limited as they were from a simultaneous military expansion by post-World War II settlements. Despite the fact that in his influential text on China's 'peaceful rise' Zheng Bijiang claimed that his country would not pursue hegemony, increased Chinese and Indian economic power *was* accompanied by military growth and both countries have recognized the importance of the maritime domain when determining their futures.[3]

The rising powers' maritime ambitions in the Asia-Pacific and Indian Ocean regions can be understood in starkly realist, geopolitical terms; according to one analysis, the assumptions and arguments of the ascendants are unmistakably Mahanian.[4] Commenting specifically on Chinese military diplomacy, the US Center for Naval Analyses offered that 'since the 1990s the People's Republic of China (PRC) has become a ubiquitous presence on the world stage'.[5] Similarly, speaking at the US Naval War College in November 2007, Rear Admiral Chopra of the Indian Navy declared that his country should 'emulate America's nineteenth century rise to sea power' as it made its way in the world.[6] The two countries are, therefore, suitable candidates for a deeper investigation of naval diplomatic activities in support of national power.

Of the two rising Asian powers, India's naval expansion has received less attention in the West, but there has been a definite shift in focus towards the maritime domain, as Waheguru Singh Sidhu and Jing-dong Yuan noted in 2003 when writing a comparative analysis of India and China:

Since the late 1970s, India has shifted its emphasis from the army to the navy. . . . Strategic intentions are to establish predominance in the Indian Ocean . . . and prevent other powers, such as China and Japan, from making inroads in the area.[7]

This assertion seems to have been upheld in a 2007 speech by Indian Defence Secretary Shri Shekhar Dutt to a New Delhi seminar on defence, security and diplomacy. Dutt stated that although securing his country's borders remained the first priority, India's area of interest now extended far beyond the confines of the subcontinent. India's security environment, he argued, 'extends from the Persian Gulf to the Straits of Malacca across the Indian Ocean'.[8] The environment he was referring to, India's self-declared 'extended neighbourhood', was clearly maritime in character and geography.[9] To exert influence over such vast swathes of the globe, by what Dutt termed 'promoting co-operation and understanding', would require a sizeable navy capable of deliberate diplomatic missions in pursuit of foreign policy objectives.[10]

During the Cold War and into the 1990s the Indian Navy's activities tended to sit at the 'hard' end of the power spectrum, with deployments centred on support to the Sri Lankan government's fight against the Tamil Tigers or, more commonly, on deterrence missions against Pakistan. As an example, in the wake of the Kargil crisis of 1999, when Pakistani forces crossed the line of control into the disputed territory, India put its navy on alert and altered the deployment plans for its Eastern and Western Fleets. This overt manoeuvring sent a signal that any 'misadventure' by Pakistan would be firmly dealt with, and India later claimed that its naval response had had a definitive effect on the outcome of the crisis.[11]

However, from around the turn of the 21st century India increasingly used its navy for soft power purposes. The Indian Navy declared that its theme for 2000 would be 'Building Bridges of Friendship'.[12] Since then it has regularly dispatched its aircraft carrier, INS *Viraat*, into the Gulf and during one 24-month period between 2005 and 2007 'around 40' Indian warships were deployed either into the Gulf or to Oman for diplomatic purposes.[13] It commenced the *Varuna* series of bilateral naval exercises with France in 2001, resumed the *Malabar* exercises with the United States in 2002, the *Indra* exercises with Russia in 2003, and *Konkan* with the United Kingdom in 2004.[14] After its non-alignment stance during the Cold War, India was using every opportunity to build amity, and not only with those states physically bordering its 'security environment', or with those sharing a colonial history. Its outreach was bigger than that.

Following the attacks of 11 September 2001 in New York and the subsequent Western-led war on terror, the Indian Navy was used to signal a small but important message. Though it did not contribute directly to the war on terror, under the banner of Operation *Sagittarius* the Indian Navy escorted high-value vessels through the Strait of Malacca choke point en route to the Middle East.[15] At Mexican request, the Indian Navy also escorted a sail training ship through the Strait in early 2002.[16] After the Cold War, during which India was viewed with semi-suspicion by the Western bloc, its navy was in the forefront of rehabilitation with the (Western) international community.

Concurrently, India developed its humanitarian assistance and disaster relief capabilities, attributes which were particularly key in its maritime area of interest. The Indian Navy played a part in the aftermath of the Sumatra earthquake and tsunami of Boxing Day 2004, a role closely watched and later emulated by China, and in 2006 INS *Rajput* became the first foreign warship on the scene to conduct relief operations after another earthquake in Indonesia.[17] On its return from the Mediterranean in 2006, a long-range sortie which showcased its expeditionary capabilities to watching parties, an Indian naval task group diverted to Lebanon to conduct a non-combatant evacuation operation from Beirut; around 2,280 Indian, Sri Lankan and Nepalese nationals were collected and taken to a place of safety.[18]

In a novel method of winning friends, from the mid-2000s the Indian Navy conducted a number of hydrographic surveys of other states' exclusive economic zones. One such deployment occurred in March and April 2007 when INS *Sarvekshak* surveyed Mauritius and then presented the completed charts to the country's prime minister in a special ceremony.[19] Of course, such activity may not be entirely altruistic and India could be set to profit from the knowledge gained. Nonetheless, both parties were content with the arrangement, and similar activities have since taken place in co-operation with the Maldives and Seychelles.

It is possible that India's non-threatening and 'independent' status is in itself an attractive proposition to the lesser developed countries in its 'extended neighbourhood', making India a partner of choice for those states lacking a national naval capability. For instance, Mozambique, on the far African shores of the Indian Ocean, requested and was afforded maritime security by the Indian Navy for a series of major events. In July 2003 INS *Ranjit* and *Suvarna* deployed there to provide seaward protection during an African Union summit in Maputo.[20] The following year INS *Savitri* and *Sujata* did the same, first during a World Economic Forum meeting and later a meeting of Afro-Pacific-Caribbean heads of state. On those occasions the Indian Navy took the opportunity to extend Indian influence further by giving medical treatment to 450 patients and training to the Mozambique Navy.[21]

India's interest in furthering its position in Africa did not end there, and in 2008 its ships deployed to the Gulf of Aden for anti-piracy patrols in parallel with the NATO deployment Operation *Ocean Shield* and, importantly, in close proximity to Chinese missions in the same region.[22]

What these examples help to show is that with the end of the Cold War, New Delhi's world view changed. No longer was the Indian Navy a 'Cinderella Service', destined for marginalization in comparison to the other armed forces, but a major weapon in its government's diplomatic arsenal.[23] Becoming a global actor required India to have a global navy and it got one.

When China is considered in greater detail, it becomes apparent that it too required a significant naval element in its 'pursuit of greatness':

> Over the past two decades, China has been steadily developing naval power, which it has regarded as a necessary attribute of great power status. As China

rises in economic power, its maritime interests similarly expand (and with it its naval power).[24]

Of course, 21st-century China differs from the contemporary, post-Westphalian West and from India in the way that its military establishment relates to other elements of government. Consequently, it differs in the way that its political establishment can be manifestly influenced by military considerations. The result is perhaps a politico-military construct reminiscent of the Cold War authoritarian East, though the PRC may be cognizant of this and slowly changing. Indeed, 'strength of numbers and the PLA's historical legacy under Mao have ensured that the Chinese military has retained a role in shaping foreign policy but its degree of influence has waxed and waned in the decades after Mao's passing'.[25] As the US Center for Naval Analyses points out:

> The most fundamental point to make is that the PLA's conduct of foreign military relations is considered to be a strategic level activity by the Chinese leadership. . . . In this regard the 'political' and the 'military' are inseparable. The PLA's military activities are viewed by both the PLA and China's civilian leadership as a political undertaking using military means for strategic reasons, not as a freestanding set of military initiatives by military professionals for explicitly military reasons.[26]

China's own 2010 white paper on national defence describes the (at least outwardly) social and developmental roles of its armed forces, roles which would be purely political activity in the West. In that respect it is more reminiscent of Gorshkov than of Mahan. Amongst its strategic objectives it lists the maintenance of social harmony, world peace and stability. Within the last point it specifically discusses its cooperative military relations, relations that are 'non-aligned, non-confrontational and not directed at any third party'.[27]

Some theorists have argued that by depicting itself in this way, as an 'inherently defensive power, China has set a standard for its behaviour at sea'.[28] It might therefore be deduced that the PLAN is being optimized for the exercise of soft, or at least smart, power in its growing role on the world stage.

In a 2007 assessment, the US Office of Naval Intelligence stated that the Chinese Navy's interaction with foreign countries had four major components: high-level exchanges, ship visits, functional exchanges and arms sales and purchases.[29] Of note, the assessment made no mention of either bilateral or multilateral exercises, a strategy which China had been already pursuing for a number of years. The Chinese themselves have described how:

> Maritime joint exercises have been held on a regular basis. In 2003 China ran a joint maritime search and rescue exercise with Pakistan, the first ever between China and a foreign country. During mutual port calls and other activities the PLAN has run bilateral or multilateral joint maritime exercises with the navies of India, France, the UK, Australia, Thailand, the US, Russia, Japan, New Zealand and Vietnam. . . . In 2007 and 2009 the PLAN

participated in multilateral joint maritime exercises organized by the Pakistan Navy. In 2007 the PLAN took part in the joint maritime exercise held in Singaporean waters within the framework of the Western Pacific Naval Symposium. In 2010 China held a joint maritime training [*sic*] with Thailand, the first ever between China and a foreign country.[30]

As American forays into Africa had been led by its Navy, so too did the PLAN take the van as China began to exercise its military forces with foreign states. Chapter 1 discussed the relative ease with which naval forces can be turned to low-level, symbolic engagement; to achieve the same results with their air and land counterparts requires a far greater expression of political will by government. As the Chinese Information Office stated above, the PLAN first exercised with Pakistan in 2003, but it was not until 2007 that the first joint military training on land was carried out.[31]

The PLAN's sudden appearance on the world stage after decades of virtual introversion did not go unnoticed and it triggered some concerns amongst other regional actors. It could have made India 'alarmist, at times almost panicky'.[32] How China then adjusted its strategy to meet regional concerns is worthy of consideration. It is interesting to note how the type of bilateral exercise conducted could in itself indicate the relative warmth of any particular relationship. Geoffrey Till has pointed out that 'in contrast to its exercises with other navies, Sino-Indian exercises have so far been largely limited to search and rescue operations'.[33] SAR, of course, is a low rung on the naval co-operation ladder, but a rung nonetheless.

A similarly low rung, but one which has historically been an effective means of gaining and exerting influence, is the port visit. During the Cold War and in the early 1990s, Chinese ships rarely visited foreign ports and when they did, the visits were exclusively confined to the Asia-Pacific region. In the period 1985–97 the PLAN made just 14 foreign visits. In contrast, in the decade after 1997 the rate of ceremonial visits increased threefold and 46 visits were made, including six to North America, five to South America, eight to Europe and three to African ports.[34] It was the beginning of an unprecedented outreach strategy.

In its analysis, the US Office of Naval Intelligence identified 1997 as the watershed for the Chinese Navy. Its increased activity starting that year and its use as a means of furthering national interests abroad was part of a deliberate attempt to underline the PRC's rise to greatness:

The first year China dispatched two task forces in a single year was 1997. It was also the first time a PLAN vessel visited South America. Indeed, this was the first time a PLAN vessel visited anywhere outside the Asia-Pacific region. The growing quantity and scope of PLAN voyages beginning in 1997 illustrates the increased foreign-policy role China assigns to its naval fleet. During those 1997 voyages, the PLAN assigned precedence to showing the Chinese flag abroad at the expense of Chinese military readiness. The overriding goal was to illustrate to the people of those countries, including overseas Chinese who visited the ships in huge numbers during port calls, that China and the PLAN were both open to the outside world and no longer just a backward coastal navy. Significantly, China simultaneously deployed its only two relatively capable, reasonably modern warships, the two new *Luhu*-class guided-missile destroyers, away from Chinese waters. The readiness of these ships to participate in some potential crisis, such as in the Taiwan Strait, was effectively subordinated to the value of sending these ships to North and South America and to three ASEAN countries.[35]

Ken Booth's prestige thesis had found a ready home in modern China.

Indian analysts were amongst the first to perceive a change of tack in China's use of the PLAN. A New Delhi analysis from 2001 noted that 'port calls to various countries signified the active role of the PLAN in the making of China's foreign policy'.[36] It also noted that when compared to earlier periods when the Chinese Navy was effectively a coastal defence force rather than an outward-looking blue-water navy, its visits had become showcases for China's long reach. In particular, it asserted that China was exhibiting the 'political and strategic resolve to contain its adversaries' through its deployments.[37] Because India had been at war with China as recently as 1962 and the two countries had been regional competitors since, it might consider itself one of the 'adversaries' to be contained.

Beyond ship visits and the occasional exercise, China also began to develop strategic dialogues with other actors that it perceived to be important in shaping the international security situation, such as the United Kingdom, Australia, South Africa and Japan.[38] The PLAN conducted joint patrols of the Beibu Gulf/Gulf of Tonkin with the Vietnamese Navy and, of course, it contributed to the multi-national counter-piracy effort off the Horn of Africa. There can be no doubt that these engagements were targeted affairs and not acts of random kindness. China itself claimed to take 'a proactive and open attitude to international escort cooperation' and by 2010 had established mechanisms for regular intelligence sharing with several countries and international organizations, including the EU, NATO, Russia, the Republic of Korea, the Netherlands and Japan.[39] As the US Center for Naval Analyses pointed out, 'China's footprint is no longer confined to the Asia Pacific region'.[40]

The PLAN foray into Horn of Africa counter-piracy operations, commencing in 2008 and continuing to this day, is perhaps the best example of this extended footprint. The destroyers *Wuhan* and *Haikou*, accompanied by their replenishment vessel *Weishan Hu*, were their country's first extra-regional deploying vessels and were able to remain on task for three months; many more similar deployments followed.[41] As well as affording the PLAN an opportunity to challenge itself at range from its home bases and to operate alongside other navies, the counter-piracy effort significantly altered how other powers viewed China. As one Indian commentator wrote, 'the Chinese Navy is here to stay for a long time to come – piracy or no piracy'.[42] A deeper, more insightful analysis, which identified a number of domestic, regional and international stakeholders in China's naval counter-piracy strategy, was offered by two Dutch academics:

The Chinese government has multiple interests at stake when it comes to addressing Somali piracy.

1   The presence of the Chinese Navy signals to the rest of the world that China is among the leading actors regarding maritime security in the Indian Ocean.

2   It contributes to Beijing's ability to protect its interests in a region of great economic importance. Both shipping lanes and the countries of the Middle East and Africa play a major part in China's external economic relations.

3   Beijing has shown its own population that it is capable of protecting Chinese property and lives from piracy attacks, and that the Chinese vessels need not rely on foreign navies for their protection. In other words, this shows that China is a great power and the leadership of the CCP [Chinese Communist Party] is taking up this responsibility.

4   The counter-piracy mission serves to underscore the fact that China – not the Taiwanese government – protects Taiwan's shipping interests. Thus the Chinese claim that Taiwan is part of China is bolstered.[43]

China appears to be self-satisfied with its naval outreach strategy, openly lauding its own achievements. Its 2010 defence white paper declared that

> the Chinese Navy has dispatched, in seven sorties, 18 ship deployments, 16 helicopters, and 490 Special Operation Force (SOF) soldiers on escort missions. Through accompanying escort, area patrol, and onboard escort, the Chinese Navy has provided protection for 3139 ships sailing under Chinese and foreign flags, rescued 29 ships from pirate attacks, and recovered nine ships released from captivity.[44]

China was telling its own people and the world of its contribution to the international community.

China had also taken note of the reputational gains to be made by fielding a credible ability to contribute to humanitarian operations. Following the West's, and India's, response to the 2006 Asian tsunami, which the PLAN had been largely powerless to mirror, it launched a new hospital ship called the *Peace Ark*.[45] Entry into the humanitarian assistance 'club' was a shrewd move for a country with a rather dubious record of human rights. As Holmes and Yoshihara have written:

> China's soft power strategy seems based on the premise that a nation can store up international good will by supplying 'international public goods' like maritime security, which benefit all nations with a stake in the international order.[46]

Though the PLAN may have begun to be optimized for soft power in pursuit of its diplomatic role, it did not ignore the harder end of the spectrum. The PRC's troubled relationship with Taiwan has already been discussed and one commentator, unconvinced by China's new 'soft' approach, went so far as to suggest that the PLAN 'now seems almost wholly, even obsessively, focused on the Taiwan problem. . . . These factors already seem to be seriously intruding into Chinese strategic thinking'.[47] However, an effective combination of soft and hard power is not impossible to achieve and the PRC was either potentially very adept at balancing both, or content to permit constructive debate over the future direction of its sea power.

When a rising power faces the existing hegemon there will inevitably a suggestion of rivalry. Leszek Buszynski identified causal relationships between the American support for Taiwan, and China's handling of its territorial disputes in the South China Sea:

> From a Chinese perspective, the U.S. naval presence in the western Pacific prevents the reunification of Taiwan with the mainland and emboldens the ASEAN claimants in the South China Sea to oppose Chinese claims.[48]

The South China, East China and Yellow Seas are rife with maritime territorial disputes involving the PRC, the Republic of China, Vietnam, the Philippines, Malaysia, Brunei and Indonesia, and over the past several decades China has been accused of bullying behaviour in the region.[49] In addition it has been suggested that China also attempted to 'alter international norms concerning freedom of navigation for military purposes and to roll back the balance of coastal state and international rights in coastal zones that were negotiated in the development of UNCLOS' to fit better with its own claims.[50] However, Lyle Goldstein of the US Naval War College China Maritime Studies Institute suggested that there had been much rhetoric or 'bluster' about the seas from the PRC:

> A stereotypical view of the Chinese Navy in the West and especially in the United States is that of a group inclined, whether by professional disposition, nationalist inclination, or bureaucratic self interest to favour aggressive naval expansion. However, the [Chinese language] sources illustrate a considerably more complex picture. There are hawkish views on the South China Sea, to be sure, but these views exist alongside more practical, cautious and even enlightened views as well.[51]

That the disparate positions, the 'hawkish' and the 'enlightened' can exist concurrently is not necessarily an indication of weakness or uncertainty in the PLAN leadership's strategy; it may merely be an indication of ongoing refinement. Naval diplomacy can exist on many levels simultaneously and by doing so offers choice and flexibility to the user.

At the more aggressive end of the scale, China built quite a track record. In 1995, for example, it seized the appropriately named Mischief Reef, an islet located 130 miles from the Philippines' Palawan Island and adjacent to the Palawan Strait, one of the region's key sea-lanes. Despite repeated Filipino requests to withdraw, China continued its military build-up in the reef and its naval forces there would be well positioned to be used to disrupt passing maritime traffic.[52] In 2004 there was posturing between China and Japan over the sovereignty of the

Senkaku (Japanese)/Diaoyu (Chinese) Islands in the East China Sea, including the deployment of a PLAN *Han* class nuclear submarine in the area.[53] In 2005 Vietnam claimed that China had started to seize its fishing boats in the South China Sea and detain their crews;[54] this escalated to a total of 17 boats and 21 fishermen detained in 2009 alone.[55] Finally, in 2010, China objected to a planned US-South Korean military exercise in the Yellow Sea, which had been organized as a response to North Korea's sinking of the South Korean *Cheonan*. Beijing criticized the participation of the USS *George Washington*, arguing that deploying an aircraft carrier to the Yellow Sea would be provocative, even though the carrier had conducted operations in the Yellow Sea earlier in the year without incident. But as with any form of communication, timing is key.

The challenge turned out to be a significant diplomatic victory for China, because though the exercise went ahead *George Washington* did not participate.[56] This could be viewed as a failure of naval diplomacy by the United States; it was later explained to the US Congress that the navy 'refrained from staging exercises in the Yellow Sea area' because of Chinese 'sensitivity'.[57]

Without doubt, as the post-Cold War period progressed, the South China Sea became a 'focal point for US-China rivalry in the western Pacific', which the USNS *Impeccable* 'incident' of 2009 ably demonstrated.[58] *Impeccable*, a tactical auxiliary general ocean surveillance (TAGOS) vessel, was challenged by a PLAN warship and five Chinese 'civilian' ships approximately 120 km south of Hainan Island, which housed a PLAN base.[59] China claimed that *Impeccable*'s presence in its exclusive economic zone (EEZ) had been a violation of domestic and international law.[60] Though the surveillance of the sea area was galling to Beijing, its legal objection was weak, for 'in short, nothing in the 1982 UN Convention on the Law of the Sea (UNCLOS) changes the right of military forces of all nations to conduct military activities in the exclusive economic zone'.[61] The Chinese ships (a government fisheries patrol vessel, a maritime surveillance service vessel of the State Oceanographic Administration and two small fishing trawlers) attempted to stop *Impeccable*'s data gathering. The fishing vessels manoeuvred to within 8 m of *Impeccable* and people on board the trawlers used a grappling hook to try to snag *Impeccable*'s towed cable and its related acoustic equipment. The vessels involved show that naval diplomacy, even that by a state, need not be limited to naval forces. '*Impeccable* left the scene in order to reduce immediate tensions but returned to the exact location several days later in the company of an American warship, USS *Chung Hoon*'.[62]

Deductions

The last three chapters have pointed out that the early post-Cold War period was one of rapid change in the global order and the resultant security situation was far from stable. While there was a notable decrease in inter-state conflict, there was a corresponding increase in what has been described as non-state or intra-state 'ethnopolitical conflict'.[63] The Cold War victors were quick to reap the peace dividend, but 'by not paying sufficient attention to places most people would characterize as obscure – Somalia, Bosnia, Kosovo, Afghanistan – the local has turned global'.[64] However, the most capable navies were well suited to respond to the emerging order, for only they regularly operated throughout the world and 'thus could probably be the only force available for ongoing, sustained deterrence – as it has been for virtually all crises'.[65]

The specific examples of naval diplomacy cited here have shown that there is little doubt that any or all of the theoretical approaches described in Chapter 2 could be applied to the post-Cold War years. As the Eastern bloc fragmented, sea power was used to garner influence and build amity with new partners. As stringent nationalism took hold in some quarters, naval forces both coerced and deterred. Opportunists, state and non-state, made use of the sea for prestige and established powers, even the hegemonic, increased their efforts to convince and persuade. Coalition or alliance building was a feature throughout, as was the inescapable truth of the value of forward presence. Rising powers, in particular India and China, have found naval expansion to be a necessary accompaniment to economic growth and global influence – ever was the case.

However, as has been alluded to, these existing approaches have not been sufficient to understand every nuance of naval diplomacy since 1991. Nor have the enduring themes, derived from the writing which provided the bedrock for the models, completely withstood scrutiny. The actions in the Adriatic and the containment of Iraq in the 1990s, for instance, were taken under mandate of the United Nations. Non-state actors such as the Tamil Tigers, Hezbollah and the organizers of the Gaza Freedom Flotilla have challenged the assumption that naval diplomacy is purely a state-centric business. America's flexing of muscles in the Taiwan Strait was as much a message to its domestic audience and Taiwan as it was to mainland China; similarly, North Korea's securitization and Russia's gain from US miscalculation of Black Sea relationships undermine the existing models' dogma that naval diplomacy is an interaction between two actors, an assailant and a victim. Nonetheless, one enduring theme does hold true: at its core, every conscious application of sea power to communicate political intent assumes rationality on the part of the audience at the receiving end.

This short qualitative analysis of immediate post-Cold War naval diplomacy has uncovered some previously ignored principles. Naval diplomacy can support an internationalist, liberal agenda; it can target multiple audiences simultaneously and it can be a tool for the non-state actor. Levels of naval co-operation and interoperability can indicate the health of an international relationship, yet even at its simplest level it can also provide a politically acceptable degree of diplomatic engagement. These principles can be taken forward into the development of a new, 21st-century model for naval diplomacy.

Notes

1 Gujral, I. K. 'The Post-Cold War Era: An Indian Perspective.' *World Affairs* 1, No. 1 (1997): pp. 44–55. www.ipcs.org/article/india-tje-world/the-post-cold-war-era-an-indian-perspective-1.html (accessed 16 January 2013).

2 Yilmaz, Muzaffer Ercan. 'The New World Order: An Outline of the Post-Cold War Era.' *Alternatives: Turkish Journal of International Relations* 7, No. 4 (2008): p. 46.
3 Bijiang, Zheng. 'China's "Peaceful Rise" to Great Power Status.' *Foreign Affairs* 84, No. 5 (2005): p. 22.
4 Holmes, James & Yoshihara, Toshi. 'China and the United States in the Indian Ocean: An Emerging Strategic Triangle.' *U.S. Naval War College Review* 61, No. 3 (2008): p. 51.
5 United States. Center for Naval Analyses. Gunness, Kristen. *China's Military Diplomacy in an Era of Change.* Conference Paper. (Arlington, VA: CNA, 2006), p. 1.
6 Holmes & Yoshihara, 'China and the United States in the Indian Ocean', p. 48.
7 Singh, Sidhu, Wahegru, Pal & Yuan, Jing-dong (Eds.). *China and India: Co-Operation or Conflict?* (Boulder, CO: Lynne Rienner Publishers, 2003), p. 60.
8 Dutt, Shri Shekhar. 'Seminar on Defence, Security, Diplomacy: India's National Interests.' Inaugural speech by the Indian Defence Secretary at the India International Centre, New Delhi, 24 February 2007. www.associationdiplomats.org/specialevents/Annual Seminars/200607/20070224DefenceSecurityDiplomacy/20070224DefenceSecspeech.htm (accessed 10 June 2013).
9 Scott, David. 'India's "Extended Neighborhood" Concept: Power Projection for a Rising Power.' *India Review* 8, No. 2 (2009): p. 107.
10 Ibid.
11 Global Security. '1999 Kargil Conflict.' Global Security. www.globalsecurity.org/military/world/war/kargil-99.htm (accessed 14 June 2013).
12 India. Ministry of Defence. *MOD Annual Report 2000–2001*: p. 33. www.mod.nic.in/reports (accessed 10 June 2013).
13 Scott, David. 'NATO and India: The Politics of Strategic Convergence.' *International Politics* 49, No. 1 (2012): p. 105.
14 Scott, 'India's "Extended Neighborhood" Concept', p. 115. The *Malabar* exercises with the United States had begun in 1992 but were suspended in 1998 following India's nuclear weapon testing programme.
15 India, *MOD Annual Report 2002–2003*, p. 26.
16 Ibid., p. 27.
17 India, *MOD Annual Report 2006–2007*, p. 32.
18 Ibid.
19 India, *MOD Annual Report 2007–2008*, p. 30.
20 India, *MOD Annual Report 2003–2004*, p. 40.
21 India, *MOD Annual Report 2004–2005*, p. 46.
22 Scott, 'NATO and India: The Politics of Strategic Convergence', p. 105.
23 Rai, Ranjit. 'Indian Navy in the 21st Century.' *Naval Forces* 24, No. 6 (2003): p. 33.
24 Buszynski, Leszek. 'The South China Sea: Oil, Maritime Claims, and US-China Strategic Rivalry.' *Washington Quarterly* 35, No. 2 (2012): p. 145.
25 Marc Lanteigne dedicates a chapter of his book to 'strategic thinking and the roles of the military.' See: Lanteigne, Marc. *Chinese Foreign Policy: An Introduction, 2nd Ed.* (Abingdon: Routledge, 2013), pp. 80–101.
26 United States. CNA, *China's Military Diplomacy in an Era of Change*, p. 2.
27 China, 'China's National Defense in 2010.'
28 Yoshihara, Toshi & Holmes, James. *Red Star over the Pacific: China's Rise and the Challenge to U.S. Maritime Strategy.* (Annapolis: Naval Institute Press, 2010), p. 150.
29 United States. Office of Naval Intelligence. *China's Navy 2007.* (Washington, DC: ONI, 2007), p. 112.
30 China. 'China's National Defense in 2010.' Information Office of the State Council of the People's Republic of China, 31 March 2011. www.china.org.cn/government/whitepaper/2011-03/31/content_22263510.htm (accessed 30 October 2012).
31 Ibid.

32 Yoshihara & Holmes, *Red Star over the Pacific*, p. 173.
33 Till, *Asia's Naval Expansion*, p. 150.
34 United States. ONI, *China's Navy 2007*, p. 117.
35 Ibid., pp. 116–117.
36 Kondapalli, Srikanth. *China's Naval Power*. (New Delhi: Institute for Defence Studies & Analyses, 2001), p. 185.
37 Ibid.
38 United States. CNA, *China's Military Diplomacy in an Era of Change*, p. 4.
39 China, 'China's National Defense in 2010.'
40 United States. CNA, *China's Military Diplomacy in an Era of Change*, p. 1.
41 Agnihotri, Kamlesh. 'Four Years of Anti-piracy Mission: Chinese Navy's Showcase Achievement.' www.maritimeindia.org/four-years-anti-piracy-mission-chinese-navy% E2%80%99s-showcase-achievement# (accessed 17 June 2013).
42 Ibid.
43 Kamerling, Susanne & van der Putten, Frans-Paul. 'An Overseas Naval Presence without Overseas Bases: China's Counter-Piracy Operation in the Gulf of Aden.' *Journal of Current Chinese Affairs* 40, No. 4 (2011): p. 138.
44 China, 'China's National Defense in 2010.'
45 Hao, Su. 'China's Humanitarian Operations Policy.' In Erickson, Andrew, Goldstein, Lyle & Li, Nan (Eds.). *China, The United States and 21st Century Sea Power: Defining a Maritime Security Partnership*. (Annapolis: Naval Institute Press, 2010), p. 243.
46 Holmes, James & Yoshihara, Toshi. 'Is China a "Soft" Naval Power?' *Jamestown Foundation China Brief* 9, No. 7 (2009): p. 5.
47 McVadon, Eric A. 'China's Navy Today: Looking toward Blue Water.' In Erickson, Andrew, Goldstein, Lyle & Lord, Charles (Eds.). *China Goes to Sea: Maritime Transformation in Comparative Historical Perspective*. (Annapolis: Naval Institute Press, 2009), p. 388.
48 Buszynski, Leszek. 'The South China Sea: Oil, Maritime Claims, and US-China Strategic Rivalry.' *Washington Quarterly* 35, No. 2 (2012): p. 147.
49 Pedrozo, Paul. 'Beijing's Coastal Real Estate: A History of Chinese Naval Aggression.' *Foreign Affairs*, 15 November 2010. www.foreignaffairs.com/articles/67007/ raul-pedrozo/beijings-coastal-real-estate (accessed 22 November 2010).
50 Dutton, Peter. 'Three Disputes and Three Objectives: China and the South China Sea.' *U.S. Naval War College Review* 64, No. 4 (2011): p. 53.
51 Goldstein, Lyle. 'Chinese Naval Strategy in the South China Sea: An Abundance of Noise and Smoke, But Little Fire.' *Contemporary Southeast Asia* 33, No. 3 (2011): p. 328.
52 Lanteigne, *Chinese Foreign Policy*, p. 136.
53 Dutton, Peter. 'Carving Up the East China Sea.' *U.S. Naval War College Review* 60, No. 2 (2007): p. 63.
54 Buszynski, 'The South China Sea: Oil, Maritime Claims, and US-China Strategic Rivalry', p. 143.
55 McVadon, 'China's Navy Today', p. 388.
56 Ibid.
57 United States. Congressional Research Service. Manyin, M., Chanlett-Avery, E., Nikitin, M. & Taylor, M. *US-South Korea Relations*. R41481. (Washington, DC: CRS, 2010).
58 Buszynski, 'The South China Sea: Oil, Maritime Claims, and US-China Strategic Rivalry', p. 139.
59 Lanteigne, *Chinese Foreign Policy*, p. 88.
60 Pedrozo, Paul. 'Close Encounters at Sea: The USNS *Impeccable* Incident.' *U.S. Naval War College Review* 62, No. 3 (2009): p. 102.
61 Ibid.

62 Dutton, 'Three Disputes and Three Objectives', p. 54.
63 Yilmaz, 'The New World Order', p. 45.
64 Simons, Anna, McGraw, Joe & Lauchengco, Duane. *The Sovereignty Solution: A Commonsense Approach to Global Security.* (Annapolis: Naval Institute Press, 2011), p. 124.
65 George, *The U.S. Navy in the 1990s*, p. 70.

7   Towards a new model for 21st-century naval diplomacy

Existing understanding of naval diplomacy, derived from the writings of historians and strategists from the 19th century to the end of the 20th century, can be plainly expressed. To reiterate, the topic is generally seen from a realist international relations perspective, it tends to be state centric and it assumes binary, mechanistic relationships which presuppose rational cognitive decision-making processes on the parts of both instigator and recipient.

However, the reality of naval diplomacy is different. Accepted wisdom needs to be challenged. Evidence demonstrates that naval diplomacy can support either realist or liberal international relations agendas; it is more often used by states than by non-state actors, but the latter are more active than might be supposed. It is rarely limited to just two parties and commonly involves multiple actors and stakeholders in the relationship. Of equal importance, naval diplomacy is more likely to be conducted on a regional basis than on a global scale. The actors involved range from military navies and coastguards to commercial organizations, NGOs and terrorist or criminal groups of all shapes and sizes. Quantitatively it is far more prevalent in the pursuit of amity than enmity, there are varying degrees of engagement and disengagement, and the act of not doing or stopping to do something that is expected can be as important as its more visible opposite. In short, there are sufficient differences between theory and reality, differences which continue to grow as the international system evolves, to prompt the construction of a new model of naval diplomacy for the 21st century.

A proposed alternative

The basic models which have already been derived in Chapter 2 from the writings of naval historians and theorists are 'foundational'. That is, they take disparate generalizations of known facts under a single framework and provide an overall insight into the topic.[1] To maintain a consistent approach, the same foundational methodology is applied in this chapter. And to start to construct a new model, some basic questions must be addressed

Why? Purpose in post-Cold War naval diplomacy

In its most straightforward form, an alternative model for 21st-century naval diplomacy should begin by posing a fundamental question. What is the *purpose* behind any particular scenario, interaction or relationship being considered? In the realist tradition the purpose of diplomacy is to be a means by which to 'act in accordance with the logic said to inhere in an anarchical system of power distributed between self-interested, self-helping, power-maximisers'.[2] It could equally be applied to revisionist actors, determined to alter the balance of power, or to those more interested in the maintenance of the status quo.[3] In short, it is about competitive advantage.

However, diplomacy is more specific than simply being a means to further self-interest. It is a multi-directional communicative tool and naval diplomacy, a niche form of diplomacy available to some actors, is the use of naval and maritime assets as communicative instruments in international power relationships to further the interests of one or more of the actors involved. The difference may be subtle, but it is there. A more liberal interpretation can also be applied to naval diplomacy, taking into account the presence and influence of international institutions and law, alliances and coalitions, non-state actors and interdependent global trade – all of which shape and constrain world politics.

Purpose in naval diplomacy, therefore, is always to communicate a message, whether that is explicit or implicit, to a single recipient or many. To understand purpose, the 'why' of any particular situation, an analyst must pose a simple triad of inter-relating questions: *What* is being communicated? *Who* is involved? And *How* is it manifested? Each question depends on the others; for example, the message to be passed must surely depend on the motivations of the actors involved, and the method of delivery will depend on the means available – North Korea, for example, will not attempt to coerce South Korea by positioning an aircraft carrier off its coast because it does not possess that capability. Similarly, when considering how to garner prestige with a potential ally, the United States may well determine to deploy an aircraft carrier on a goodwill visit because it possesses many.

Figure 7.1 below shows the basic elements of a foundational model of 21st-century naval diplomacy. *Purpose* sits firmly at the centre with the triad of *What, Who* and *How* bounding it. Each question can be explored further according to its constituent parts to provide a framework for comprehension and a tool for analysis.

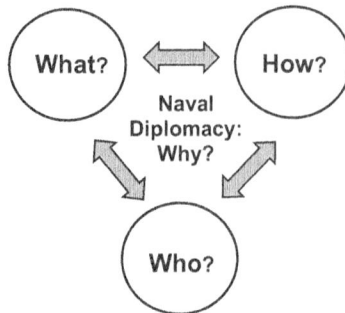

Figure 7.1 The basic elements of 21st-century naval diplomacy

What? Basic communication theory

During the Cold War a theory of communication was developed which became known as the 'message influence model'. It was based on Shannon and Weaver's *The Mathematical Theory of Communication*, published in 1949, and was originally devised to explain telephony. However, the model was found to be instructive in other fields and came to be developed and applied to describe all human communication.[4] According to the message influence model, a source will transmit a message and the message will be subsequently received, understood and acted upon by its audience. Diagrammatically, it can be represented as in Figure 7.2.

As can be seen from Figure 7.2, message influence is highly simplistic and has been criticized as 'an outdated, twentieth century [. . .] model that is no longer effective in the complex global war of ideas'.[5] It assumes that there is no outside interference to the message being sent, that the audience is always a passive recipient and it offers no contextualization. It also indirectly suggests that communication only occurs when a message is being deliberately transmitted. Of course, in reality communication is a constant and often subconscious process taking place through ongoing actions, deeds and words.[6] Nonetheless, the model does provide a useful introduction to the communications process and is remarkably consistent with the contemporaneously produced concepts of naval diplomacy developed in the Cold War. That is, the 'assailant' (source) uses naval means (the message) to reach the 'victim' (the audience).

Writing in the aftermath of the Second World War, Paul Kecskemeti produced a significant article on communication and influence. Though admittedly writing about the experiences of totalitarian propaganda during the war, Kecskemeti's work is nevertheless transferable to other spheres and ages and says much about the approach of 'forcing' a message to an audience through repetition: 'Public opinion control is the suggestive effect of constantly repeated stimuli: what you say often enough will in the end come to be believed'.[7] The implication of this assertion for sea power is that a steady drumbeat of preventive deployments, presence in areas and regions deemed to be of national interest, and ongoing demonstrations of credibility and capability could lead to a general acceptance of the instigator's 'message'. The global activities of the world's most powerful navies, from persistent presence in the Arabian Gulf to the strategic deterrence posture

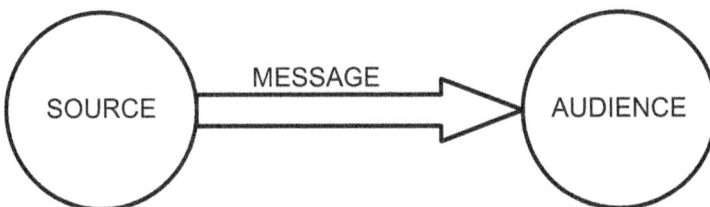

Figure 7.2 A simplified representation of the message influence model

practiced by the USN supports this premise – the world has come to believe that the Western naval powers dominate the seas because that is the image that has been presented to them over decades. To challenge that belief an actor is faced with a difficult task, having to overcome both reality and perception.

However, towards the end of the 20th century the message influence model was overtaken in prominence as researchers developed alternative perspectives on complex, multiple audience communications which better reflected the 'real' world. An influential work written in the 1990s described communication as a complex system requiring the interpretation of actions, thoughts, motivations and intentions.[8] A decade later, researchers at the Arizona State University Consortium for Strategic Communication built on this work and introduced the 'pragmatic complexity' model. Pragmatic complexity adopted a systems approach in which the whole is more than the sum of its parts, where it is not necessary to have an independent source or audience, and where actors are 'locked into a relationship of simultaneous, mutual interdependence'.[9] In addition, it might be assumed to take into account the difficult question of who controls the medium being used: it is striking how the same event can be described very differently in different parts of the global media, and striking how much faith respective audiences put into their source of choice. There is no doubt, for example, that the 2006 sinking of the Israeli ship *Hanit* was portrayed very differently on Hezbollah's TV channel *Al Manar* than in the Israeli news media. Today's explosion of social media, where people tend to follow and be followed by like-minded individuals and where alternative points of view are dismissed as fake, merely adds to the complexity.

Pragmatic complexity therefore attempts to do something which message influence does not – it attempts to interpret reality. Clearly, in such a model uncertainty and ambiguity may develop which could either assist or hinder the parties involved in the messaging process. The pitfalls of uncertainty are self-evident, but there are also potential benefits of ambiguity in diplomatic communication, ambiguity which may allow the originator to claim that the interpretation of a message was not that which was meant:[10]

> Ambiguity is often prompted by the need to take multiple audiences into account. Explicit and unambiguous signalling, while desirable vis-à-vis one category of receivers, might have disastrous effects on the sender's relations with another category of receivers. In diplomatic signalling the potential audiences may be both international and domestic.[11]

The lessons for naval diplomacy are worthy of consideration. The means in use may be ambiguous; a flotilla's deployment may be interpreted very differently in the minds of the parties involved. To the deployer it may be a message of friendship; to the neighbour it could be seen as a bid for prestige; to the primary target – or indeed to another state not intended as a target at all – it could be considered a threat. Similarly, any means of communication, including naval diplomacy, could be temporal; that is, it could 'highly time and condition sensitive. Messages that work one week may not work the next'.[12] The timing of naval deployments therefore, must be cognizant of other factors, as the case study of Exercise *Sea Breeze* in the Black Sea discussed in Chapter 4 demonstrated. In that example the purpose of the exercise was ambiguous – to the United States it was a bilateral endeavour aimed at friendship; to Russia it was a NATO encroachment into its area of influence and interest; to Ukraine it was a stepping stone to potential membership of the Western Alliance. In addition, its timing and location were ill-considered – Russo-Ukraine relations were at a low ebb, a BLACKSEAFOR exercise (involving Russia) was about to start, and *Sea Breeze* was centred on the ethnically Russian area of the Crimea, rather than on the less controversial port of Odessa as it had been in previous years.[13]

Finally, there is the prospect of deliberate disinformation in communication and messaging, in which one party's intent is portrayed as something else to the target audience. This could be a tactic by the source of the message in order to hide its true intentions, or it could potentially be a calculated misportrayal by the media, the target audience itself or a third party. As Holmes, Winner and Yoshihara noted when discussing the challenges facing the ascendancy of the Indian Navy in the 21st century, India's well-considered strategy of benign, non-intrusive outreach to fellow maritime nations in the Indian Ocean could be impeded by misperception or disinformation.[14] Who might be the instigator of such disinformation could be deduced by an appreciation of the winners and losers of the tactic; an analysis of all of the stakeholders involved and not just the primary participants would therefore be warranted.

When considering naval diplomacy, therefore, the question of 'what' relates directly to 'why', the purpose, and it proves to be neither straightforward nor consistent over time. When applying the findings of this book, naval diplomacy should be viewed as messaging either degrees of amity or enmity or both, and its purpose determined in terms of the effects identified in the chronological survey of incidents in the Appendix: coercion, deterrence, picture building, prestige, reassurance, co-operation, attraction or assistance – or a combination of any number of them. There might also be unintended consequences or systemic side effects of diplomatic activity at sea which could be visible to a participant or observer but, equally, might be hidden or unrecognized at the time.

Who? Basic stakeholder theory

The next question in the simplified proposed model is 'who' is involved. Chapter 2 discussed how existing realist models assumed the presence of a rational actor at the heart of the decision-making process. However, it also discussed how the reality is often more complex and that there will inevitably be a number of actors consciously or unconsciously party to any given situation. These stakeholders must be taken into account in any analysis; stakeholder theory, therefore, should be understood.

Stakeholder theory originated in the world of business studies. In what is commonly seen to be a landmark publication, R. Edward Freeman challenged the accepted view of the commercial corporation.[15] In his *Strategic Management: A Stakeholder Approach*, Freeman questioned the simplistic 'production view of the firm', which placed corporations in the centre of the process of turning raw resources from suppliers into products for customers.[16] Diagrammatically, it could be shown as in Figure 7.3.

As can be seen, the production view of business is not dissimilar to the simple message influence model found in basic communication theory or the assailant-victim model of naval diplomacy and many recognizable shortcomings are shared. However, the theory, though useful in furthering understanding, simply does not reflect reality and Freeman proposed an alternative perspective which attempted to describe how businesses really work and the interconnections between the active and passive actors involved. He developed the concept of business 'stakeholders', whom he defined as the 'wide range of groups who can affect or are affected by a corporation'.[17] Examples of such groups included owners, government, political groups, the financial community, suppliers, activists, customers, unions, employees, trade association and competitors.[18] They can be shown diagrammatically in a rudimentary 'map', as in Figure 7.4.

It is clear that stakeholder theory has wider applicability than just the world of business, and since Freeman's work first appeared in 1984 it has been used in economics, political science, education and the environmental sciences.[19] As the World Bank has suggested, stakeholder theory has wide applicability and is relevant to not only to the subject for which it was derived, but also to international relations.[20] One writer took the international relations point further, proposing that although the bilateral model of international discourse may still survive, it is increasingly challenged in the globalized world by the myriad of interconnected interests: 'The older state-based form of diplomacy exists alongside emergent forms, one label for which might be multi-stakeholder diplomacy'.[21] This is an argument that could be compared directly with that made in Chapter 2, which suggested that in the maritime domain modern, or industrial, naval forces might have to co-exist with and operate alongside the post-modern navies of states which fully embrace globalization. It is another example of shifting emphasis in the post-Cold War global order. The changes are evolutionary rather than revolutionary.

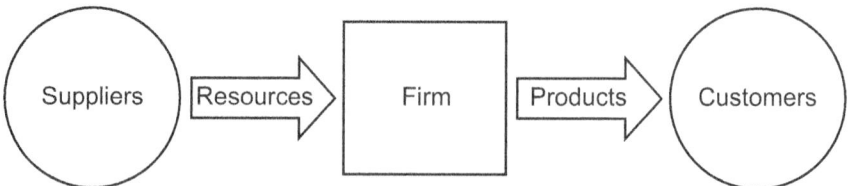

Figure 7.3 The production view of the firm

Source: From Freeman

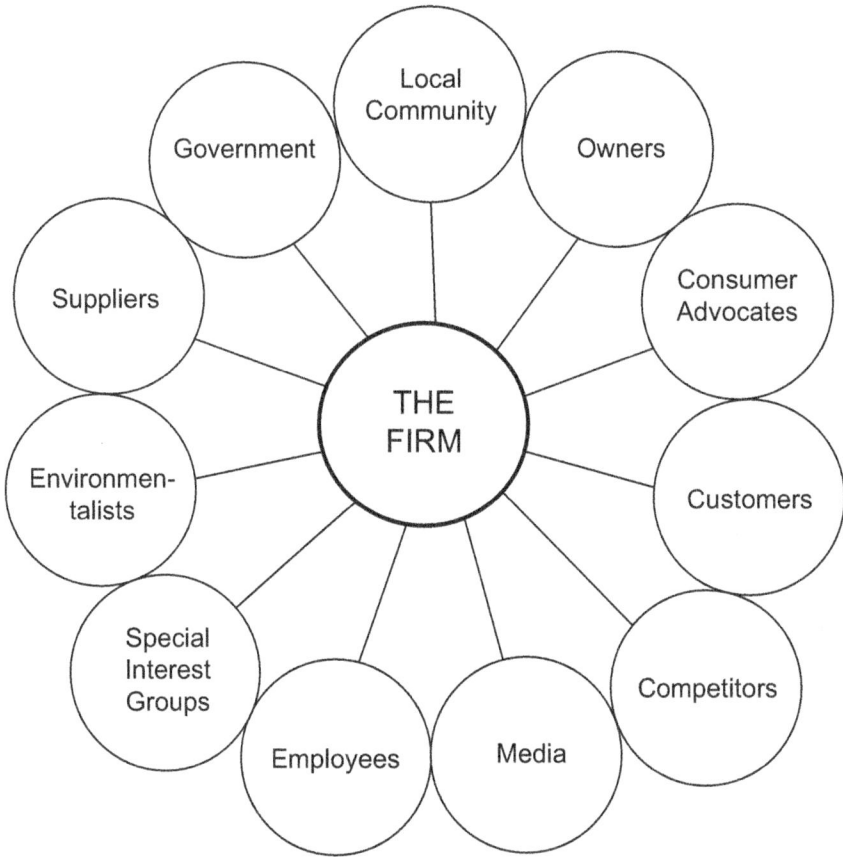

Figure 7.4 Stakeholder mapping[22]
Source: From Freeman

Of course, stakeholder theory has not been without its critics. It has variously been accused of impracticality because of its excessively broad definition of stakeholders over whom an organization may have little or no control,[23] and of undermining the basic principles of capitalism in favour of 'ethical values'.[24] Some commentators have argued that though stakeholder theory might 'prove useful in identifying interests', for other purposes its claims were 'overblown'.[25] However, 'identifying interests' is an important factor in non-warfighting sea power, and one that has traditionally been under-researched. There are rarely (if ever) just two parties involved in naval diplomacy, and a credible mechanism to understand the roles played by other direct or indirect participants would be useful. Adapting Freeman's definition, one might assume the stakeholders in this context to be the wide range of actors who can affect or be affected by naval diplomacy.

Self-evidently, not all stakeholders in any given situation carry equal weighting – there will inevitably be a hierarchy of influence and significance.

Building on Freeman's map, Lynda Bourne and David Walker devised what has become known as the 'stakeholder circle', showing not only the actors who affect or could be affected by a corporation but also their relative influence (Figure 7.5).

It is apparent from the diagram that Bourne and Walker continued to place the firm or corporation at the centre of their 'map', but they situated the other stakeholders in one of three expanding concentric circles representing the firm's internal actors, external directly affected actors and then those who may be indirectly affected; influence was deemed to decrease as distance from the centre increased. Put another way, functional proximity to the rational decision-making body was deemed to be an indicator of influence over it. The three groups might also be called primary, secondary and tertiary stakeholders.

Though the term had not been coined at the time, a form of stakeholder analysis was conducted in the classic 1969 article on the Cuban Missile Crisis by Graham Allison. Allison challenged the assumption of a single 'rational, unitary decision-maker' in government.[26] Instead he suggested alternatives to the rational actor model, which acknowledged 'the fact that a government consists of a conglomerate of semi-feudal, loosely allied organizations, each with a substantial life of its own'.[27] He also pointed out that even then leaders do not sit on top of 'monolithic groups' but are subject to bureaucratic politics and competitive

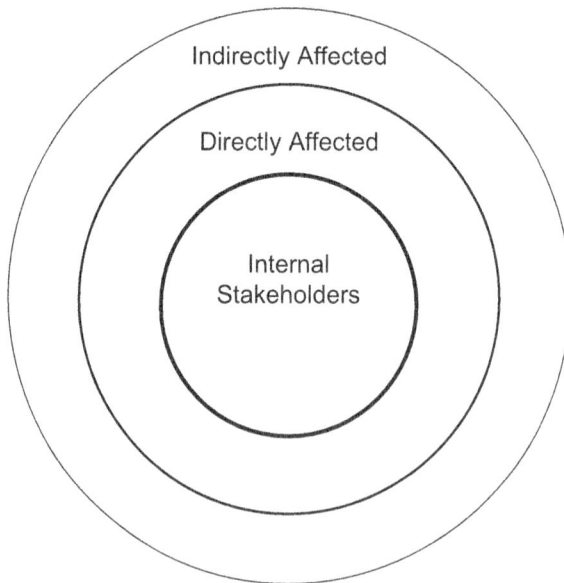

Figure 7.5 Stakeholder circle[28]
Source: From Bourne and Walker

bargaining.[29] These could be considered the internal stakeholders in Bourne and Walker's circle. Allison delved deeply into the make-up of government machinery to avoid oversimplification; the same level of analysis can, of course, be applied to non-government and non-state stakeholders in other conflict or diplomatic, communicative engagement scenarios.

When stakeholder theory has been applied directly to a post-Cold War military context, however, it has predominantly been within a discussion of morality and ethics. For example, an article in a US Marine Corps press publication in 2013 applied stakeholder theory to counter-insurgency, identifying the local population, non-governmental organizations and the media as stakeholders in a conflict, and then encouraging active troops to display empathy the various audiences.[30]

As with the application of basic communication theory, the general principle of determining the primary, secondary and tertiary stakeholders in any given communications moment is reasonable and useful in the study of naval diplomacy. If, as has been claimed, power and influence can result from 'connectedness', then analysis of connectivity must be able to provide a valuable insight into the nature and effectiveness of that power.[31] In terms of naval diplomacy, understanding which actors are involved, their motivations and their relationship to each other can result in better application or, alternatively, circumvention of the means.

The study of naval activity in the Adriatic Sea in the 1990s is an interesting case of multiple actors with various motivations operating singly, in concert or both at different times. Mapping their 'connectedness' could provide insight into purpose. In that example it might be reasonably assumed that one of the primary stakeholders was the Serbian state – but who were the others? Though 14 countries eventually contributed maritime forces to the Adriatic, most did so intermittently as members of supra-state organizations such as NATO and the WEU who in turn were operating under the remit of the United Nations.[32] International organizations, therefore, particularly multinational military alliances, were the primary stakeholders facing Serbia and their constituent members were influential but secondary stakeholders. Motivations varied but the contributing states were participating as much to prove their commitment as trusted allies and partners (and, for their domestic audience's consumption, as responsible members of the international community) as they were to simply counter Serbian aggression in the Balkans and enforce UN Security Council Resolutions. It was, in effect, a low-risk strategy of demonstrating 'action'.

Other former Yugoslavian states were also secondary or tertiary stakeholders affected by the activity at sea. Some other non-participating but interested third-party states, such as Russia, were also tertiary stakeholders. Serb sponsored or affiliated groups in Croatia and Bosnia-Herzegovina, though not directly involved on the maritime front, were certainly affected by the blockade and should be considered. Domestic and international audiences were clearly also part of the mix, as were those commercial organizations with an interest in seaborne trade with the former Yugoslavia or in the Adriatic region more generally. Figure 7.6 is a simple attempt to place these actors in a stakeholder circle.

Maritime Contributing States
UN
Former Yugoslav States
Serb-Sponsored Groups

Tertiary

Secondary

Serbia
NATO
WEU

Primary

Other Regional Actors
Domestic Audiences
Wider Int Community
Non-state Maritime Interest Groups
Commercial Actors

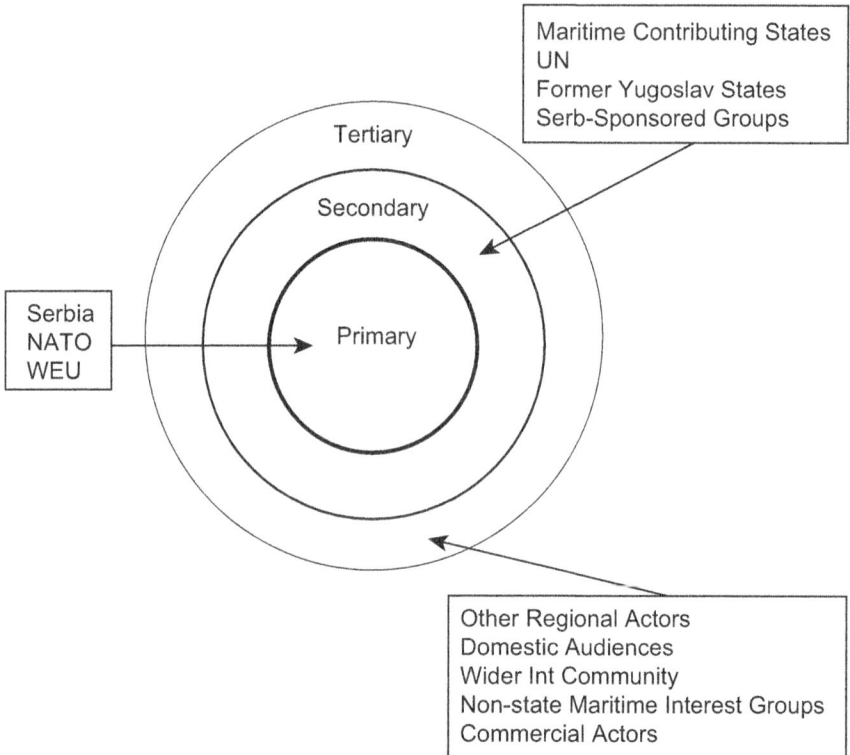

Figure 7.6 Adriatic 1990s stakeholder circle

In developing a 21st-century model of naval diplomacy, it is clear that primary, secondary and tertiary audiences and their interconnectedness should be all be included, acknowledging however that such mapping is always a subjective and inaccurate science. Actors may include the direct participants but also the international, regional or domestic communities, including alliances and international institutions, or even a different part of the initiator's own government, along with multinational corporations and non-governmental organizations who may sit in one or more audience categories depending on the scenario.

Approached this way, it is apparent that the ability to contribute to, to affect or to be affected by naval diplomacy is not necessarily a function of either scale or type of actor involved. Naval diplomacy is not the sole preserve of the blue-water military navy, but an opportunity (or threat) for regional, adjacent force projection, coastal or even token navies and coastguards, and a range of supra-state or non-state actors and audiences from NGOs to commercial corporations and local populations.

How? **Ways and means**

Finally, the third leg of the triad of the proposed model is 'how' naval diplomacy is manifested. Writing in 2011, J. J. Widen stated that 'to categorize different kinds of operations in naval diplomacy, that is functional definitions, is not sufficient'.[33] The implication is that by describing naval diplomacy in terms of its ways, the context may be missed and the strategic argument consequently lost. However, although such categorization may not be 'sufficient', it is essential. Naval historians have produced volumes on the tactical employment of sea power; those tactical activities are indispensable pixels in the greater, strategic picture.

Christian Le Mière questioned whether maritime diplomatic events could ever be classified beyond groupings based on underlying purpose, as each incident appears unique. However, he did go on to categorize some tactical methods into the kinetic (i.e. those involving physical force) and the non-kinetic, suggesting that the degree of force employed gave a useful guide to intentions.[34] This approach is in keeping with Sir James Cable's, whose definitive, purposeful, catalytic and expressive modes referred to the threat or actual use of force. From this perspective, explicitness of message would appear to be hinged in part on explicitness of method.

Le Mière's question of whether functional classification is possible can be addressed by the analysis of empirical evidence. It is true to state that of the examples of naval diplomacy cited in this book, few if any share identical tactics. Nevertheless, they can be grouped by their general ways and means. One approach to do this is to use the method of categorizing activity according to the widely accepted (in official doctrine and academic literature) attributes which grant navies particular advantage. For instance, the British doctrinal attributes of access, mobility, lift, reach, versatility, poise, resilience and leverage are still lauded as the 'ways' in which the Royal Navy achieves its 'ends'.[35]

However, as Chapter 1 stated, those attributes have largely gone unchallenged and may not be an appropriate prism through which to view the contemporary maritime operating environment. The trait of versatility, for example, arguably requires breadth of capability and is therefore questionable when applied to small and token navies or coastguards. The US Navy is certainly versatile but the navy of, say, the Republic of Ireland, with its rather limited focus on patrolling its territorial seas and immediate area of 'jurisdiction', could not be viewed as particularly flexible in its offer of political choice to the Irish state.[36] By comparison, the Irish Army, though small, has operated nationally and globally in peace support missions since 1958 and is therefore more of a diplomatic tool.[37] Perhaps relative versatility amongst and between maritime, land and air armed forces is partly a function of scale, and therefore the assumption of particular advantage may only be valid for larger, multi-role navies with extra-regional reach. Ireland's Navy made a foray into this more recently, deploying to the Mediterranean as part of the EU Naval Force combating people smuggling and human trafficking there.[38]

Similarly, technological change could bring into doubt the longevity of other 'enduring' attributes. The development of anti-access/area denial capabilities (A2AD), for example, might challenge the notion of poise, as Iran demonstrated in early 2015 with its very public demonstration of a missile attack against a mock-up of a US aircraft carrier.[39] This is perhaps an outlet for a different form of naval diplomacy, in which relatively weak naval powers can challenge the relatively strong by overtly targeting perceived 'strengths' and turning them into critical vulnerabilities. North Korean ballistic missile 'tests' in 2017 offer another example.

Additionally, in the information age the high seas are rapidly losing their monopoly as the world's only global commons. The new global commons of cyberspace is increasingly a manoeuvre environment of choice for state and non-state actors alike, with its advantages of reach and penetration, low cost and plausible deniability.[40] Similarly, unmanned aerial systems are increasingly persistent and resilient (though still significantly short of naval platforms), and consequently picture building, the gathering of intelligence or generation of domain awareness, may be better conducted in future from the air or from space than from the sea. One writer applied some traditional maritime thinking to the military use of space and determined that it fits very well.[41] There may be other comparable parallels to draw as technology advances.

There may also be legal, societal or ethical challenges to the naval attribute of access. As the example in the next chapter shows, Greenpeace's presumption of an unfettered use of the high seas was not shared by Russia in 2013, when MY *Arctic Sunrise* became the subject of state-led duress. Nor was Israel's assumption of freedom of maritime manoeuvre shared by Hezbollah in 2006. As the boundaries between state and non-state, and between the functions of naval activity become ever more 'fuzzy', long-held beliefs about a rules-based order and what can be done, by whom, to whom and where, may need to be recalibrated.[42] The point is not merely the applicability to naval diplomacy, but the perception of the value of naval forces relative to other instruments of power.

There remain, however, many proponents of naval power and this is not the place to predict its complete demise, but there are compelling arguments for its adaption. Christopher Layne, for instance, suggested a change in American grand strategy after the Cold War. He argued that as the sole world power the United States could afford to sharply reduce the size and role of its ground forces while simultaneously increasing 'overwhelming naval presence'. He called his strategy 'offshore balancing'.[43] Whether it could ever be a practical strategy for the United States or any other country is debatable, but the point is that it was suggested by a credible academic. There are at least some commentators who believe that naval power, if applied correctly, can be sufficiently robust to be the basis for contemporary strategy.

In discussing the 'how' of naval diplomacy, therefore, analysis through functional definitions of specific tactics or operations should not be attempted solely on the basis of debatably passé concepts. Though they have up until now stood the test of time, the attributes which gave advantage in the 19th and 20th centuries might not remain such unique selling points in the 21st century and, as a result, complementary alternatives should be sought. To do just that, the quantitative and qualitative evidence provided in the Appendix and the earlier case studies might be used to identify a number of methods, practiced by both state and non-state actors alike, by the relatively powerful and relatively weak, and applicable irrespective of scale. Rather than group them according to kinetic force as Le Mière did (and thereby implicitly reinforcing the definition of naval diplomacy as an *act* as opposed to a means of *communication*), the classification of tactics, of 'how', as movable points along Nye's spectrum of soft and hard power is more appropriate and accurate.

At the soft end of the spectrum, for instance, actors might pay goodwill visits, gift or sell arms, or engage in simple, intermediate or complex capacity-building exercises to forge amity. They may conduct basic operations together or, ultimately, work towards and achieve interoperability at the highest end of warfighting capabilities. To express enmity they may protest (as may a secondary or tertiary stakeholder), arrest, interdict or poise near an offending location. At the very hardest end of the scale they could blockade, mount physical strikes or occupy sovereign seas, property or territories. All of these can be found across the hundreds of examples cited in this book. Of course, at the most aggressive end, where the distinction between the 'limited' force of naval diplomacy becomes blurred with the more fulsome version of major combat operations, the interpretation of tactics and functions requires even greater scrutiny. What may appear 'limited' to one actor may appear to be extreme to another. The mapping of the differences between limited force and physical conflict, if indeed they exist at all, is certainly an area worthy of further research.

Clearly, there may be a close correlation between the 'how' and the 'what' of naval diplomacy. For example, if the message to be passed is one of enmity through coercion then a credible and explicit tactic could be to mount a limited physical strike by naval air, surface or submarine capabilities. Likewise, communicating amity through assistance following a natural disaster might naturally mean the provision of help or aid. However, that correlation is not always the case. The tactics themselves are not necessarily exclusive and are often used in combination, supporting the hypothesis that naval diplomacy is not and never has been a binary endeavour. There are times when identical tactics could be used be used to express very different messages, resulting in very different effects. For example, exercises between actors might be an initial foray into friendship or co-existence, as many Arab-Israeli interactions have been, or they may be means to improve interoperability between close allies such as the United States and United Kingdom. They might even be a demonstration of capability targeted against a third party, as in the series of US-South Korean *Team Spirit* exercises aimed in significant part at the deterrence of North Korea.

This chapter proposes a series of 11 tactics, evident in and derived from the examples of naval diplomacy described earlier, which together cover a broad spectrum of from the use of hard power to softer effects. They range from the overtly hostile, such as the hard power tactic of occupying territory or property which has been rare in the immediate post-Cold War maritime environment, to the benign, such as the ages-old goodwill visit, sitting at the soft end of the scale and a very commonplace occurrence. But even these opposite end tactics, instinctively associated with the military navies of recognized states, have potential for alternative manifestations. A form of dissent could see non-state groups attempting to occupy that which does not legally belong to them; the Movement for the Emancipation of the Niger Delta (MEND), for example, seized Nigerian ships in 2009 and, as will be discussed later, Greenpeace have temporarily occupied (if not controlled) oil platforms in their campaigns at sea.[44] Similarly, port visits may be the stock-in-trade of warships but they are also conducted by coastguards and, of course, commercial companies. An interesting variation on the latter is the case of an attempt by campaigning groups and council members opposed to Arctic drilling to prevent the Royal Dutch Shell Company from using and visiting the port of Seattle.[45]

Between these tactics are others such as the use of physical strike to inflict punitive damage at or from the sea. As Hezbollah, the Tamil Tigers and the Mumbai terrorist attackers of 2008 have shown, the use of strike is most definitely not the preserve of state actors. Nor, as New Zealand has shown in its anti-nuclear testing stance, is protest the preserve of the non-state actor. Similarly, the implementation of formal or informal blockades by state or non-state actors; the various modes of interdiction and protection, which are vital policing components of maritime security; the provision of aid (itself very much a multi-stakeholder affair); and, the varying degrees of engagement and disengagement that are central to exercises and interoperability between actors, are all tactics employed in 21st-century naval diplomacy.

The list is not exhaustive but it is representative. Though they are shown in Figure 7.7 at intervals along the hard/soft spectrum, their relative place need not be permanently set. They are also portrayed as common verbs, non-unique expressions of definite actions; they are therefore independent of specific technological capabilities which will inevitably change over time, but they remain functions or roles which have been inherent, at least to some degree, in sea power throughout history. They also differ from Cable's descriptive approach which emphasized an assailant's intent as the referent object.

In sum, the 'how' of naval diplomacy, the actions or tactics employed by all of the actors involved, can be categorized and such categorization, when considered alongside stakeholder analysis and communicative aims, aids understanding. Together, 'what', 'who' and 'how' help to determine of purpose and are therefore an essential part of the development of a model or framework for the analysis of naval diplomacy.

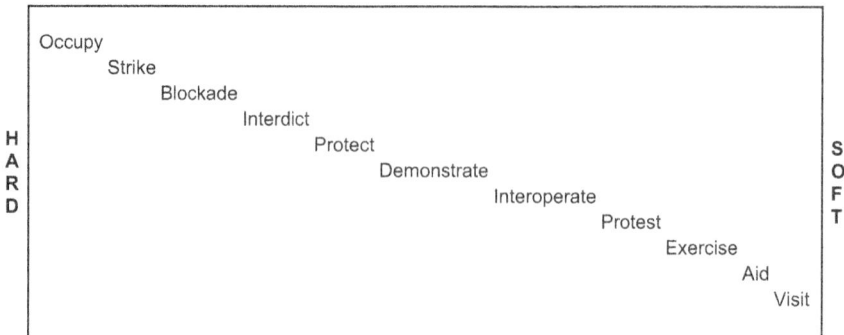

Figure 7.7 Tactics employed in naval diplomacy

A foundational model for 21st-century naval diplomacy

Figure 7.1 was a simplistic, diagrammatical representation of three points which might be considered in the contemporary study of naval diplomacy and its purpose: *what, who* and *how*. By expanding on those points, which can be taken in any order, and developing second- and third-order levels of analysis, a more comprehensive foundational model for 21st-century naval diplomacy may be determined.

Figure 7.8 shows a new model for naval diplomacy in the post-Cold War global order, but one which could also be used to analyse historical scenarios from any period. The enduring *what, who* and *how* questions are given substance by subordinate questions of enmity and amity, of hard and soft power tactics and of target audience analysis. The suggested building blocks of those are effects, stakeholders and ways and means derived from both theory and evidence. Of course, they could be added to or removed as the analyst requires.

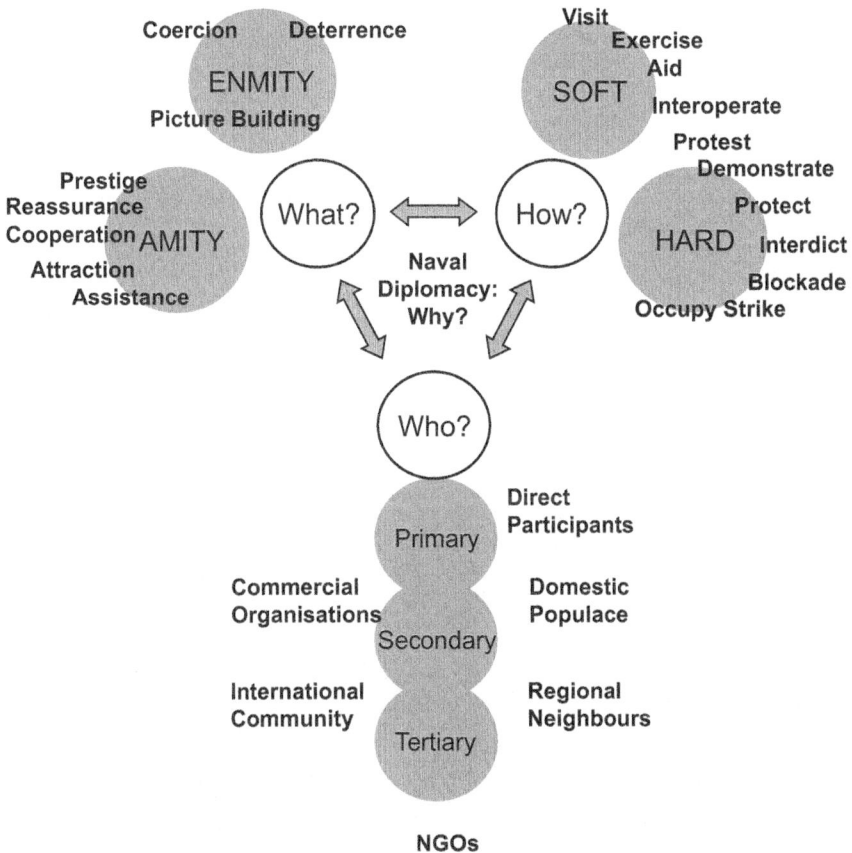

Figure 7.8 A foundational model of 21st-century naval diplomacy

Notes

1 Clarke, Kevin A. & Primo, David, M. 'Modernizing Political Science: A Model-Based Approach.' *Perspectives on Politics* 5, No. 4 (2007): pp. 742–743.
2 Sharp, Paul, *Diplomatic Theory of International Relations*. (Cambridge: Cambridge University Press, 2009), p. 54.
3 Mearsheimer, John. 'Structural Realism.' In Dunne, Tim, Kurki, Milja & Smith, Steve (Eds.). *International Relations Theories: Discipline and Diversity, 3rd Ed.* (Oxford: Oxford University Press, 2013), p. 79.
4 Tatham, Steve. *Strategic Communication in Conflict and the Concept of Non-kinetic Informational Effect in Military Operations with Special Reference to the British Experience in the Historical Context, Its Contemporary Application in Afghanistan and in Future*. PhD Thesis. University of Southampton, 2011, p. 101.
5 Corman, Steven, Trethewey, Angela & Goodall, Bud. *A 21st Century Model for Communications in the Global War of Ideas*. (Phoenix, Arizona: Consortium for Strategic Communication, Arizona State University, 2007), p. 2.
6 Tatham, *Strategic Communication*, pp. 101–102.
7 Kecskemeti, Paul. 'Totalitarian Communications as a Means of Control: A Note on the Sociology of Propaganda.' *Public Opinion Quarterly* 14, No. 2 (1950): p. 226.
8 Luhmann, Niklas. *Social Systems*. (Stanford: Stanford University Press, 1995), pp. 137–143.
9 Corman, Trethewey & Goodall, *A 21st Century Model for Communications*, p. 10.
10 Jonsson, Christer & Hall, Martin. *Communication: An Essential Aspect of Diplomacy*. Paper prepared for the 43rd Annual ISA Convention, New Orleans, 23–27 March 2002: p. 5.
11 Ibid., p. 6.
12 Tatham, *Strategic Communication*, p. 106.
13 Global Security. 'Sea Breeze.' www.globalsecurity.org/military/ops/sea-breeze.htm (accessed 14 December 2014).
14 Holmes, James R., Winner, Andrew C. & Yoshihara, Toshi. *Indian Naval Strategy in the 21st Century*. (Abingdon: Routledge, 2009), p. 72.
15 Morphy, T. 'Stakeholder Theory.' www.stakeholder.com/stakeholder-theory.htm (accessed 27 January 2014).
16 Freeman, R. Edward. *Strategic Management: A Stakeholder Approach*. (Cambridge: Cambridge University Press, 2010), p. 5.
17 Ibid., p. 1.
18 Ibid., p. 55.
19 World Bank. 'What Is Stakeholder Analysis?' World Bank. www1.worldbank.org/pub licsector/anticorrupt/PoliticalEconomy/PDFVersion.pdf (accessed 9 April 2014).
20 Ibid.
21 Hocking, Brian. 'Multi-Stakeholder Diplomacy: Forms, Functions and Frustrations.' In Kurbalija, Jovan & Katrandjiev, Valentin (Eds.). *Multistakeholder Diplomacy: Challenges and Opportunities*. (Msida, Malta: Diplo Foundation, 2006), p. 14.
22 Ibid., p. 25.
23 Morphy, 'Stakeholder Salience.'
24 Mansell, Samuel F. *Capitalism, Corporations and the Social Contract: A Critique of Stakeholder Theory*. (Cambridge: Cambridge University Press, 2013), p. 3.
25 Orts, Eric W. & Strudler, Alan. 'Putting a Stake in Stakeholder Theory.' *Journal of Business Ethics* 88, No. 4 (2009): p. 605.
26 Allison, Graham. 'Conceptual Models and the Cuban Missile Crisis.' *The American Political Science Review* 63, No. 3 (1969): p. 694.
27 Ibid., p. 698.
28 Bourne, Lynda & Walker, David. 'Project Management and the Stakeholder Circle.' *International Journal of Managing Projects in Business* 1, No. 1 (2008): p. 126.

29 Ibid., p. 707.
30 Murat, Geoffrey. 'Ethics and Irregular Warfare: The Role of Stakeholder Theory and Care Ethics.' In Connelley, Carroll & Tripodi, Paolo (Eds.). *Aspects of Leadership Ethics, Law and Spirituality*. (Quantico, VA: Marine Corps University Press, 2012), pp. 39, 45, 54.
31 Hafner-Burton, E., Kahler, M. & Montgomery, A. 'Network Analysis for International Relations.' *International Organization* 63, Summer (2009): p. 559.
32 NATO. 'NATO/WEU IFOR Final Fact Sheet.' 2 October 1996. www.nato.int/ifor/general/shrp-grd.htm (accessed 21 February 2013).
33 Widen, J.J., 'Naval Diplomacy – A Theoretical Approach.' 4 (2011), p. 717.
34 Le Mière, *Maritime Diplomacy in the 21st Century*, pp. 50–51.
35 UK, *British Maritime Doctrine, 4th Ed.*, pp. 2–1 to 2–6.
36 The Republic of Ireland currently has eight patrol vessels which operate predominantly 'through Ireland's jurisdiction.' See: Ireland. 'Defences Forces Ireland.' www.military.ie (accessed 24 March 2015).
37 Ibid.
38 European External Action Service. 'Irish Ship "LÉ Niamh" Joins Operation SOPHIA.' https://eeas.europa.eu/headquarters/headquarters-homepage/34392 (accessed 22 February 2018).
39 Gady, Franz-Stefan. 'In A2/AD Showcase, Iranian Navy Sinks *Nimitz* Carrier Mock-Up.' *The Diplomat*. http://thediplomat.com/2015/02/in-a2ad-showcase-iranian-navy-sinks-nimitz-carrier-mock-up/ (accessed 24 March 2015).
40 United States. Department of Defense. *Cyberspace Operations*. Joint Publication 3–12(R). (Washington, DC: DoD, 2013).
41 Klein, John J. 'Corbett in Orbit: A Maritime Model for Strategic Space Theory.' *U.S. Naval War College Review* 57, No. 1 (2004): pp. 66–69.
42 Till, Geoffrey, *Seapower: A Guide for the Twenty-First Century, 3rd Ed.* (Abingdon: Routledge, 2013), p. 225.
43 Layne, Christopher. 'From Preponderance to Offshore Balancing.' In Art, Robert & Waltz, Kenneth (Eds.). *The Use of Force: Military Power and International Politics*, 6th Ed. (Oxford: Rowman & Littlefield, 2004), p. 292.
44 *Jane's Defence Weekly* 46, No. 16 (2009): p. 19.
45 Beekman, Daniel & Bernton. 'City to Study Whether It Can Block Base for Shell Drilling Fleet.' *Seattle Times*, 9 March 2015. www.seattletimes.com/seattle-news/politics/city-to-study-whether-it-can-block-base-for-shell-drilling-fleet/ (accessed 29 March 2015).

8 Applying naval diplomacy in today's world

As was stated in the introduction, using the same evidence to both create and test a theory is not a valid approach – it exacerbates the risk of confirmation bias. Therefore, whereas the basis of the new model for 21st-century naval diplomacy lies in the events which took place in the decades immediately following the end of the Cold War, the cases chosen to test it are selected from outside that period. The theoretical framework is tested against a renowned example of naval diplomacy from the height of the Cold War and then applied in today's world, against a further three examples from the period 2011–15. These final three examples represent state-on-state confrontation, the involvement of non-state actors, and transnational concerns, respectively. They were selected for their diversity rather than their resemblance to any 'typical' example of naval diplomacy of the past century. Each test case is divided into two brief sections: the first provides historical and geopolitical context by outlining key events; the second provides a short analysis based on the triad of questions described in Chapter 7. Of course, other cases could be chosen for examination and while the model takes into account new developments, the fact that it draws on ideas and literature from naval theory and other academic disciplines means that it could also be used to reconsider earlier periods.

A re-evaluation of the USS *Pueblo* incident

The USS *Pueblo* incident is one of the most oft-cited examples of Cold War naval diplomacy. Cable covers it extensively and it has spawned a number of memoirs, books and articles.[1] It is included here precisely because it is well known and has been exhaustively studied. Though there are many analyses they habitually differ in detail and emphasis with few, if any, containing all aspects of the incident. Consequently the test in this example is to determine whether the foundational model provides an adequate framework for comprehension, by organizing a logical research agenda to capture pertinent details.

The widely accepted narrative of events describes how in early 1968 USS *Pueblo*, an intelligence gathering ship, was on patrol in the East Sea off the coast of North Korea. By 22 January of that year it had become clear that *Pueblo*'s presence was known to North Korea after it had been passed by a patrol craft and approached and then circled by two North Korean fishing vessels. *Pueblo* was unescorted, the United States having made the assumption that she would be safe in international waters, an assumption which with hindsight turned out to be unwise.[2] A day later, on 23 January, another patrol boat approached *Pueblo* at high speed, ordered her to heave to and threatened to open fire if she did not comply. Within the hour a further three patrol vessels had joined the first and two North Korean MiG-21 fighter aircraft were overflying the area. *Pueblo* attempted to depart from the scene at her maximum speed but could not outrun the faster North Korean vessels. The North Korean craft fired on *Pueblo* and one of the aircraft fired warning shots into the sea. Left with little choice, *Pueblo*'s commanding officer surrendered his ship and followed the patrol boats into the port of Wonsan.[3]

During the intense diplomatic negotiations which followed the capture of USS *Pueblo*, confessions of spying were obtained and the ship's crew were regularly photographed and appeared in the domestic press. Eventually, in December 1968, in exchange for a US acknowledgement of the validity of the confessions and an admission that the ship had been seized in North Korean territorial waters, the crew were released.[4]

Taken as an isolated example of naval diplomacy, the *Pueblo* incident is ostensibly an altercation between North Korea and the United States. Indeed, Cable describes it as such in his analysis. However, to fully appreciate the situation the wider context must be understood. In this respect a 2009 analysis by Giseong Lee on US coercive diplomacy against North Korea gives a good background to the situation leading up to the capture of *Pueblo* and to the interwoven relationships involved. For instance, North Korea had attempted, and failed, to assassinate the South Korean president three days earlier, Pyongyang was experiencing difficult and complex relationships with both the USSR and China, and the United States was giving unquestioning support to South Korea. Similarly, in his classic Cold War work, John Lewis Gaddis (without reference to the *Pueblo* incident) discusses the Soviet-North Korean relationship and concludes that the former disliked the latter but could not let it fail for fear of a perceived American 'victory' in the region.[5] For its part, China (North Korea's longstanding if, at times, reluctant ally) played no direct physical role but was mindful of its own influence within the communist world and provided tacit support to Pyongyang.[6] Of no lesser importance, Lee situates the confrontation in the Cold War in Asia and, crucially, alongside the ongoing Vietnam War and approaching Tet Offensive.[7] By the time of the *Pueblo* incident President Johnson's White House was already under intense pressure to unwind American commitments in South East Asia, which the additional demands of an unfolding situation off the Korean coast can have done little to ease.[8]

In the context of the time, it has been widely argued that there was an underlying assumption in Washington that all incidents, wherever they occurred, were connected with the broader Cold War and must, therefore, be orchestrated by Moscow. It would have been incomprehensible for US decision makers in Washington to think that North Korea could have acted alone against the United States and *Pueblo*.[9] Indeed, recently released contemporary testimony shows that the US House Armed Services Committee was briefed that it was 'reasonable to assume . . . that the documentation captured from the *Pueblo* has been turned over to the Soviets and possibly the CHICOMS [Chinese Communists]'.[10] Of course, the fact that documentation was turned over does not necessarily mean that North Korea acted at Moscow's behest when first seizing the ship.

Sir James Cable ignores these factors in his analysis, though he does discuss the American assumption that despite Cold War rhetoric surveillance vessels operating on the high seas would not be directly interfered with by the other side; a convention had evidently evolved between the United States, the USSR and their allies, the violation of which would upset the strategic balance.[11] As with all communicative relationships there is inherent risk in assuming the norms and perceptions of one participant necessarily apply to the others. The US Navy reassessed its policy of sailing surveillance ships unescorted after the *Pueblo* incident but found the cost of providing protection prohibitively high. By mid-1969 the US chief of naval operation, Admiral Thomas H. Moorer, recommended decommissioning all 'spy' ships; within six months they had been removed from service.[12]

Cable also chose not to mention the subsequent manoeuvring by the various stakeholders in his textual analysis. Instead, he reports the late January 1968 USN deployment of three aircraft carriers into the Sea of Japan and the February 1968 Soviet deployment of cruisers and destroyers to the same area as entirely separate incidents in his chronological index.[13] As has been discussed in relation to Cable's analysis of the Falklands conflict, in any analysis there will inevitably be a subjective assessment of the temporal boundaries of any incident. Timescales matter, particularly when considering the effectiveness of any action, and this can then skew subsequent statistical or comparative analysis.

In contrast, in their analysis of Soviet naval diplomacy Dismukes and McConnell considered the *Pueblo* incident to be, in part, a message of support from North Korea to North Vietnam at a time when practical assistance to Hanoi from the USSR and China was all but absent.[14] In addition they describe how the Soviet Union was reluctant to jeopardize progress in its improving relationship with North Korea and thus responded negatively to a US request for assistance in negotiation. However, they also point out how the only overt Soviet display of support for North Korea, the deployment of ships to the area, occurred several weeks into the incident when it was apparent to all sides that US naval presence in the region was reducing.[15] This clearly suggests that the Soviet target audience was North Korea and, perhaps, its own domestic populace – though the time lag could also have been a carefully considered signal of reassurance to the United States that no further confrontation was wanted. That account differs slightly from that given by David Winkler in his book *Cold War at Sea* which describes how the Soviet intelligence gathering ship *Gidrolog* attempted to physically block the passage of USS *Enterprise* in the Sea of Japan as the latter was making its way towards the stricken *Pueblo*.[16]

Nonetheless, returning to Lee's analysis of the incident, there is another strong argument which suggests that the primary political motive for the incident was domestic rather than international. Lee states that North Korea 'largely ignored the ship's intelligence value' and exploited the incident for domestic propaganda.[17] The North Korean population needed a 'boost' and he contends that the discovery of USS *Pueblo* presented a relatively easy target of opportunity for Pyongyang to portray the regime as heroically resisting a powerful external threat and that opportunity was grasped.[18] The actions which followed were then impulsive reactions to a developing international situation based on differing interpretations of events in different national capitals.

It is clear that there are many and varied interpretations of the *Pueblo* incident suggesting that there were a range of factors and motivations at play. Applying the foundational model to the incident may assist in providing retrospective understanding. First, when attempting to establish 'what' communicative message was being conveyed, one might determine that there were many and that they changed in emphasis and priority as time went on. Initially, the United States was actively embarked on a process of picture building against North Korea – primarily indicative of a state of enmity between the two countries, but also a positive message of reassurance to the South. Subsequently, North Korea's interference with *Pueblo* on the high seas indicates enmity in a coercive, yet limited form.[19] Later, as the situation developed, both the United States and North Korea exploited the incident to boost their own credibility and 'masculinity' with their domestic audiences and the USSR gave half-hearted reassurance to its client state but was careful not to push its superpower rival too far when doing so.

The stakeholders in the *Pueblo* incident, of course, are numerous. The primary participants were clearly the governments, armed forces and in particular the navies of the United States and North Korea, and members of the civilian maritime community of the latter. Secondary state audiences included the Soviet Union and South Korea, but China, North Vietnam, Japan and the international community as a whole could be considered at the tertiary level. Linkages between each were not necessarily direct, but there may well have been a lot of 'dotted lines'. Finally, as already stated, domestic constituencies and populations – in North Korea, the United States and USSR – had to be satisfied and these may be placed in the secondary or tertiary fields with equal validity at different times during the crisis. In fact, once the incident had transitioned from the high seas to the airwaves, domestic audiences then became the primary targets in the political manoeuvring taking place.

The 'how' of the incident is more apparent. In terms of Nye's spectrum of behaviour, the physical means employed by all players tended to the 'hard' end. The United States poised with *Pueblo* and again with its aircraft carrier flotilla after the event, as did the USSR with their deployment of cruisers and destroyers. North Korea's action was one of interdiction while other regional actors watched with interest but did not take an active, physical role. The United States used the best capability it had for picture building and intelligence collection, but due to resource constraints (particularly given its commitments to fighting the war in Vietnam) and some erroneous assumptions based on an altogether different context (i.e. the Cold War against the Soviet Union), it chose not to protect *Pueblo* with other warships. North Korea's tapestry of fishing vessels to report and patrol boats to interdict, however, represent an impressive degree of coordination of the sea power available to the state, something which Soviet Admiral Sergei Gorshkov would undoubtedly have recognized.

The *Pueblo* incident has been much written about and few of the considerations raised above are new. However, as a vehicle for comprehension the new model provides a viable framework for this Cold War cause célèbre. Compared to the traditional, often narrow, approaches, it provides a wider, more satisfactory approach to the analysis of the incident and opens up alternative avenues of research[20] Of course, the purpose of the new foundational model is to assist in both the comprehension and analysis of cases such as this, but it does not necessarily lead to just one result; two analysts could quite conceivably use it to reflect on a particular incident and end up with two or more quite different accounts of the same event. In this case the model does aid comprehension but does not necessarily provide new insight into why the incident occurred.

The case of the Senkaku/Diaoyu/Diaoyutai Islands

Japan, the People's Republic of China and Taiwan all lay claim to a grouping of uninhabited rocks and islands in the East China Sea. The Japanese name for the islands is Senkaku, China refers to them as Diaoyu and Taiwan calls them Diaoyutai. The three states competing for sovereignty all see military and economic advantages to the resolution of the dispute in their favour.[21]

Historically, following annexation by the Ming dynasty in the 16th century, the islands had been part of China but were largely considered unimportant by Peking/Beijing. They were annexed by Japan in 1885, with Tokyo claiming that they had effectively been ungoverned and not under the control of any state up until that point. Over half a century later, after the Japanese surrender at the end of the Second World War, the islands were placed under US administration and remained so until 1971.[22] Taiwan made a claim for the islands in 1959 but took no further action.

Alessio Patalano, commenting in 2013 on the main protagonists in the territorial dispute, wrote that the Senkaku/Diaoyu/Diaoyutai Islands were not a significant issue throughout much of the Cold War, because China was attempting to consolidate its land borders and Japan was concentrating on its economic development.[23] To that analysis can perhaps be added Taiwan's preoccupation with self-preservation and quest for international acceptance. Throughout the Cold War and immediately afterwards, therefore, it was most likely domestic politics, rather than international or inter-regional relations, which periodically raised the profile of the East China Sea territorial disputes. In support of this argument Patalano put forward the view that

> The impact of domestic politics on these [territorial] disputes derives from the import of sovereignty for national political authorities in terms of both domestic legitimacy and international status.[24]

However, economic factors also added to the islands' strategic importance and provided considerable motivation for increased activity in support of the various claims which became apparent from the 1990s onwards. A 2013 report for the European Union Library discussed the economic importance of the East China Sea shipping lanes.[25] Patalano similarly noted that the region is structurally a maritime system in which the sea is central to trade and commerce, military power and political influence.[26] Some commentators have also questioned whether the East China Sea dispute is connected with the possibility of oil and gas deposits in the region;[27] it is estimated that mineral reserves in the disputed zone could be as much as 100 billion barrels of oil and 2 trillion cubic feet of gas.[28] This is a huge amount and is a comparable quantity to the reserves already exploited and estimated to remain in the North Sea which have provided significant economic value to the United Kingdom and Norway. Control of the islands is therefore a very attractive proposition to each of the parties concerned over and above their traditional rhetoric and their indulgence of popular domestic opinion.

Direct interaction over the islands sovereignty took place periodically throughout the immediate post-Cold War period. In 1994, for example, Hong Kong–registered vessels protested against Japanese sovereignty after Tokyo proclaimed an EEZ around the islands. Several Hong Kong vessels were blocked by Japanese patrol boats, some protesters jumped into the sea and one drowned.[29] In 1998 Chinese protesters landed on the islands and clashed with the Japanese coastguard; in 2000 Chinese People's Liberation Army (Navy) vessels exercised near the islands, and in 2004 Japanese patrol boats were again involved in an altercation with Chinese fishing vessels.[30] According to official Japanese sources two Chinese oceanographic research ships entered territorial waters off the islands in 2008, and in September 2010 bilateral relations between China and Japan were exacerbated when a Chinese fishing vessel deliberately collided with a Japanese coastguard ship.[31]

It is interesting to note that each of the claimants employed different maritime activity in connection with the disputed islands. Until 2012 China had sent naval vessels adjacent to Senkaku/Diaoyu/Diaoyutai but had never ventured into their territorial waters to 'avoid antagonizing relations with Japan'.[32] However, throughout the 2000s China had increased its constabulary and maritime enforcement efforts in the region through the Coastguard, Maritime Safety Administration, China Maritime Surveillance, the General Administration of Customs and the Fisheries Law Enforcement Command, each of which, along with commercial fishing vessels, effectively represented state interests.[33] It is clear China did not always rely on the 'official' PLAN for its at-sea diplomacy. Echoes of Gorshkov's multi-stranded approach to maritime and naval diplomacy, which he described in *Seapower of the State*, can again be heard.

On the other hand, Japanese maritime activity centred almost exclusively on its Maritime Self-Defence Force and coastguard, which regularly patrolled the East China Sea but also undertook capacity building and assistance activities with regional neighbours.[34] These activities were designed to consolidate the Japanese position as a good neighbour and indirectly strengthened their customary sovereignty claim on the international stage.

However, the diplomatic dispute escalated significantly in 2012 when the Japanese government purchased the islands from their private owners. The move, ironically intended to be de-escalatory in Japan, was deemed provocative in China and resulted in mass protests in some Chinese cities.[35] Such 'protests' under an authoritarian regime are potentially orchestrated centrally by the state and might therefore be seen as a carefully considered signal in their own right, rather than as a consequence of naturally occurring public opinion. Taiwan subsequently launched an East China Sea Peace Initiative and, though it did not withdraw its own claim to the islands, resolved to seek a diplomatic solution to the issue. In return, Japan rewarded Taiwan with access to surrounding waters for its fishing vessels.[36] China, in contrast, deployed 'paramilitary forces' to the area, and in January 2013 the confrontation escalated further when a Chinese naval vessel locked its fire control radar – usually considered to be a highly aggressive act as it indicates preparations to opening fire – onto a Japanese destroyer.[37] The situation was such that some in the West thought that it 'could lead to conflict'.[38]

In November 2013, China announced the creation of an Air Defence Identification Zone (ADIZ) above the islands, a move which Japan labelled 'unilateral escalation' of the dispute.[39] Taiwan expressed 'regret' at the creation of the ADIZ and promised that its military would take measures to protect Taiwanese national security if necessary. Following the declaration of the ADIZ, Chinese ships then repeatedly sailed into Japanese claimed, and internationally recognized, territorial waters.[40] Japan's principal ally and security guarantor, the United States, publicly backed Tokyo and dispatched two B-52 bombers from Guam to overfly the ADIZ without notifying Beijing.[41] It also promised support should conflict occur while at the same time stressing that it had no position on the specific boundary/sovereignty issue.[42]

Applying the new foundational model to the Senkaku/Diaoyu/Diaoyutai dispute and beginning with a stakeholder analysis, it can be seen that there are two primary state actors involved: China and Japan, the principal claimants to sovereignty of the islands. Alongside these, the United States and Taiwan may be considered secondary players, as could the domestic audiences of each of the major protagonists. Tertiary actors include those East Asian regional states with their own maritime sovereignty disagreements with China, particularly those in the South China Sea such as Vietnam, the Philippines and Malaysia. The plethora of non-state actors concerned include fishermen and the commercial shipping corporations with an interest in maritime security in the region.

Tactics used range from the employment of maritime soft power by Japan to support their own claim including port visits, exercises and capacity building, to China's hard power approach through orchestrated civil and naval protest, poise and temporary occupation. The declaration of the ADIZ could be considered a limited form of blockade and also suggests that further, more aggressive action could follow.[43] The US Navy's Seventh Fleet, effectively a permanently deployed fleet-in-being poised in Japan, can also be factored into the equation.

The resultant messaging between the stakeholders, therefore, exhibits the characteristics of every trait identified in earlier chapters. There is coercion (by China and Japan, of each other), deterrence and reassurance (by the physical presence of Japanese naval and coastguard vessels, by the US Seventh Fleet and by the Chinese ADIZ), picture building and the pursuit of prestige by all parties, and co-operation, attraction and assistance (particularly on the part of Japan and Taiwan). Whether in that respect the new model offers a useful framework for analysis or a mere itemized checklist is perhaps debatable. However, in conjunction with the stakeholder analysis and tactical appreciation, the model as a whole is applicable to this example and can be used to help determine purpose. The purpose for China and Japan was sovereignty. For the United States, Taiwan and the tertiary stakeholders it was the maintenance of the status quo and ongoing maritime security in the region.

Greenpeace, Russia and the Arctic

In 2010 Greenpeace commenced its 'Save the Arctic' campaign. Its objectives were to secure international agreement to create a global sanctuary in the uninhabited and sparsely habited areas around the North Pole and to ban offshore oil drilling and industrial-scale fishing in Arctic waters.[44] The physical manifestations of the campaign were often in the form of at-sea protests against energy exploration companies. Amongst their protests, Greenpeace list action against Cairn Energy off Greenland, against Royal Dutch Shell in the Beaufort Sea, and against Rosneft and its concessions, Statoil, ExxonMobil and ENI, in the Barents and Kara Seas. For each, Greenpeace claim the protests had been conducted peacefully and safely.[45]

In August 2012 Greenpeace began protesting against the *Prirazlomnaya* oil platform operated in the Pechora Sea by the Russian state-controlled energy company Gazprom. The platform was situated on the Russian continental shelf and within the Russian Federation's Exclusive Economic Zone and since 2011 Russian authorities had declared a three nautical mile 'safety zone' around it. The first protest involved several activists suspending themselves from the sides of the platform in order to draw public attention to the dangers *Prirazlomnaya* posed to the environment, particularly if it suffered an oil spill.[46] Later, in August 2013, Greenpeace had an altercation with Russian authorities after attempting to sail its ship, MY *Arctic Sunrise*, into the Northern Sea Route through the Arctic without permission.[47]

However, it was in September 2013 that Greenpeace again mounted a protest against Gazprom and the *Prirazlomnaya* platform with the intention of scaling the structure and unfurling a banner below its main deck.[48] Greenpeace launched inflatable boats from *Arctic Sunrise* to carry activists to the platform and they were intercepted by inflatable craft from the Russian coastguard vessel *Ladoga*. Collisions between the inflatables and violence ensued including, Greenpeace claimed, the firing of weapons from the coastguard boats.[49] The crew of *Prirazlomnaya* also intervened, using water hoses to stop activists climbing the rig. Two

Greenpeace members were arrested and taken on board *Ladoga*.[50] The following day *Arctic Sunrise* was boarded by Russian coastguard personnel via helicopter while outside Russian territorial waters and outside the three-mile rig safety zone, but inside the Russian EEZ. The ship, and 30 crew members of 19 different nationalities, were detained and taken to the port of Murmansk with accusations ranging from piracy to hooliganism to terrorism levelled at the protesters.[51] Much of the action was then replayed in the world's media.[52] By mid-October an estimated 1.5 million emails had been sent to Russian embassies worldwide, demanding the release of the so-called Arctic 30.[53]

Perhaps it was inevitable given the human interest story unfolding between Greenpeace and the Russian state that some commentators would argue that much of the media coverage at the time focused on the welfare of those individuals arrested and not on the potentially more important matters of the legal and institutional frameworks governing the Arctic.[54] The UN International Tribunal for the Law of the Sea heard the case of the arrest of *Arctic Sunrise* and in November 2013 ordered its release.[55] The Netherlands, as the flag state of the ship, provided a surety of 3.6 million euros and by early December all activists had been freed.[56] Nonetheless, *Prirazlomnaya* remained active in the Arctic and mineral exploitation continued.

This example of diplomatic play at sea is important because the principal protagonists were, initially, non-state actors, albeit on the Russian side much more closely connected to the state than oil companies in the West would normally be assumed to be. Very rapidly, however, both state support and international opinion was brought to bear to affect both sides in the dispute. Applying the new model here, it is best to again start with an attempt to identify the stakeholders. Greenpeace was certainly a primary actor, but it is a non-governmental organization which derives much of its 'power' from its global mass membership, who might then be considered an important, though nebulous, secondary audience. Moreover, Greenpeace does have a headquarters in the Netherlands and its ship, MV *Arctic Sunrise*, was also registered there. In the days and weeks following the arrest of MV *Arctic Sunrise* and the 'Arctic 30', the Netherlands became Greenpeace's *de facto* state sponsor.

In the opposing camp Gazprom was superficially a multinational corporation with business interests worldwide and its own economic network of suppliers and customers, many of them states. Nonetheless, its origin lay within the USSR Gas Industry Ministry and the Russian state remains its majority shareholder.[57] Russia, therefore, with a navy and coastguard at its disposal, was a key interlocutor and the source of Gazprom's authority and power at sea. As the situation developed it became a difficult task to differentiate the actions and tactics of Gazprom from those of the Russian government. Russia should therefore be considered a primary stakeholder, and Greenpeace would have been keenly aware of this when they began their campaign. It is not always clear where the non-geographical boundaries of a state lie.

Greenpeace's aims were clearly stated. At the strategic level they wished to see an end to drilling in the Arctic, and in 2012–13 they communicated their objective to raise global awareness. To do so they balanced an amity agenda of appealing to popular environmentalism through non-violent but sometimes 'risky' action against an adversarial posture towards their target for change. Both were necessary if they were to achieve their goal. Their tactics, then, were similarly a combination of hard and soft techniques, from physical protest and coercive behaviour, to picture building (gathering evidence and publicizing Gazprom's activities and their inherent dangers) and attraction to their cause. Throughout, the prestige associated with Greenpeace as a respected campaigning NGO was critical.

Gazprom and Russia had a different challenge. Their commercial activities were not illegal and when confronted by Greenpeace they attempted to achieve their aim of continuing mineral exploitation through visible law enforcement means. The coastguard initially poised in the vicinity of *Prirazlomnaya* to act as a deterrent to MY *Arctic Sunrise*. Once deterrence failed, Russia turned to interdiction and arrest, both to deal with the immediate situation and, perhaps, to send a message about any future attempt by Greenpeace or another organization intent on preventing drilling. Russia's actions were undoubtedly at the hard end of the spectrum and they did little by way of public diplomacy to appease the international community. It is probable that the external, international audience was far less important to Moscow than its own domestic constituency and its economic goals. The Russian strategic narrative, consistent over centuries, is one of external plots, pressures and threats which need strong, centralized government to counter. Heavy-handedness has become its norm.

This example shows that diplomatic activity at sea is not always a zero-sum game. Both Greenpeace and Russia/Gazprom achieved their short-term objective. Drilling was not stopped but global awareness was certainly raised and public sympathy undoubtedly lay with the protesters. Is this naval diplomacy? Cable would not have chosen to include this incident in his catalogue of incidents because it would not fit his limited criteria of state actors, 'assailants', 'victims', winners and losers. However, it is included here because it is an expression of power-play at sea fitting the definition given in Chapter 1, and it can be analyzed through the framework of the new foundational model.

Transnational concerns and ballistic missile defence

The final example to test the new model has been selected precisely because it did not fit the generally accepted mould of traditional naval diplomacy. The majority of case studies in the existing literature and, in fact, the majority of examples cited in this book consist of discrete incidents with clear beginnings, middles and ends. The transnational concerns over ballistic missiles and the (primarily American) network of defences around the globe, however, are different and reflect that much activity takes place in the grey area between overt war and supposed peace. They represent an ongoing diplomacy in which picture building, deterrence, coercion, reassurance, assistance, prestige and more can be readily identified. If the model is able to provide an analytical framework for the naval element of such scenarios, then it would prove to be a valuable methodological tool.

Ballistic missiles are not a new phenomenon. The Second World War German V2 rocket was a ballistic missile, and the United States, United Kingdom, France, Russia and China all employ ballistic missiles as delivery mechanisms for their nuclear deterrents. Pakistan, Iran, Syria, Israel and North Korea can also be added to that list. The attractiveness and utility of ballistic missiles to those who have them rests on two factors – their ability to carry a high-effect payload (either nuclear, biological, chemical or conventional) and, most importantly, on the degree of difficulty in defending against them. Flight profiles make conventional air defence sensors and weapons systems unsuitable counters – conceptually, intercepting a ballistic missile at any stage of its trajectory is akin to 'hitting a bullet with a bullet'.[58]

Ballistic missiles are often seen as symbols of national prestige and scientific competence and are thus a tempting investment for the ambitious power, whether that is a state or a non-state actor. Importantly, they have diplomatic value in terms of deterrence and coercion and military value because of their psychological, political and kinetic impact.[59] Tactical and symbolic use of ballistic missiles is not uncommon: Iraq used them in the First Gulf War, North Korea has fired them into the Sea of Japan, Syria has seen them used extensively in its civil war, but to use them at the inter-regional or inter-continental strategic level, such as against centres of population or points of critical national infrastructure during a period of tension or confrontation has, to date, been held in reserve. For instance, during a potential turning point in the Syrian civil war in 2013 when it appeared that Western powers might resort to military intervention, the Assad regime did not use ballistic missiles against third parties, despite having the capability to do so.

It is in this context that ballistic missile defence (BMD) can become both a military and diplomatic tool. BMD is high on the US defence agenda and has traditionally enjoyed broad bipartisan support in the US Congress.[60] The United States uses a series of bilateral arrangements with Turkey, Israel, Japan and the United Arab Emirates for mutual advantage and forms the bedrock of NATO BMD capability in Europe.[61] The first level of NATO BMD, the Active Layered Theatre Ballistic Missile Defence System (ALTBMD), was declared to be at 'interim capability' at the NATO summit in Chicago in 2012.[62] It consists of situational awareness systems in Germany, a mobile radar site in Turkey and a naval element, a US Navy Aegis warship (the weapon 'shooter' in the architecture) stationed in the eastern Mediterranean. ALTBMD is synonymous with the US European Phased Adaptive Approach (EPAA), which contributes not only to European NATO but also to the protection of the continental United States from long-range ballistic missiles.[63]

Despite its role in underwriting ALTBMD, the United States is keen for partner states to 'shoulder more of the burden' in European defence; BMD is a hugely expensive enterprise with all elements of an integrated system costing billions of dollars. The Netherlands has plans to upgrade four of its air defence frigates with long range early warning radars as its contribution and Spain permits the basing of four US Aegis ships at Rota on its southern coast.[64] There is therefore a complex mix of international interests incorporating elements on land and at sea, operational contributions, logistic support and forward presence by allies. In addition, there is the message to potential belligerents with ballistic missiles that such an attack would be fruitless and, by inference, result in a costly retaliation to no useful end. BMD, in essence, provides deterrence by denial and assumes rationality on the part of the actors involved.

One pillar of the new model's triad has already been discussed. The '*what*', those communicative messages associated with ballistic missiles and the defence against them, are complex but largely unambiguous. The international actors fielding the weapons do so for reasons of prestige, reassurance, deterrence and coercion. Those involved in BMD likewise pursue deterrence, coercion and, potentially, an element of prestige, but they also aim to build alliances, assist and co-operate with their backers and reassure junior partners.

It is probable that BMD also carries with it a degree of securitization.[65] The financial cost of defensive systems can be of such magnitude that investment in them becomes attractive only when a very real ballistic missile threat is perceived. The Japanese investment in direct (Aegis warships) and indirect (permitting US basing) BMD in the face of North Korean unpredictability perhaps exemplifies this approach.

The '*who*' and '*how*' are equally apparent. Though weapon proliferation cannot be dismissed, those state and non-state actors in possession of ballistic missiles are believed to be known and those involved in countering them are, at present, limited to state actors who are identifiable through their association with the network of the BMD 'shield'.[66] Secondary and tertiary stakeholders include those states and organizations which feel disadvantaged by the presence of offensive or defensive systems in their own areas of concern or interest (examples here could include Russian concern at American BMD systems in eastern Europe) and those who wish for a role but who have not yet been able to obtain systems (such as South East Asian states within range of North Korean missiles). Forward presence, cooperative agreements, logistical support, procurement of interoperable systems, protest and demonstrations of capability are commonly used tactics amongst both offensive and defensive ballistic missile actors.[67] In many cases, consistent with the particular advantages of naval forces in diplomatic activity outlined in Chapter 1, participating in the maritime component of BMD may be more politically acceptable to the states involved than fully committing to its land-based element. The framework developed in the new model enables both comprehension of such factors and analysis of motives. By doing so it is a useful tool for the study of 21st-century naval diplomacy.

An alternative prism

'Assailant-victim' models of naval diplomacy are simply not appropriate in the 21st century. The centrality of the nation state, of mechanistic relationships and the focus on coercive rather than cooperative action that are common in many existing commentaries on the subject are only now beginning to be challenged by navalists in the globalized, post-modern era in which we live.

Of course, there is a large literature re-examining the importance of the nation state in the post-Cold War world, and of the place of force. Some, for example, have predicted a coming system which they call a 'great power society', comprising not states but of 'non-unitary actors' focused on maximizing wealth. Such a system would not settle conflict through force or threats, but through negotiation and compromise.[68] Terrorism, environmental politics, the globalization of trade, the significance of inter-governmental and non-governmental organizations and the importance of international law, are yet more issues set to challenge 'traditional' concepts of naval diplomacy today and in the years ahead. This book does not argue that these assertions of global transformation must be accepted in their entirety – we have not yet seen the 'end of history' – but it does support the idea that the global order has evolved over the last quarter of a century, is continuing to evolve, and that these changes will affect sea power.

Consequently, this chapter has attempted to scrutinize naval diplomacy through a new prism. Building on the earlier conclusion that existing frameworks were inadequate means of capturing the realities of post-Cold War activity at sea, it adopts an interdisciplinary approach involving basic communication and stakeholder theories, to apply an alternative, foundational model from the evidence of the real world. Using its definition of naval diplomacy as a communicative endeavour, it has derived a new framework in which the questions of *what* is being communicated, *who* is involved and *how* it is being done can be posed. It has suggested themes by which amity and enmity may be expressed, it has demonstrated how actors affecting and affected by naval diplomacy may be identified and their connectedness and relative influence plotted, and it has outlined a series of non-unique tactics or means which may be available to maritime stakeholders to achieve their aim.

However, the book does not set out to claim that the new model that it proposes is the only viable approach to the study of contemporary naval diplomacy. Indeed, history is replete with attempts to construct generalizations and 'law-like principles' about international politics and relations from the detection of patterns.[69] Different approaches are equally valid but the foundational model developed here attempts to articulate a practical representation of naval diplomacy based not only in theory but also in the reality of events since the end of the Cold War.

Notes

1 See, for example: Lerner, Mitchell B. *The Pueblo Incident: A Spy Ship and the Failure of American Foreign Policy.* (Lawrence, KS: University Press of Kansas, 2002); and, more recently, Cheevers, Jack. *Act of War: Lyndon Johnson, North Korea and the Capture of the Spy Ship Pueblo.* (New York: Penguin, 2013). Comments on the *Pueblo* Incident also appear in works discussing wider naval diplomacy such as Dismukes, Bradford & McConnell, James (Eds.). *Soviet Naval Diplomacy.* (New York: Pergamon Press, 1979), pp. 119–123; and in books on Cold War sea power such as Winkler, David F. *Cold War at Sea.* (Annapolis: Naval Institute Press, 2000), pp. 37, 58–62.
2 Till, Geoffrey. *Seapower: A Guide for the Twenty-First Century, 3rd Ed.* (Abingdon: Routledge, 2009), p. 232.

3 This short narrative of events is a précis of Lee, Giseong, *U.S. Coercive Diplomacy towards North Korea*. PhD Thesis. University of Aberdeen, Aberdeen, 2009, pp. 97–98 (itself a summary of primary and secondary sources) in addition to the works cited above.
4 U.S. House Armed Services Committee, Special Subcommittee on the USS. *Pueblo, Inquiry into the USS Pueblo and EC-121 Plane Incidents*. HASC No. 91–92. (Washington, DC: US Government Printing Office, 1969), p. 1628.
5 Gaddis, John Lewis. *The Cold War*. (London: Penguin, 2005), pp. 130–131.
6 Relations between the Chinese Communist Party and the Communist Party of the Soviet Union had been strained for some years and Sino-Russian competition between 1965 and 1969 centred on their relative influence in communist countries. See Ball, S. J. *The Cold War: In International History 1947–1991*. (London: Arnold, 1998), p. 138.
7 Lee, *U.S. Coercive Diplomacy towards North Korea*, pp. 99–103.
8 Caridi, Ronald J. *20th Century American Foreign Policy: Security and Self-Interest*. (Englewood Cliffs, NJ: Prentice-Hall, 1974), p. 357.
9 Lerner, *The Pueblo Incident*, pp. 99–100, 137; Lee, *U.S. Coercive Diplomacy towards North Korea*, p. 105; Dismukes & McConnell (Eds.), *Soviet Naval Diplomacy*, p. 119.
10 United States. U.S. House Armed Services Committee. *Memorandum for the Record on the Secret Pueblo Hearings of the House Committee on Armed Services*. DOCID 4121701. (Washington, DC, 15 January 1969). (Approved for release by NSA 27 May 2014. Transparency Case #63391.)
11 Cable, James. *Gunboat Diplomacy 1919–1991: Political Applications of Limited Naval Force, 3rd Ed.* (Basingstoke: Macmillan, 1994), p. 26.
12 Winkler, David F. *Cold War at Sea*. (Annapolis: Naval Institute Press, 2000), p. 37.
13 Cable, *Gunboat Diplomacy, 3rd Ed.*, p. 196.
14 Dismukes & McConnell (Eds.), *Soviet Naval Diplomacy*, p. 119.
15 Ibid., pp. 119–121.
16 Winkler, *Cold War at Sea*, p. 58.
17 Lee, *U.S. Coercive Diplomacy towards North Korea*, p. 101.
18 Ibid., pp. 99–100.
19 Interestingly, the limited coercion employed by North Korea stopped short of sinking USS *Pueblo*. It is reasonable to assume that Pyongyang was aware of the precedent set in the USS *Liberty* incident of the previous year (1967) in which that 'spy' ship was subject to Israeli torpedo and aircraft attack while monitoring radio transmissions in international waters during the Six-Day War; the United States did not retaliate. (See: Till, *Seapower, 3rd Ed.*, p. 232; Cable, *Gunboat Diplomacy, 3rd Ed.*, p. 195.)
20 Cable described the incident as definitive with North Korea as the 'assailant' and the United States as the 'victim.'
21 European Union. Library of the European Parliament. Vutz, Cornelia. *The East China Sea Territorial Dispute: Senkaku, Diaoyu, or Tiaoyutai Islands?* (Library Briefing, 29 July 2013), p. 1.
22 Ibid.
23 Patalano, Alessio. 'Sea Power, Maritime Disputes, and the Evolving Security of the East and South China Seas.' *RUSI Journal* 158, No. 6 (2013): p. 51.
24 Ibid.
25 EU, *The East China Sea Territorial Dispute*, p. 2.
26 Patalano, 'Sea Power, Maritime Disputes', p. 49.
27 Lanteigne, Marc. *Chinese Foreign Policy: An Introduction, 2nd Ed.* (Abingdon: Routledge, 2013), p. 55.
28 EU, *The East China Sea Territorial Dispute*, p. 2.
29 Japan. 'Defense of Japan.' Japanese Defense White Paper 2011. www.mod.go.jp/e/publ/w_paper/2011.html (accessed 23 May 2013).
30 Global Security. 'Senkaku/Diaoyutai Islands.' www.globalsecurity.org/military/world/war/senkaku.htm (accessed 17 June 2013).

31 Japan, Defense White Paper 2011. In addition, Lanteigne, *Chinese Foreign Policy, 2nd Ed.*, p. 3; also, Pedrozo, Paul. 'Beijing's Coastal Real Estate: A History of Chinese Naval Aggression.' *Foreign Affairs*, 15 November 2010. www.foreignaffairs.com/arti cles/67007/raul-pedrozo/beijings-coastal-real-estate (accessed 22 November 2010).
32 Patalano, 'Sea Power, Maritime Disputes', p. 52. This does not include the claim that oceanographic research ships entered the territorial waters in 2008, discussed above.
33 Ibid.
34 Ibid., p. 53.
35 BBC. 'China Establishes Air Defence Zone over East China Sea.' 23 November 2013. www.bbc.co.uk/news/world-asia-25062525 (accessed 31 March 2014).
36 EU, *The East China Sea Territorial Dispute*, p. 5.
37 Patalano, 'Sea Power, Maritime Disputes', p. 48.
38 Till, Geoffrey. *Asia's Naval Expansion: An Arms Race in the Making.* (London: Rout-ledge, 2012), p. 149.
39 BBC. 'Q&A: China-Japan Islands Row.' 27 November 2013. www.bbc.co.uk/news/world-asia-pacific-11341139 (accessed 31 March 2014).
40 BBC, 'China Establishes Air Defence Zone over East China Sea.'
41 USA Today. 'US Sends B-52s over Chinese Claimed Water.' 26 November 2013. www.usatoday.com/story/news/world/2013/11/26/japan-china-senkaku-islands/3746771/ (accessed 24 July 2014).
42 The Guardian. 'Obama Says U.S. Will Defend Japan in Island Dispute with China.' www.theguardian.com/world/2014/apr/24/obama-in-japan-backs-status-quo-in-island-dispute-with-china (accessed 27 June 2014).
43 Though the Air Defence Identification Zone may not constitute a legal blockade under Article 42 of the UN Charter, it has been discussed in those terms in the popular media. See, for example: BBC. 'Why China Air Zone Raises Risk.' 26 November 2013. www.bbc.co.uk/news/world-asia-25086345 (accessed 31 March 2014).
44 Greenpeace. 'Save the Arctic.' www.savethearctic.org/ (accessed 24 March 2014).
45 Greenpeace. *Statement of Facts Concerning the Boarding and Detention of the MY Arctic Sunrise and the Judicial Proceedings against All 30 Persons on Board.* (Amster-dam: Greenpeace International, 19 October 2013), p. 2.
46 Kramer, Andrew E. 'Greenpeace Activists Climb Russian Oil Rig.' *New York Times*, 24 August 2012. www.nytimes.com/2012/08/25/world/europe/greenpeace-activists-climb-russian-oil-rig-in-arctic-ocean.html?_r=1& (accessed 24 March 2014).
47 Depledge, Duncan & Dodds, Klaus. 'No "Strategy" Please, We're British.' *RUSI Journal* 159, No. 1 (2014): p. 29.
48 Greenpeace, 'Statement of Facts Concerning MY Arctic Sunrise', p. 4.
49 It is worthy of note that different states employ different types of Coastguard. In the UK, for example, the Maritime Coastguard Agency's role is predominantly limited to marine safety and search and rescue. At the other end of the scale the US Coast-guard has a military role in wartime. (See: Till, *Seapower, 3rd Ed.*, pp. 314–316; Speller, *Understanding Naval Warfare*, pp. 153–154. The Russian Coastguard could be described as tending towards the paramilitary in its execution of constabulary tasks.
50 Greenpeace, 'Statement of Facts Concerning MY Arctic Sunrise', pp. 4–9.
51 ITAR-TASS. 'Greenpeace Case: 30 Arctic Sunrise Crewmembers Detained.' 25 Sep-tember 2013. http://en.itar-tass.com/greenpeace-ship-arctic-sunrise-case/701253 (accessed 24 March 2014); Zylstra, Ashton. 'Piracy or Hooliganism: Detention of the Arctic Sunrise.' *Matters of Russian and International Law* 9, No. 10 (2013): p. 10.
52 See, for instance: Rosenberg, Steve. 'Russia "Seizes" Greenpeace Ship after Arctic Rig Protest.' BBC, 23 September 2013. www.bbc.co.uk/news/world-europe-24170129 (accessed 24 March 2014).
53 Greenpeace, 'Statement of Facts Concerning MY Arctic Sunrise', p. 14.
54 Depledge & Dodds, 'No "Strategy" Please, We're British', p. 29.

55 United Nations. International Tribunal for the Law of the Sea. 'Case No. 22: The Arctic Sunrise Case (Kingdom of the Netherlands v. Russian Federation), Provisional Measures.' www.itlos.org/index.php?id=264 (accessed 24 March 2014).

56 Zylstra, 'Piracy or Hooliganism', p. 15.

57 Gazprom. 'About Gazprom.' www.gazprom.com/about/history/chronicle/1989-1995/ (accessed 27 June 2014).

58 United States. Congressional Research Service. Rinehart, Ian E., Hildreth, Steven A. & Lawrence, Susan V. *Ballistic Missile Defense in the Asia-Pacific Region: Cooperation and Opposition*. R43116. (Washington, DC: CRS, 2013), p. 8.

59 Chaudhary, Upendra. 'Why Countries Go for Ballistic Missiles?' *Indian Defence Review* 13, No. 2 (1998). www.indiandefencereview.com/print/?print_post-id=5367 (accessed 20 February 2014).

60 Masters, Jonathan & Bruno, Greg. 'Council on Foreign Relations.' US Ballistic Missile Defence. www.cfr.org/missile-defense/us-ballistic-missile-defense/p30607 (accessed 3 February 2014).

61 NATO. 'Ballistic Missile Defence Brief.' www.nato.int/cps/en/natolive/topics_49635.htm (accessed 15 March 2014).

62 Tigner, Brooks. 'Nato Announces Interim BMD Capability But Still Faces Daunting Schedule.' Jane's International Defense Review 45, No. 6 (2012): p. 6.

63 United States. 'Missile Defence Agency.' www.mda.mil/ (accessed 14 March 2014).

64 United States. US Navy. 'Navy Names Forward Deployed Ships to Rota, Spain.' www.navy.mil/submit/display.asp?story_id=65393 (accessed 28 June 2014).

65 As previously stated, 'securitization' is a hypothesis which suggests that a state might exaggerate the threat against it in order to legitimize its subsequent actions. See: Waever, Ole. 'Securitization and Desecuritization.' In Lipschutz, Ronnie (Ed.). *On Security*. (New York: Columbia University Press, 1995), pp. 46–86.

66 United States. White House. *National Policy on Ballistic Missile Defense Fact Sheet*. National Security Presidential Directive 23, 20 May 2003. (Washington, DC: White House, 2003).

67 United States. Congressional Research Service. O'Rourke, R. *Navy Aegis Ballistic Missile Defense (BMD) Program: Background and Issues for Congress*. RL33745. (Washington, DC: CRS, 2010), pp. 3, 7, 9.

68 Goldreiger, James & McFaul, Michael. 'A Tale of Two Worlds: Core and Periphery in the Post-Cold War Era.' In Buzan, Barry & Hansen, Lene (Eds.). *International Security Volume II: The Transition to the Post-Cold War Security Agenda*. (London: Sage, 2007), p. 284.

69 Graham, Cheryl M. *Deterrence Revalidated: An Investigation of the Practice and Application of Deterrence in the Post-Cold War World*. PhD Thesis. University of Aberdeen, Aberdeen, 2010, p. 23.

Conclusion

This book set out to look at old ideas and see if they were still relevant in the 21st century. But what were the ideas? If the body of work by the various theorists, practitioners and commentators is combined, it can be seen that both qualitative and quantitative approaches were put to use. Mahan never used the term 'naval diplomacy', but he did describe various acts which might be classified as such today. Cable took a dataset of over 100 naval incidents over seven decades of the 20th century and analyzed them to support his hypothesis. Those writings and others can be used to construct models which can then aid the analysis of particular scenarios, and that has not changed.

However, the introduction posed a series of questions, and some hypotheses were proposed which, when answered, would address the place and utility of naval diplomacy in the post-Cold War global order. It is time to return to these questions and provide some conclusions:

1   What is naval diplomacy? How does it differ from or build upon other forms of military/defence diplomacy?

It was determined in Chapter 1 that diplomacy is a communicative process that seeks to further the interests of an international actor, and not just through codified discourse. Bargaining, lobbying and non-verbal communication are the norms of human interaction and an integral part of diplomatic practice. The process need not be limited to recognized states and there are numerous examples of international institutions, multinational corporations, non-governmental organizations and *de facto* territorial administrations which partake in diplomatic dialogue.

The concept of niche diplomacy was then introduced, which refers to actors in possession of particular strengths, relative to other actors, bringing them to bear in their power relationships. The employment of military forces in pursuit of political advantage short of war would therefore be a form of niche diplomacy by those with appropriate capabilities, particularly the militarily strong, which could be applied along a spectrum of behaviour from the 'hard' (deterrence and coercion, up to and including kinetic force) to the 'soft' (the range of outreach and engagement now commonly referred to as defence diplomacy). From time to time weaker actors might also resort to the employment of military forces to communicate their messages, either through choice, including at times when the stronger actor is politically more constrained in its use of the military instrument, or because they believe they have no better alternative at their disposal. The subtle or limited use of military force could even enhance its effectiveness over an overt threat or ultimatum as a policy instrument for both the strong and the weak.

Land and air forces can be, and of course are, used as diplomatic instruments at specific points along the sliding scale of operations, but it is naval forces which offer the greatest choice to those wielding them. The particular advantages of flexibility, presence without commitment, political leverage, reach and sustainability make naval forces ideally suited to the task of international communication. These attributes may not necessarily endure forever, but they have stood the test of time until now. Naval forces are not the hammers of the toolbox, able to bang home a nail; they are the wrenches, able to tighten or loosen as the situation dictates.[1] Instinctively, navies and their people know this; as Roger Barnett wrote in his book with the intriguing subtitle *Why Navies Think Differently*,

> whereas controls over visitors from other countries are imposed on land and permission must be obtained for overflight of another international state, the open seas are available for use by all. This near absence of political control means that the legal regimen for the high seas tends to be modest in scope. The politically uncontrolled nature of the oceans [. . .] makes the maritime environment unique.[2]

The terms 'naval' and 'maritime' are used variously by commentators to describe at-sea activity, including diplomatic, communicative engagements. Etymologically, 'maritime' has its roots in 'of the sea', whereas the meaning of 'naval' is found in 'of ships' or 'of navies', that is fleets of ships. Although the activities under investigation in this book take place in the maritime environment, they are more properly characterized by the tools of their delivery – the fleets of ships, submarines and, at times, aircraft which actors employ. Therefore, although both terms are acceptable, 'naval' is arguably more accurate when applied to the diplomatic use of sea power.

The book, consequently, supports the first hypothesis described in the introduction. Naval diplomacy is a subset of general diplomacy and will be used as a means of communication by maritime states in pursuit of their national interest. More specifically, it can be defined as the use of naval assets as communicative instruments in international power relationships to further the interests of the actors involved.

2   What are the traditional models of naval diplomacy? Who conducts it, how, with what aim and against whom?

The temporal classification of naval diplomacy into pre-Cold War, Cold War and post-Cold War periods is purely a construct of this book. It was done because the accepted theories largely emanated from the bipolar geopolitical world of the

Cold War and therefore did not necessarily fully account for that which went before or that which would come afterwards.

Reviewing other periods reveals different interpretations of the utility of naval forces in peacetime or, at least, when not engaged in total war. In the 19th and early 20th centuries, for example, writers focused on the deterrent effect of navies, on the 'status' that they could embody and on their usefulness in building international relationships and alliances.

Cable's hierarchy of *definitive, purposeful, catalytic* and *expressive* modes, which ranged from hard to soft power and from the highly effective to the token, became a standard in the Cold War. However, other Cold War commentators returned to familiar themes of coercion, non-coercive influence and alliance building, always with one eye on the prestige value of naval power. It was the post-Cold War, post-modern commentators who widened the debate, bringing into focus a continuum of hard to soft power effects through coercion, protection, persuasion and assistance.

Nonetheless, whether 'classical', Cold War or 'post-modern', the models or frameworks for naval diplomacy display a number of enduring themes. First, the earliest models are based in the *realist* or *liberal realist* theoretical traditions of international relations. Classical naval writers such as Mahan and Corbett saw their advocacy of sea power, including the use of force in peacetime, as a means to further the interests of the user at the expense of the recipient. Similarly, observers of the Cold War protagonists, including Sir James Cable with his 'strong and weak', 'assailant and victim' themes, speak directly to realism.

Second, and closely linked to the realist tradition, each model is essentially *state centric*. Though the post-Cold War, 'post-modern' commentators place less overt emphasis on the state, couching their words in terms such as 'globalism' and acknowledging the importance of institutions, international law and coalitions, the state remains the basic unit of discourse. Mike Mullen, for instance, did not propose his vision of a 1,000-ship navy or global maritime partnership for altruistic reasons. He wanted the United States, his country, to be at the heart of it and to lead it.

Third, each model is based on a mechanistic methodology in which one 'side' does something and the 'other side' reacts. That the models rely on this action-reaction process between the (primarily) state actors involved means that they are essentially *binary* in nature.

Fourth, and following on from the previous three observations, the realist, state-centric, binary models of naval diplomacy are all outcome based and they thus demand that decisions be made. In Schelling's theory of arms and influence, success depends on the individual's assumption of rationality and on the individual's accuracy of prediction of outcomes. In other words, the models are based on attempts to manipulate the *cognitive* process: 'actions are chosen for both their immediate effect and for the effect they have on the other player's choice'.[3]

Existing models, then, can be described as event-based approximations of state actors' use of the 'spare capacity' inherent in military navies when not at war to influence other state actors. The hypotheses that existing models were conceived in the Cold War and are products of their time, and that they assume a binary, mechanistic relationship between the actors involved, are supported by the research.

3   What, if anything, is new in the post-Cold War era? Have 'globalization' and the perceived increasing importance of non-state actors affected naval diplomacy? Has the incidence of naval diplomacy changed over time?

Globalization did not begin with the fall of the Soviet Union, but the cross-border flow of goods and services, the transnational nature of political decision-making, the interdependence between states and the proliferation of problems requiring global rather than local solutions all increased pace after 1991.[4] The examples of naval diplomacy cited in this book might prove useful to some readers and researchers but they are inevitably incomplete overviews. However, they do show that it is the most capable navies which are best suited to respond to the emerging global order. Opportunists, both state and non-state, also make use of the sea to further their aims and rising powers, particularly China and India, have found naval expansion to be a necessary accompaniment to economic growth and global influence. As Simon Serfaty stated when introducing the idea of a post-Western world, it is 'not about the decline of the West, but the ascendency of everyone else'.[5]

The book has also shown that naval diplomacy is primarily but not exclusively carried out by states and that the appetite of non-state actors to become involved in international communication on the global seas appears to be increasing. As a 2009 US Naval Institute *Proceedings* article which discussed the 'contested commons' stated: 'There is a consensus that rising state and non-state powers, combined with continued globalization, will put great pressure on the international system as a whole'.[6] That pressure will inevitably need to be managed, but not necessarily through force. The instruments of sea power are used numerically more for the purpose of amity than they are to express enmity; however, at the 'harder' end of the spectrum of operations there is little discernible difference in the desired outcomes of incidents before, during or after the Cold War. At the 'softer' end of the scale there are degrees of engagement which, when considered objectively, can be used to judge the health of any particular international relationship. However, the impact of disengagement, or proactively *not* doing something, should not be underestimated. Navies are and have always been used for symbolic purposes and that symbolism perhaps approached a new zenith in the post-Cold War era with an international doctrine of humanitarianism and friendly co-operation fuelled by public opinion informed in turn by global media coverage.

In summary, the principles of naval diplomacy have in all probability changed little over time but, as hypothesized, its use is more prevalent than the literature suggests. If we look to the future we may start to see new aspects of an old role: ballistic missile defence at sea, theatre security co-operation, the enforcement of no-fly zones, forward presence, freedom and navigation operations and global fleet stations are already new forms of naval diplomacy. Others will follow. The hypothesis that naval diplomacy spans a broad spectrum from hard to soft power can certainly be supported but, as the strategies of the major sea powers testify, there is always advantage to be had from a 'decided preponderance at sea' – a Mahanian phrase which is every bit as valuable in peacetime as it is in war, now as a century ago.[7]

4   Are the existing models for naval diplomacy still valid? To what extent do they require revision? Do they appropriately encompass likely target audiences (potential adversaries, potential allies and domestic audiences)?

The existing models of naval diplomacy, due to their limited scope, particularly their state-centrism and relative focus of hard power effects, are not sufficient to understand every nuance of the naval diplomacy practiced either at their time of conception nor since 1991. In fact, many of the examples of cited in this book would not have qualified for inclusion in Cable, Luttwak or Booth's theoretical frameworks, but they are nonetheless valid uses of sea power.

In addition, the enduring themes outlined above have not completely withstood scrutiny through the analyses presented in the book. The actions in the Adriatic and the containment of Iraq in the 1990s, for instance, were taken under the mandate of the United Nations and not by states acting in isolation. Non-state actors such as the Tamil Tigers, Hezbollah, the organizers of the Gaza Freedom Flotilla and Greenpeace have challenged the assumption that naval diplomacy is purely a nation state's business. As Yezid Sayigh wrote in 1998, 'strategic coercion involving non-state actors is likely to be part of inseparable, continuous adversary relationships rather than one-off episodes'.[8] The United States' flexing of muscles in the Taiwan Strait in the mid-1990s was as much a message to its own domestic audience and to Taiwan as it was to mainland China. Similarly, North Korea's securitization and Russia's gain from US miscalculation of Black Sea relationships, especially that with Ukraine, undermine the existing models' doctrine that naval diplomacy is a binary, mechanistic interaction between an assailant and a victim. Even so, one enduring theme does hold true: at its core, every conscious application of sea power to communicate political intent assumes rationality on the part of the audience at the receiving end; the difficulty can be identifying that audience.

The real world examples used show that incidents of naval diplomacy are seldom limited to just two parties. In a significant number of cases three or more actors are involved and, often, there is also a plain intent to send a message to the domestic, regional or international community. A case in point could be the Persian or Arabian Gulf at any time in the last few decades. Are Western powers there to contain? To reassure? To build relationships? To protect oil supplies? Is it true to assert that 'my enemy's enemy is my friend?' Who is doing what, to whom or with whom is not necessarily a straightforward question to answer. There are numerous examples described in this book which show the complexity of international relations and the corresponding intricacy of naval diplomacy. Any attempt to describe the incident in bilateral terms between any of the actors would be unsophisticated and erroneous.

From these findings it is concluded that the existing understanding of naval diplomacy is insufficient. As the hypothesis presented in the introduction stated, an alternative foundational model, not based solely on events, but drawing on basic communication and stakeholder theories, is therefore required.

5   Can a new model be constructed? If so, what should be its key tenets?

A new foundational model for naval diplomacy has been proposed which takes into account the strengths and shortcomings of previous frameworks and the realities of contemporary sea power. To provide a framework for comprehension and a vehicle for determining purpose, the *why?* of naval diplomacy, the model asks three basic and interdependent questions – *who? what?* and *how?* – before expanding to second- and third-order levels of analysis through the application of basic communication theory, basic stakeholder theory and the common understanding of naval roles and methods, particularly those 'composite' missions and tactics derived from the available evidence. Different theoretical approaches are equally valid, but the foundational model developed in this book is an attempt to construct a practical framework based not only in theory but also in the reality of events in recent history. It is not presented as *the* model for naval diplomacy in the 21st century, but as *a* model which may complement those which have gone before in order to provide a useful, alternative tool for analysis in future.

As the implications below explain, the final hypothesis posed in the introduction, that understanding of contemporary naval diplomacy can aid the development of appropriate force structures and capabilities of maritime states, can be supported. However, there is more. Though developed for the study of naval diplomacy, the simple interdisciplinary approach taken in the construction of the model in this book may make it useful for other purposes. It could certainly be applied in the study of other areas of military, defence or diplomatic activity such as peacekeeping operations, international development and the provision of foreign aid. It may assist in the understanding of conflict resolution by unpicking the constituent parts of any dispute. It may also be pertinent to trading relationships, particularly technology proliferation, and their impact on security.

Implications

It would reveal a certain degree of hubris for a book of this nature to make extravagant or excessive claims for the implications of its findings. Conversely, it would be remarkable if it had yielded none at all. Through the scrutiny of existing literature on naval diplomacy, the use of examples from the immediate post-Cold War era and the construction of a new analytical model, an alternative perspective has been developed which could aid future understanding of national and international security responses. For instance, naval deployments could be more effectively targeted; foreign activity at sea could be better understood and, if necessary, countered; and the ability of non-state actors to further their own interests, or to support national or even supra-national interests from the sea could be better harnessed. The implications of this work can be addressed in three broad and overlapping categories: its contribution to theoretical debate, its meaning for policymakers and, finally, its utility for practitioners.

In the course of researching for this book it has been acknowledged that Sir James Cable's *Gunboat Diplomacy* is a widely accepted, standard discourse on the topic, particularly in its treatment of the coercive element of naval diplomacy. A contribution to theoretical development, therefore, has been to take Cable's framework forward into the post-Cold War global order. No other known work has applied Cable's methodology and categorization to post-1991 events, and certainly not for the number and range of examples (over 500 from all parts of the world) examined in Chapter 3 and detailed in the Appendix. Whilst providing a continuation of Cable's work into the 21st century, the book has also challenged its validity, especially its widely accepted notions of state-centricity, 'action-reaction' processes and ready dismissal of 'soft' power methods.

Other novel contributions to theoretical development include the challenge to the widely accepted series of 'enduring' naval attributes, the association of securitization with naval diplomacy, and the application of multi-disciplinary concepts such as basic communication and basic stakeholder theories to its core principles. These may spark further debate.

Sir James Cable announced in his final edition of *Gunboat Diplomacy* that 'coercive diplomacy will be less costly and less of a risk than war'.[9] This book supports that assertion and extends it to include the range of other possible activities beyond hard power effects carried out by state actors. Naval diplomacy is, and will continue to be, a cost-effective use of sea power in peacetime and is not merely 'less risky' than war, but could actually reduce the risk of war. This is a point that policymakers should be cognizant of and the book's examples could contribute to understanding and consequently facilitate evidence-based decision-making for those who work in the policy arena.

By using practical evidence to inform decisions rather than relying on potentially skewed, politically motivated assessments, policymakers should be better able to make logical choices which will in turn lead to better value for money and eventually more successful pursuit of their interests at and from the sea. The book may assists in this by its layered *what?, who?* and *how?* framework, connecting message with audience, tactic with platform and, ultimately, purpose with outcome.

For nation states, a better understanding of naval diplomacy would help to inform investment decisions which will inevitably be made according to scale of national ambition. As an example, it could be used to support a proposition that a state with limited military capability or resource should invest in, say, hydrographic survey ships to provide a niche service for its region, if such a thing were lacking. Alternatively, it may be determined that a state with global aspirations should invest in hospital ships or disaster relief capabilities if it sought to extend its international influence through non-coercive means and shed any legacy image of a poor human rights record. Of course, the diplomatic role is not necessarily the defining mission of navies and these insights must be assessed alongside other requirements, particularly the military 'war-fighting' and constabulary roles of naval forces.

Similarly, the evidence base could be used to suggest procurement of multi-purpose rather than single role platforms, given the range of tasks and the unpredictability of employment which navies commonly face. Paradoxically, greater specialization has historically meant higher unit costs, therefore fewer hulls and consequently fewer opportunities to demonstrate forward presence. The quantity versus quality debate, prevalent in much contemporary naval commentary, could be fed from the examples cited in the Appendix.

Both persistent forward presence and infrequent, targeted deployments have purpose and reason, but which works better? How to employ a navy is undoubtedly a question which has vexed policymakers for generations, and there are no straightforward answers. However, subject to a more refined determination of 'success' criteria, the book may be able to provide some data on the relative merits of deployment type when considering diplomatic messaging and assist in planning based on outcome, rather than simply founded on ease of delivery. In short, there is a rich seam of evidence to assist decision-making on acquisition, force structures and deployment priorities.

For non-state actors the research may be similarly useful. It captures numerous cases of non-state actors attempting to communicate enmity and amity through various means, but their incidence is still not as ubiquitous as that of nation states. Understanding the nature of the maritime 'global commons' and the possibilities inherent in its use as a communication medium could fuel growth in this area of activity.

Finally, all decision makers could call on the evidence and the new model to better understand the actions of others. Is another actor's deployment a signal of amity or enmity, is it aiming its message at its competitors or its own population, and is the demonstration of high levels of interoperability with a third party a thing of concern? Again, the book may not directly provide the answer, but it could provide a framework within which to logically ask the right questions.

For practitioners, the book and its findings might be used in a number of ways. First, the sheer scale of naval diplomatic activity could be acknowledged and its principles incorporated into future doctrine, education and training. For too long the ability to engage in naval diplomacy has been seen as a 'free good' born of military sea power.[10] This does not necessarily need to be the case. For instance, appreciating that the strategic purpose of a bilateral exercise is at least in part the existence of the exercise itself and not just the quality of the tactical training it offers, could be a valuable insight to those involved and ultimately lead to improved outcomes. Arab-Israeli exercises, for example, fall into this category, as do US-South Korean exercises undertaken in full view of Pyongyang, and US-Japanese shows of strength in the South and East China Seas.

Second, practitioners will continue to question whether post-modern navies can sustain the full spectrum of operations that they took for granted in the past. The diplomatic utility of military forces does depend on credibility and capability, but as force structures change and navies, certainly in the West, reduce in size, the necessary combination of credibility and capability may well be achieved through partnerships, coalitions and alliances. In the future there could be a real need for closer co-operation and greater collaboration to further self-interest – the '1,000-ship navy' aspiration offered one such vision; there may be similar initiatives in future, and they may not all be friendly. This book can be used to identify those actors already embarked on this process of global or regional maritime partnership and, importantly, to ascertain which rung they occupy on the engagement 'ladder'. Likewise, it could indicate where comparable opportunities lie for other actors considering similar moves. By understanding intent, practitioners can more effectively acknowledge their own strengths and vulnerabilities and spot those of competitors.

Third, harnessing the communicative element of the political war for ideas will play an increasing part in conflict in future. This is a point articulated in the comments of David Ayalon, Israel's deputy foreign minister during the Gaza Freedom Flotilla encounter in 2010, who said: 'As you know, today the war is in the screens. This is a political war, a PR war and also a legal warfare'.[11] In practical terms, this means that practitioners should incorporate their strategic communication messages into each stage of the planning process for routine and bespoke deployments and determine the best means to deliver them. The use of the media, including new or social media channels, to maximize and target the communicative element of naval diplomatic activity employment, would be a logical progression of business, and this research could, through its incorporation of basic communication theory and espousal of target audience analysis, prompt such considerations.

This book has largely concentrated on the diplomatic activities of the seven or eight most capable 'military' navies of the day. The more detailed study of smaller coastal navies and coastguards may reveal different patterns; conversely, it might confirm the series of enduring principles and deem them applicable to all shapes and sizes of force and in all corners of the globe. Such research would be a logical next step.

The selected examples revealed a trend of increasing activity at sea by non-state and semi-state actors. Greater analysis of the range of actors engaged and the type of activity they practice would be valuable. This could include but should not be limited to the study of semi-governmental bodies, non-governmental organizations, multinational corporations, independent research authorities, fishing communities, criminal organizations, terrorist or paramilitary groups and those who use the sea for leisure purposes. As an example, future research could ask whether there is a communicative, environmental campaigning element to the activities of the latter group when they mount 'expeditions' to the Southern Ocean and Antarctica. If so, how does it work and how well is it received? If such expeditions grew in size and number, how would the international community react? This would not be a study of tourism but a study of messaging at sea.

Multinational acquisition projects and the 'gifting' of naval platforms have been briefly discussed and they may also offer a rich vein for further analysis. If the type of exercise or activity practiced is an indicator of the health of the relationship between the actors involved, then the same would almost certainly apply to the degree of collaborative procurement and joint technological development carried out between actors. Highly technical and specialist industries such as aerospace, weaponry and advanced warship design and construction are commonly developed by multinational consortia, suggesting close, trusting relationships. Is there evidence that these politico-industrial partnerships translate into politico-military alliances? What of defence sales to potentially hostile competitors? France's 2014 decision to stop the export of amphibious shipping to Russia after the latter's adventurism in Ukraine is an interesting diversion.

Finally, there is a tendency to equate naval diplomacy with the overt presence of surface warships, typified by Edward Luttwak's advocacy of 'visibility' over 'viability' and Sir James Cable's repeated dismissal of submarines as useful diplomatic instruments.[12] The reality, as this book has shown, is different. It is not just about 'gunboats'. To achieve a greater fidelity in understanding this difference the type of platform (submarine, aircraft carrier, frigate or patrol vessel) used could be mapped against the type of activity practiced to determine whether or not there is an optimum configuration to express amity or enmity, soft or hard power, or to reach the desired target audience. The impact of technology could also be better understood as it pertains to naval diplomacy; was Robert Gates wrong? Do you actually need 'a billion-dollar warship' if you are to impress, educate and attract another actor to your cause?

The common denominator of all these things is, of course, the measure of effectiveness of any particular example. Perhaps the most difficult question which needs to be addressed is that of the definition of success and failure in naval diplomacy. Frustratingly it has been, and remains, intangible.

Notes

1 The hammer and spanner analogy was first used by Sir James Cable. See: Cable, James. *Gunboat Diplomacy 1919–1991: Political Applications of Limited Naval Force, 3rd Ed.* (Basingstoke: Macmillan, 1994), p. 147.
2 Barnett, Roger. *Navy Strategic Culture: Why the Navy Thinks Differently.* (Annapolis: Naval Institute Press, 2009), p. 32.
3 Schelling, Thomas C. *Arms and Influence* (2008 Edition). (New Haven: Yale University Press, 2008), pp. 3–5.
4 Hay, Colin. 'International Relations Theory and Globalization.' In Dunne, Tim, Kurki, Milja & Smith, Steve (Eds.). *International Relations Theories: Discipline and Diversity, 3rd Ed.* (Oxford: Oxford University Press, 2013), p. 294.
5 Serfaty, Simon. 'Moving into a Post-Western World.' *Washington Quarterly* 34, No. 2 (2011): p. 8.
6 Flournoy, Michele & Brimley, Shawn. 'The Contested Commons.' *U.S. Naval Institute Proceedings* 137, No. 7 (2009): p. 18.
7 Mahan, Alfred, T. *The Influence of Sea Power Upon History, 1660–1783.* (Mineola, NY: Dover, 1987), p. 82.
8 Sayigh, 'A Non-state Actor as Coercer and Coerced', p. 212.
9 Cable, *Gunboat Diplomacy, 3rd Ed.*, p. 146.
10 There was an erroneous assumption in many Western post-Cold War navies that preparation for 'high-end' war fighting meant that 'lesser' roles such as peace support,

humanitarian assistance and diplomacy could be automatically achieved. Costly experience showed that this was not the case and each required doctrine, planning, training and refinement.

11 Tatham, Steve, *Strategic Communication in conflict and the concept of non-kinetic informational effect in military operations with special reference to the British experience in the historical context, its contemporary application in Afghanistan and in future*. PhD Thesis. University of Southampton, Southampton, 2011, p. 178. The quote is attributed to Ayalon, David, 'Reactions to Raid on Flotilla', by Beckerman, Gal, *New York Jewish Daily*, 2 June 2010.

12 Luttwak, Edward, N. *The Political Uses of Sea Power*. (Baltimore: Johns Hopkins University Press, 1974), p. 39; Cable, *Gunboat Diplomacy 3rd Ed.*, p. 71. See also Widen, J.J. 'Naval Diplomacy – A Theoretical Approach.' *Diplomacy and Statecraft* 22, No. 4 (2011): p. 728, which describes naval platforms, 'large surface warships especially', as the 'perfect' vehicles for representing their country.

Appendix

Chronological index of incidents of naval diplomacy

Incidents of naval diplomacy 1991–2010

Key

Cable classification

D	(Definitive):	the act or threat of force which possessed a definitive purpose apparent to both sides.
P	(Purposeful):	less direct; limited naval force applied in order to change the policy or character of a foreign government.
C	(Catalytic):	'lends a hand' to act as a catalyst in a situation the direction of which has yet to be determined.
E	(Expressive):	where warships are employed to emphasize attitudes or to make a point.
–	(No entry):	incidents which Cable would not have categorised as gunboat diplomacy and would not have listed in his index.

Composite classification

The major outcomes specified by existing models of naval diplomacy, shown in Chapter 2:

Coercion, Deterrence, Co-operation, Prestige, Reassurance, Picture Building, Attraction, Assistance.

Date	Principal Actors	Description	Cable Classification	Composite Classification
1991				
January	US Somalia	USS *Guam* and *Trenton* conduct Non-Combatant Evacuation Operation (NEO) from Somalia, taking 281 people of 30 nationalities to a place of safety[1]	D	Assistance
January	UK Libya US Iraq	Britain deploys HMS *Ark Royal* to the Mediterranean to poise off Libya, freeing US aircraft carriers to deploy to the Gulf[2]	P	Co-operation/ Deterrence
January	US Iraq	US CVN conducts air strikes against Iraqi forces, as part of the commencement of *Desert Storm* hostilities following Iraq's invasion of Kuwait in August 1990[3]	D	Coercion
January to February	Australia US UK Iraq	The Australian Defence Force contribution to Op *Desert Storm* includes incorporating HMAS *Brisbane* and *Sydney* into a USN battle group. A medical team also serve in the US Hospital Ship *Comfort*[4]	E	Co-operation
February	US Iraq	Following *Desert Storm* the US poises amphibious shipping in the Arabian Gulf with 18,000 Marines afloat[5]	P	Coercion
February	Italy Libya	Italy stations its corvette *Danaide* off Libya during Exercise *Mare Aperto*[6]	E	Coercion
February	US UK Saudi Arabia Iraq	Iraqi naval threat to Western and regional interests rendered ineffective by US, UK and Saudi air strikes[7]	D	Coercion
February	Australia Greece	RAN deploys HMAS *Perth* to the Mediterranean in support of the 50th anniversary of the WWII campaigns in Greece and Crete[8]	E	Reassurance/ Prestige
March	USSR NATO	Soviet forces continue to withdraw from Eastern Europe and streamline structures, but Soviet Navy continue to update capabilities, exempt from defence wide cuts[9]	–	Prestige

Month	Actor	Event	Code	Category
March	US, Iraq, Int Community	Ships and aircraft from USN carriers begin to enforce sanctions and a no-fly zone over southern Iraq[10]	–	Deterrence/Reassurance
March	Australia, Indonesia	RAN conducts its largest ever fisheries surveillance operation in its northern waters and apprehends 35 Indonesian vessels fishing illegally[11]	P	Deterrence
April	Germany, Iraq	Germany commits five MCMVs and two support ships to the Gulf in its first out-of-area NATO deployment[12]	E	Co-operation/Prestige
April	Australia, Indonesia	HMAS *Launceston* and *Wollongong* pay goodwill visit to Ambon in Indonesia for an ANZAC Day service[13]	E	Attraction/Prestige
April	Japan, Iraq, Int Community	Japanese Security Council and Cabinet make decision to send minesweepers to Gulf; six depart at the end of the month and return in October[14]	E	Prestige/Co-operation
May	Australia, Solomon Islands, Tonga, Philippines	An Australian vessel visits Honiara to host a sea day for local VIPs and media from the Solomon Islands and Tonga. Separately, a ship visits the Philippines for another sea day[15]	E	Prestige/Co-operation
May to June	UK, Bangladesh	RFA *Fort George* and Royal Marine units conduct Op *Manna*, providing flood relief in Bangladesh following a cyclone[16]	–	Assistance
June	Iran, US	Two Iranian speed boats exercising in central Gulf fire on USS *La Salle*[17]	P	Coercion
July	UK, Grenada	HMS *Ambuscade* is diverted to Grenada to reassure the island's prime minister, who feared civil unrest[18]	P	Reassurance
July	USSR, Germany, NATO	The Soviet Union withdraws its final warships from former East German bases[19]	C/E	–
August	USSR	Warships blockade Tallinn in Estonia during a coup attempt to overthrow President Gorbachev[20]	C	Coercion
August	USSR, Vietnam	Soviet ships in the Indian Ocean temporarily relocate to Vietnam before coup attempt in Moscow[21]	C	Coercion/Reassurance
September	Australia, Philippines	Following volcanic eruptions in the Philippines, HMAS *Swan* and *Westralia* visit and carry out repair work[22]	–	Assistance

(Continued)

Date	Principal Actors	Description	Cable Classification	Composite Classification
September	USSR Finland	An unidentified submarine violates Finnish territorial waters[23]	E	Picture Building
September	NATO USSR	NATO conducts a series of naval exercises in the North Atlantic (*Vendetta, Strong Nut, North Star*)[24]	C/E	Deterrence/ Prestige
September	UK France	The UK and France look to collaborate on a new nuclear submarine project[25]	–	Co-operation
September	NATO	NATO considers establishment of standing naval force in the Mediterranean[26]	C/E	Attraction/ Prestige/ Co-operation
October	USSR Int Community	Soviet Union announces that half of its Pacific Fleet submarines will be scrapped, then redeploys two SSGNs from the Northern Fleet to the Pacific[27]	E	–
October	France China Taiwan	China protests after France sells six frigates to Taiwan[28]	–	Deterrence/ Co-operation
October	UK Egypt	UK and Egypt conduct a week-long bilateral naval exercise and port visit; only the third such exercise since the 1956 *Suez Crisis*[29]	E	Co-operation
October to March 1992	UK Haiti	HMS *Amazon* stands ready off Haiti to conduct NEO after military coup[30]	P	Assistance
November	South Korea North Korea Int Community	The first global deployment of the Republic of Korea Navy. Two frigates visit Portsmouth[31]	E	Prestige
November	UK Yugoslavia	The UK stations a warship in the Adriatic to assist with problems arising from the Yugoslav civil war[32]	C/E	Picture Building/ Reassurance
December	USSR Int Community	The Russian aircraft carrier *Kuznetsov* passes through the Turkish Straits for trials in the Mediterranean[33]	E	Prestige

1992

			P/C	
January	US South Korea North Korea	The US and South Korea announce the cancellation of Exercise *Team Spirit* 92 on condition that North Korea honours its pledge to allow inspection of nuclear facilities; the inspections were completed by the IAEA[34]	P/C	Co-operation/Coercion
March	US Kuwait Iraq	An amphibious exercise, *Eager Mace* 92, is held in Kuwait, timed to coincide with the deployment and unloading of strategic pre-positioning ships (*Active Fury* 92) based in Diego Garcia. The exercises become annual events[35]	E	Deterrence/Reassurance
March	CIS Int Community	CIS Black Sea Fleet deploys to the Mediterranean for the first time since the end of the USSR[36]	E	Prestige
March	India US UK France	India announces its plans for more naval exercises with the established blue-water navies of US, UK and France[37]	–	Co-operation/Prestige
April	NATO	STANAVFORMED officially formed, providing a permanent NATO naval presence in the Mediterranean[38]	E	Picture Building/Co-operation/Prestige
May	UK Kuwait	UK amphibious exercises involving HMS *Beaver* and 40 Cdo RM in Kuwait; the first UK/Kuwait exercise since the Gulf War[39]	E	Reassurance/Deterrence
May	Croatia Int Community	The first independent Croatian warship is launched[40]	–	Prestige
May	CIS NATO	The CIS intelligence gathering ship, *Ekvator*, shadows STANAVFORMED; the first CIS AGI activity since the end of the USSR[41]	E	Picture Building
May to November	UK Int Community	The RN deploys the *Orient* 92 task group, led by HMS *Invincible*. It visits numerous European, Middle and Far East ports and exercises with other navies in an attempt to demonstrate Britain's ability to operate at range for a prolonged period[42]	E	Prestige/Co-operation/Attraction
June	Taiwan South Africa	Three Taiwanese ships (two destroyers and a tanker) visit South Africa[43]	E	Co-operation/Prestige

(*Continued*)

Date	Principal Actors	Description	Cable Classification	Composite Classification
June	CIS Sweden	Sweden complains that two CIS submarines have violated its territorial waters; the USSR had a long history of incursions into Swedish waters which they claimed were US and UK submarines conducting 'tests'[44]	E	Picture Building/Coercion
June	WEU NATO Yugoslavia	The WEU and NATO commence operations in the Adriatic to monitor the movement of shipping in the Yugoslav civil war[45]	C/E	Picture Building/Reassurance
July	UK France	The fishery protection vessel HMS *Brecon* is dispatched to protect British fishing vessels off the Isles of Scilly following a clash with a French trawler[46]	P	Deterrence/Reassurance
July	France Germany	Franco-German ties 'deepen' following bilateral naval exercise FAUVES 92 in the Mediterranean[47]	E	Co-operation
July	US Yugoslavia	USN ships and aircraft from US carriers begin to contribute to the enforcement of sanctions against Yugoslavia[48]	C/E	Picture Building/Reassurance
July	South Africa Kenya Int Community	Two South African Navy fast attack craft visit Mombasa; it is a rare example of a apartheid era SAN visit to a 'black African' country and follows the visit of the Kenyan President to South Africa in June[49]	E	Attraction
July	Australia Fiji	Australia gifts two patrol boats to Fiji following the normalization of relations, which were severed after the 1987 coup[50]	C/E	Co-operation/Attraction
July	Georgia Int Community Black Sea Co-operation project	Georgian President Eduard Shevardnadze calls for 'limit and quota' to the number of warships in the Black Sea; the former Soviet Black Sea Fleet had been divided between Russia and Ukraine[51]	—	—
July	South Africa Angola Int Community	South Africa deploys its support ship *Tafelberg* to Luanda to assist in UN election monitoring in Angola[52]	C	Assistance
August	India Int Community	The Indian Navy conducts its 'biggest ever' exercise in the Bay of Bengal, involving 15 ships[53]	E	Prestige

Month	Countries	Event		Category
August	Russia Ukraine	Russian and Ukrainian Presidents agree to joint control of the former Black Sea Fleet[54]	E	Co-operation
August	UK West Indies	HMS Cardiff and Campbeltown conduct relief operations in the West Indies after Hurricane Andrew[55]	–	Assistance
August	NATO WEU Yugoslavia	Western naval forces start to concentrate in the Adriatic as the former Yugoslavia disintegrates[56]	C	Deterrence/Reassurance
August	China Taiwan	Taiwanese trawlers report a number of boardings by unmarked patrol craft of Chinese design. One trawler is fired upon. Taiwan denounced the patrol craft as 'pirates' and China denied responsibility[57]	P	Coercion
September	Sweden Russia	Sweden attacks an unidentified submarine contact in its territorial waters during a naval exercise; the submarine is believed not to have been hit[58]	D	Picture Building/Deterrence
October	Russia Iran Int Community	Three Russian Kilo class submarines leave Latvia for Iran. The sale resulted in protests from the US, UK and other Western states[59]	–	Co-operation/Attraction
October	US Russia	A Russian Helix helicopter lands on a US warship in the Gulf during interoperability exercises[60]	E	Co-operation
October	India ASEAN	In an attempt to 'calm nerves' over its regional expansion, India invites ASEAN countries to join a naval exercise for the first time. ASEAN had traditionally been an economic not a security agreement. Only Singapore responded positively[61]	C/E	Co-operation/Attraction
November	US Bahrain Russia Iran	The US sends the submarine Topeka to Bahrain, for the first routine maintenance in the Gulf. Understood to be messaging to Russia and Iran following the sale of the Kilo class submarines[62]	E	Co-operation/Reassurance/Deterrence
December	US Pakistan	The US threatens not to renew leases on eight frigates unless Pakistan fulfils its non-proliferation 'Pressler amendment'[63]	E	Coercion
December	US Iraq	The US redeploys its Gulf carrier to Somalia for Operation *Restore Hope*. In its absence Iraq escalates pressure on UN weapons inspectors and begins violations of the southern no-fly zone[64]	–	–

(Continued)

Date	Principal Actors	Description	Cable Classification	Composite Classification
December to June 1993	Australia Somalia US Int Community	The RAN provide strategic sea lift, logistic, communication, intelligence and air support in Somalia as part of the US-led Op *Restore Hope*[65]	C	Co-operation/ Picture Building
1993				
January	Sri Lanka LTTE	The Liberation Tigers of Tamil Eelam (LTTE – 'Tamil Tigers') claim to have built 'suicide submarines' for attacks against Sri Lankan government forces[66]	–	Prestige/ Coercion
January	France UK WEU Yugoslavia	The Adriatic deployment is strengthened and stands at 14 ships[67]	P/E	Co-operation/ Picture Building/ Reassurance
March	Australia ASEAN	Australia invites ASEAN countries to join the naval exercise *Kakadu*; Malaysia, Singapore and Thailand send ships. Indonesia sends observers[68]	E	Co-operation/ Attraction
March	Australia Dom Community	HMAS *Geelong* pays a series of visits to Aboriginal communities in the Tiwi Islands and Arnhem Land as part of a Customs and Navy awareness campaign[69]	–	Reassurance
March	UK France	During a dispute over fishing rights off Guernsey a French vessel is arrested. Later, HMS *Blazer*, a university RN unit, is boarded by French fishermen in Cherbourg in protest at UK action[70]	P	Coercion
March	Australia Fiji	HMAS *Derwent* becomes first RAN ship to visit Fiji since coup of 1987[71]	–	Attraction
May	Iran Int Community	Iran conducts a naval exercise involving more than 100 vessels including, for the first time, a Kilo class submarine[72]	E	Prestige/ Deterrence

Date	Countries	Description	Code	Category
May to June	Russia US UK Int Community	Russia deploys numerous vessels in a 'show of presence'. Three Krivak class to the Mediterranean; one Krivak to Norway; one Sovremenny to New York; one Sovremenny to the UK[73]	E	Prestige
June	US Iraq	The USN fires Tomahawk missiles at Iraqi intelligence service HQ from its ships in the Gulf and Red Sea. The use of force is in retaliation for a plot to assassinate former President Bush during a visit to Kuwait in April[74]	D	Coercion
July	Russia China	Russia deploys a flotilla from its Pacific Fleet to the East China Sea following PLAN arrests and harassment of Russian cargo ships in disputed waters[75]	P	Coercion/Reassurance
September	Poland Denmark Germany Russia	Plans are announced for a joint Polish, Danish and German naval exercise in the Baltic. Poland wishes to join NATO but Russia objects[76]	C/E	Co-operation/Attraction/Coercion
September to December	UN UK US Haiti	UN maritime interdiction operations commence off Haiti following the removal of President Aristide in 1991[77]	D/P	Coercion
October	US Somalia	The US announces its decision to send the aircraft carrier Abraham Lincoln and other ships to Somalia[78]	P	Prestige/Coercion
October	US Haiti	Following unrest, the US president orders USN to enforce a blockade of Haiti. By the following April 712 vessels had been boarded[79]	D	Coercion
December	Russia Kuwait	Russia and Kuwait hold their first joint naval exercise; up until this point Russia had only exercised with Western navies in the Gulf[80]	E	Attraction/Co-operation
December	Australia Malaysia	HMAS Canberra and Perth visit Langkawi island in Malaysia for an international maritime and space exhibition; defence and trade ministers attend. Diving teams then assist Royal Malaysian Police in search and recovery of body of missing crewman who had fallen overboard from a ship[81]	–	Co-operation/Attraction

(*Continued*)

Date	Principal Actors	Description	Cable Classification	Composite Classification
1994				
January	Australia Kiribati Pacific Islands	Australia hands a patrol boat to Kiribati as part of an ongoing co-operation programme with small Pacific Ocean island states. No weapons are included but the gift is made to help patrol EEZs[82]	–	Co-operation/Attraction
February	Poland Netherlands	Poland and the Netherlands sign an agreement for joint exercises, personnel and technology exchanges and hydrographic collaboration[83]	–	Co-operation
February	Russia NATO	Russia decides not to join the PfP but allocates the frigate *Pomar* to a NATO SAR exercise[84]	E	Co-operation
March	South Korea North Korea US	The US and South Korea agree to suspend the *Team Spirit* 94 exercise after North Korea agrees to IAEA inspections of nuclear facilities[85]	P/C	Coercion/Co-operation
April to May	NATO Int Community	Around 100 NATO vessels take part in Exercise *Resolute Response* to practice defence of sea lines of communication in the Atlantic[86]	E	Prestige/Deterrence
May	Yugoslavia NATO WEU	Yugoslav Navy ships interfere with an action by NATO/WEU warships conducting Operation *Sharp Guard* in the Adriatic; the NATO/WEU ships were attempting to board a vessel suspected of violating the embargo[87]	D/P	Coercion
May	US North Korea	The US announces that its aircraft carrier *Independence* will be kept within one week's sailing time of North Korea, to respond to any crisis if necessary[88]	P/C	Deterrence/Reassurance
June	UK Russia	The Russian Kilo class submarine No. 431 visits Portsmouth[89]	E	Prestige/Reassurance
June	UK South Africa	The South African warship *Drakensburg* joins the Joint Maritime Course off Scotland. It is the first time the RN and SAN have exercised together since 1974[90]	E	Co-operation/Attraction
June	Indonesia Dom Community	Indonesia sends a ship to strengthen its patrols around East Timor[91]	D	Coercion

Month	Actors	Event	E/P	Category
June	NATO PfP Russia	Exercise *Baltops* 94 takes place involving 35 ships from 15 countries, including Russia[92]	E	Co-operation
June	Russia Int Community	The Russian cruiser *Kerch* becomes the first to pass through the Turkish Straits into the Mediterranean since 1991[93]	E	Prestige
June	Russia North Korea US	The Russian and US navies conduct a joint exercise near Vladivostok, just 70 km from North Korea[94]	E	Co-operation/ Coercion
June	Australia Indonesia	HMAS Swan and Torrens visit Indonesia for Australia Day and to support Indonesian trade initiative[95]	–	Prestige
July	US North Korea	The USN deploys two mine countermeasures vessels to the Western Pacific to enhance its capabilities against North Korea[96]	E	Deterrence/ Reassurance
July	US Haiti	The USS *Inchon* amphibious ready group deploys to Haiti, to be ready to evacuate entitled personnel if necessary[97]	P	Assistance
July	Colombia Venezuela	Colombia and Venezuela agree to co-ordinate naval effort to counter drug trafficking, arms smuggling and illegal mining[98]	–	Co-operation
August	Australia Indonesia	The Australian and Indonesian navies jointly exercise their surveillance procedures[99]	E	Co-operation/ Picture Building
August	US Romania	The Romanian defence minister announces his country's intention to join the PfP during USS *Tortuga's* visit[100]	E	Attraction/ Co-operation
August	UK Argentina	The Argentinian sail training ship *Libertad* visits Dartmouth at the UK's invitation[101]	E	Reassurance/ Co-operation
September	Japan Russia	Negotiations take place for the first ever Russian/Japanese exercise; it will be maritime SAR[102]	–	Co-operation
September	US South Korea North Korea	The US and South Korea declare that in the event of a crisis on the Korean peninsula the headquarters of the USN 7th Fleet will move from Hawaii to South Korea[103]	–	Reassurance/ Deterrence
September	Sri Lanka LTTE	The Tamil Tigers destroy the Sri Lankan Navy's largest ship, *Sagarawardene*, by ramming it with small boats filled with explosives[104]	–	Coercion

(Continued)

Date	Principal Actors	Description	Cable Classification	Composite Classification
September	Australia Solomon Islands	RAN provides a secure environment for the conduct of the Bougainville Peace Conference[105]	C	Reassurance
October	Germany	The German Navy transfers its fast attack craft flotilla from Schleswig-Holstein to Warnemünde in the former East Germany[106]	–	Reassurance
October	US Iraq	In the absence of a USN aircraft carrier in the Gulf, Iraq moves 80,000 troops towards Kuwait. A sizeable US naval force including the aircraft carrier *George Washington*, the amphibious ship Tripoli and the 18th MEU, then reposition into the Gulf and poise off Iraq. The RN stations its *Armilla* Patrol in the Northern Gulf. Iraq backs down[107]	P	Deterrence/ Reassurance
October	Turkey US Greece Italy Romania Russia Ukraine	Exercise *Maritime Partner* takes place in the Black Sea[108]	E	Co-operation/ Attraction
October	China Taiwan	The PLAN rehearse an amphibious assault off Taiwan at a time when diplomatic relations seem possible[109]	P/C	Coercion
November	Thailand US North Korea China	Thailand turns down a US request to pre-position ships in Thai territorial waters; the pre-positioning was aimed at North Korea but Thailand does not want to offend China[110]	–	–
November	US South Africa	USS *Gettysburg* and USS *Halyburton* become the first USN ships to visit South Africa since 1967[111]	E	Co-operation/ Attraction
1995				
January	Canada Spain	Canadian Navy commences Operation *Ocean Vigilance*, monitoring fishing activity off the Grand Banks of Newfoundland. The operation would last for two years during the turbot fishing dispute with Spain[112]	P	Deterrence/ Reassurance/ Picture Building

Month	Countries	Event	Code	Purpose
January	China / Philippines	China seizes the disputed Mischief Reef 130 miles from the Philippines[113]	D	–
January	Norway / Latvia / Estonia / Lithuania	Norway donates three *Storm* class fast patrol vessels; one each to the Baltic republics[114]	–	Attraction/ Co-operation
January	Australia / France	Australia suspends RAN visits to French Pacific territories following French nuclear testing programme[115]	–	Coercion
February	UK / Sierra Leone	HMS *Marlborough* stands by off Sierra Leone to conduct NEO if required after internal rebellion[116]	P/C	Deterrence/ Reassurance
February	US / Int Community / Somalia	An international naval force of 26 ships from six countries poises off Mogadishu during withdrawal of US ground troops (Op United Shield)[117]	P	Deterrence/ Reassurance
February	US / Albania	The first US-Albanian exercise takes place, a SAR exercise involving USS *Ponce*[118]	E	Co-operation
March	Australia / Indonesia / Malaysia / Singapore / Thailand	A naval exercise, *Kakadu* II, takes place in the Timor and Arafura Seas as part of Australia's outreach to the countries of South East Asia[119]	E	Attraction/ Prestige/ Co-operation
March	Australia / Papua New Guinea	HMAS *Flinders* conducts survey of Rabaul Harbour to determine impact of volcanic eruptions and establish safe navigation routes[120]	–	Assistance/ Attraction
March	Israel / Mauritania / Morocco / Algeria / Tunisia / Oman / Egypt / Saudi Arabia / UAE / Yemen / Bahrain / Kuwait	A groundbreaking Israeli-Arab naval exercise planned to take place off Tunisia as part of the Middle East peace process. It involves SAR and 'incidents at sea' exercises[121]	E	Co-operation

(Continued)

Date	Principal Actors	Description	Cable Classification	Composite Classification
March	US China	USS *Bunker Hill* visits China. It is the first USN visit to the country since the suppression of the pro-democracy movement in 1989[122]	E	Attraction
April	Sri Lanka LTTE	The Tamil Tigers sink two warships. SLNS *Sooraya* and *Ranasura*, at the *Trincomalee* naval base, hours after the failure of peace negotiations[123]	–	Coercion
April	UK West Indies Haiti	HMS *Monmouth* patrols near the Turks and Caicos to intercept and deter illegal Haitian immigration[124]	P	Deterrence/Picture Building
May	Russia Australia	HMAS *Sydney* visits Vladivostok; the first Australian warship to visit Russia[125]	E	Attraction
June	NATO Bulgaria Romania	NATO's STANAVFORMED conducts a SAR exercise with Bulgarian and Romanian navies, within their territorial waters[126]	E	Co-operation/Attraction
June	US India	Exercise *Malabar* II takes place in an attempt to strengthen Indo-US relations[127]	E	Co-operation
July to October	Netherlands Int Community	The RNLN promotes Dutch industry during its *Fairwind* 95 deployment, visiting Egypt, the UAE, Singapore, Indonesia, China and South Africa[128]	–	Prestige
July	US Int Community	The USN reactivates its 5th Fleet in Bahrain to command naval operations in the Gulf region; it had been disbanded in 1947[129]	–	Prestige/Reassurance
July	South Africa Angola Botswana Malawi Mozambique Namibia Swaziland Zimbabwe Zambia Lesotho Tanzania	The Southern Africa Development Community form a Maritime Standing Committee under South African Chairmanship, with the aim of increasing naval and maritime co-operation in the region. South African ships visit Mozambique and Tanzania[130]	–	Co-operation

August	Australia / Indonesia	A flotilla of six Australian warships visits Jakarta to celebrate the 50th anniversary of Indonesian independence[131]	E	Attraction
August	UK / Montserrat	HMS *Southampton* stands by and then provides assistance to Montserrat during and after volcanic eruption[132]	–	Assistance/ Reassurance
August	China / Taiwan	China conducts air and maritime exercises in the East China Sea following a heightening of tensions with Taiwan[133]	P/E	Coercion
September	New Zealand / France / Int Community	HMNZS *Tui* is deployed to the Mururoa Atoll to demonstrate against French nuclear testing in the Pacific and to support the 'Protest Flotilla' which had sailed from New Zealand[134]	E	–
October	Thailand / US	The US trains Thai Navy pilots in preparation for Thailand's acquisition of Harrier aircraft from Spain[135]	–	Attraction/ Co-operation
October	Iran / Int Community	Iran conducts an amphibious exercise, *Great Khaibar*, near the Strait of Hormuz[136]	E	Coercion/ Prestige
October to November	China / Taiwan	China conducts further air and maritime exercises in the East China Sea, signalling its displeasure at Taiwanese posturing. In addition, an amphibious landing exercise is conducted on Dungshan Island, south of the Taiwan Strait and with similar geography to Taiwan itself[137]	P/E	Coercion
December	France / South Africa	The French Navy make a goodwill visit to Durban, South Africa[138]	E	Attraction
December	India / UAE	The Indian Navy and UAE conduct a naval exercise in the Gulf; the Indian ships then visit the UAE[139]	E	Co-operation/ Attraction
December	US / China / Taiwan	The USS *Nimitz* carrier battle group makes passage through the Taiwan Strait, the first to do so since 1979[140]	P/E	Coercion/ Deterrence/ Reassurance
December to January	Russia / US	A Russian Akula class nuclear submarine operates off the north-western US, tracking Trident class submarines. The US assessment is that the Russian Navy is reasserting its capabilities after a lengthy period of budget constraints[141]	E	Prestige/Picture Building

(Continued)

Date	Principal Actors	Description	Cable Classification	Composite Classification
1996				
January	Russia Int Community	The Russian aircraft carrier *Kuznetsov* and its battle group enters the Mediterranean in the first major out-of-area deployment since 1991[142]	E	Prestige
January	US UAE	A naval and marine exercise, *Iron Magic Iron Siren 96*, takes place in the Gulf[143]	E	Co-operation/Reassurance
February	UK Argentina	HMS *Northumberland* conducts presence and deterrence operations against illegal fishing by Patagonian vessels off South Georgia[144]	P	Deterrence/Picture Building/Reassurance
February	Netherlands Belgium	The Dutch and Belgian fleets join under a single operational command, 'Admiral Benelux' (ABNL)[145]	—	Co-operation
February	Greece Turkey US	Greek Navy commandos raise a flag on an uninhabited island 4 nm from the Turkish coast (in Greek: Imia; in Turkish: Kardak). Turkey responds by deploying three frigates, one destroyer and three attack craft. Greece then counters with two frigates, one destroyer and three attack craft. Both sides raise their alert states on the island of Cyprus. The three-day confrontation ends following US diplomatic pressure – Greece removes its flag and Turkish forces withdraw[146]	D	Coercion
February	Sweden Singapore	Sweden enters an agreement to train Singapore submariners[147]	—	Attraction
February	US South Korea North Korea	The US and South Korea cancel their annual *Team Spirit* exercise for the third consecutive year, but they do conduct a naval exercise, *Valiant Usher*, in the Yellow Sea[148]	C/E	Coercion
March	India Singapore	India and Singapore conduct a series of naval exercises[149]	E	Co-operation
April	US UK Liberia	US warships and UK auxiliary poise off Liberia to conduct NEO if required[150]	P	Assistance/Reassurance

Month	Countries	Description	E/P	Category
May	UK, US, Russia	The RN hosts Russo-UK-US naval exercises which culminate in a boarding exercise off Portsmouth[151]	E	Co-operation
May	US, Philippines, China	The US and Philippines hold a naval exercise. It had been postponed from 1995 because of tensions caused by Chinese missile tests near Taiwan[152]	E	Co-operation
June	Turkey, Israel	Turkey and Israel announce plans for naval exercises[153]	E	Co-operation/Attraction
June to July	UK, Denmark, Greenpeace	RN warships monitor confrontation between Danish fishing vessels and Greenpeace in the North Sea[154]	–	Picture Building/Deterrence
July	Greece, Israel	Greece and Israel announce plans for naval exercises; Greece also aims to 'dampen' its criticism of Israeli co-operation with Turkey[155]	E	Co-operation/Attraction
July	Japan, Russia	The first visit by Japanese Maritime Self-Defense Force ships to Russia, to celebrate the 300th anniversary of the Russian Navy at Vladivostok[156]	E	Attraction
September	Japan, South Korea	The Japanese training ships Kashima and Sawayuki visit South Korea. It is the first visit by the JMSDF to Korea since the end of WWII[157]	E	Attraction
September	Egypt, Saudi Arabia	The Egyptian and Saudi navies exercise together in the Red Sea. Tensions between the two countries had been high but recently improved[158]	E	Co-operation/Reassurance
September	North Korea, South Korea	A North Korean mini-submarine runs aground off South Korea during a suspected attempt to infiltrate a reconnaissance team; the crew are all found dead with shots to the head[159]	P	Picture Building
September	China, Japan	Hong Kong protest vessels invade seas near Senkaku/Diaoyu Islands after the Japanese proclamation of an EEZ. Several protesters are blocked by Japanese patrol vessels and jump into the sea; one is drowned[160]	P	Coercion
October	Taiwan, China	Taiwan conducts a one-day amphibious landing exercise involving 80 ships and 13,000 personnel[161]	P/E	Deterrence
October	UK, Croatia, NATO	HMS *Nottingham* patrols the coast of Croatia in support of the NATO operation[162]	P	Picture Building/Deterrence

(*Continued*)

Date	Principal Actors	Description	Cable Classification	Composite Classification
1997				
January	US Syria	US cruisers position in the Mediterranean to monitor Syrian Scud missile firings[163]	P	Picture Building/ Deterrence/ Reassurance
January	UK Int Community	RN commences *Ocean Wave* deployment, sending 17 ships and submarines to Middle East and Asia-Pacific in support of UK political interests by demonstrating continuing ability to deploy an effective force for a significant period[164]	E	Prestige/ Attraction
January	Australia Japan	Australia announces that the RAN would seize Japanese vessels caught fishing in Australian EEZ after failure to reach agreement on quotas[165]	–	Coercion
March	Bangladesh India Maldives Saudi Arabia	India, the Maldives and Saudi Arabia are visited by Bangladeshi ships[166]	E	Attraction
March	UK Albania	HMS *Birmingham* and *Exeter* stand by off Albanian port of Durres to conduct NEO during internal unrest[167]	P	Deterrence/ Reassurance
March to April	South Africa Brazil Argentina Uruguay	South Africa hosts *Atlasur* naval exercises with South American countries[168]	E	Co-operation/ Attraction
April	Russia Ukraine	Russia and Ukraine hold their first exercises together since the division of the Black Sea Fleet[169]	E	Co-operation
April to June	China Int Community	Three Chinese Navy ships deploy across the Pacific and visit various ports in North and South America[170]	E	Attraction/ Prestige
May	Canada Brunei	HMCS *Huron* becomes the first Canadian ship to visit Brunei[171]	E	Attraction

May	UK Malaysia FPDA	—	During the Five Power Defence Agreement (FPDA) Exercise *Flying Fish* in the South China Sea, Capt. Bopal of the Royal Malaysian Navy embarks in HMS *Illustrious* and assumes command of the maritime forces. It is the first time that a foreign maritime component commander has commanded from RN ship[172]	Co-operation/ Attraction
May	Indonesia Singapore	P/E	Indonesia and Singapore conduct co-ordinated anti-piracy patrols in the Malacca and Singapore Straits[173]	Co-operation
May	France South Africa	P/E	Fish poaching becomes a problem and France offers to help to patrol the waters around Prince Edward Island, beyond the endurance of South African patrol boats[174]	Co-operation/ Attraction
June	Sri Lanka LTTE	—	The Sri Lankan Navy attacks and sinks a number of Tamil Tiger boats[175]	Coercion
June	UK Sierra Leone	P	UK auxiliary poises off Sierra Leone during internal unrest[176]	Reassurance/ Assistance
June	UK China Int Community	E	HM Yacht *Britannia*, patrol vessels and frigate in Hong Kong for handover to China. *Ocean Wave* task group poises over the horizon[177]	Prestige/ Reassurance
August	Sri Lanka LTTE	—	Sri Lanka sinks two and damages 12 Tamil Tiger boats in an engagement[178]	Coercion
September	UK Int Community	E	The British *Ocean Wave* deployment and returns to the UK after eight months away and visits to 20 countries[179]	Prestige
September	South Africa Namibia	—	Two South African warships operate from Namibia as part of a memorandum of understanding on maritime co-operation in the region[180]	Co-operation
September	Australia China	E	HMAS *Perth* and *Newcastle* visit China in order to strengthen military ties between the two countries[181]	Attraction
October	Iran US	P	Iran conducts a ten-day naval exercise in the Gulf in response to the announcement of USS *Nimitz* deployment to the region (the deployment was, in turn, a response to an Iranian cross-border raid into Iraq)[182]	Coercion/ Deterrence

(Continued)

Date	Principal Actors	Description	Cable Classification	Composite Classification
October	Turkey Greece	The Greek minesweeper *Avra* steams over the 'narrowly submerged' Turkish submarine, *Yildiray*, in international waters in the Aegean Sea. The submarine was visible with masts protruding the surface. Turkey calls the incident a 'hostile act'[183]	P/E	Coercion
October	France South Africa	A South African task group in the Indian Ocean conducts a SAR exercise with French forces on the island of Reunion[184]	E	Co-operation
October	UK Ukraine Poland	HMS *Campbeltown* acts as host ship in Odessa for UK Secretary of State for Defence to conduct trilateral defence talks with Ukraine and Poland[185]	E	Prestige/ Attraction
October	UK Congo	HMS *Monmouth* and RFA *Orangeleaf* stand by off Congo during deteriorating political situation in the country[186]	P/C	Assistance/ Deterrence
November	Indonesia Australia Germany	Naval exercise takes place between Indonesian, Australian and German warships in the Java Sea. The German ships then pay a goodwill visit to Indonesia[187]	E	Co-operation/ Attraction
November	Malaysia Philippines	Malaysia and the Philippines conduct a nine-day anti-piracy exercise called *Sea Malphi*[188]	E	Co-operation
November	New Zealand Papua New Guinea	The RNZN leads a Truce Monitoring Group in Bougainville. It is the largest multinational deployment in the South Pacific since WWII[189]	P/E	Co-operation/ Reassurance
December	Sweden Singapore	Six Singapore sailors take part in a Swedish mine countermeasures exercise[190]	–	Co-operation
1998				
January	China US	China and the US sign a Maritime Consultative Agreement aimed at preventing incidents at sea[191]	–	Co-operation
January	US Kuwait Iraq	US amphibious forces complete a month-long exercise with Kuwait, *Eager Mace 98*[192]	E	Deterrence/ Reassurance

Month	Countries	Code	Description	Category
January	Israel, Turkey, US	C/E	Israel, Turkey and the US hold a one-day exercise in the Eastern Mediterranean called *Reliant Mermaid*. The exercise is SAR based and is viewed as an attempt to deepen the relationship between the region's two non-Arab states. The Egyptian foreign minister warned of a 'counter-balance' to the relationship[193]	Co-operation/ Reassurance
January	Greece, Georgia	–	Greece transfers a coastguard vessel to Georgia after a co-operation agreement. It is followed by a visit by the Georgian foreign minister to Greece; Georgia's first ever to a NATO country[194]	Attraction
January	US, UK, Iraq	P	The US deploys USS *Independence* and the UK deploys HMS *Invincible*, both aircraft carriers, to the Gulf because of the growing Iraq crisis[195]	Coercion/ Reassurance
February	Sri Lanka, LTTE	–	The Tamil Tigers sink two Sri Lankan naval vessels off the Jaffna peninsula	Coercion
March	Sierra Leone, UK	P/E	HMS *Monmouth*, followed by HMS *Cornwall*, visit Sierra Leone in a show of support for the restored democratic government[196]	Reassurance
March	Fiji, Australia, France	–	France and Australia help Fiji to monitor its EEZ after spending cuts forced its Navy to end patrols for the rest of the year[197]	Attraction
March	China, Ukraine, Int Community	–	The uncompleted aircraft carrier *Varyag* is bought from Ukraine by an unknown company based in Macau; it is suspected that the Chinese government is behind the deal[198]	Prestige
April	US, UK, Saudi Arabia, Pakistan, Iran	E	A four-country, four-day MCM exercise takes place off Qatar, simulating the clearance of a mined Strait of Hormuz[199]	Co-operation/ Deterrence/ Reassurance
April	US, UK, Canada, Netherlands, Iran	E	An anti-submarine warfare exercise, USWEX 98, is conducted in the Gulf by four Western powers; aimed at demonstrating capability to Iran[200]	Co-operation/ Deterrence/ Reassurance
April	Russia, Ukraine	E	Russia and Ukraine hold joint exercises in the Black Sea off the Crimean peninsula[201]	Co-operation

(Continued)

Date	Principal Actors	Description	Cable Classification	Composite Classification
April	Iran Int Community	Iran holds its first exercises with its new Kilo class submarines. Ex *Ettihad* (Unity) takes place from Bandar Abbas and through the Strait of Hormuz to Chah Bahar. It aims to demonstrate Iranian maritime power to neighbouring countries[202]	E	Prestige
May	Argentina Chile	Argentina and Chile announce naval exercises to be conducted later in the year. It is a significant development in military ties following years of high-level distrust[203]	–	Co-operation
May	India Bangladesh Indonesia Singapore Sri Lanka	Ex *Madat* 98 (meaning 'Help'), a five-day SAR exercise, takes place[204]	E	Co-operation
May	France NATO	France joins the annual *Baltops* exercise/deployment to the Baltic Sea for the first time in its 26-year history[205]	E	Co-operation/ Attraction
May	Australia India Pakistan	Australia announces suspension of RAN visits to, and exercises with, India and Pakistan following series of nuclear tests on Indian subcontinent[206]	–	Coercion
June	China Int Community	China deploys its first 'air capable' ship (*Shichang*) to Australia, New Zealand and the Philippines.[207]	E	Prestige
June	UK Guinea-Bissau	HMS *Cornwall* is withdrawn from an exercise with the South African Navy to stand by for a NEO off Guinea-Bissau if fighting in the country intensifies[208]	P	Reassurance/ Deterrence/ Assistance
June	NATO Bulgaria Romania Georgia Ukraine	Ex *Co-operative Partner* 98, a PfP exercise, takes place in the Black Sea[209]	E	Co-operation/ Attraction
June	US Croatia	Joint US-Croatian exercises take place following the visit of USS *Kauffman* to Dubrovnik[210]	E	Co-operation/ Attraction

June	India Iran Kuwait Saudi Arabia Oman Pakistan US	India attempts to counter Pakistani and American influence in the Gulf by holding its first exercises with Iran and Kuwait and a one-day exercise with Saudi Arabia and Oman. It is seen as an assertion of Indian foreign policy independence after US attempts to isolate Tehran[211]	C/E	Prestige/ Attraction/ Co-operation
June	Australia Indonesia	RAN deliver food and medical supplies to drought affected areas of Irian Jaya[212]	–	Assistance
June	North Korea South Korea	A North Korean submarine violates South Korean waters and is arrested[213]	P	Picture Building/ Deterrence
July	Portugal Guinea-Bissau	The Portuguese ship *Vasco da Gama* evacuates diplomatic staff from its former colony[214]	D	Assistance
July	Portugal Angola Guinea-Bissau	The foreign ministers of Portugal and Angola meet Guinea-Bissau rebels on board *Vasco da Gama*; government officials are invited but fail to turn up[215]	C/E	Prestige/ Reassurance
July	Russia Japan	Russia and Japan hold their first joint naval exercise (SAR). The Japanese destroyers *Kurama* and *Hamagiri* then visit Vladivostok[216]	E	Co-operation/ Attraction
July	UK Syria	HMS *Marlborough* and RFA *Fort Victoria* visit the Syrian port of Latakia; it is the first contact between the armed forces of the two countries since 1986[217]	E	Attraction/ Co-operation
August	Argentina Chile	Argentina and Chile conduct a joint naval exercise off Isla de los Estados; it is salvage based[218]	E	Co-operation
August	US China	US warships *John S. McCain* and *Blue Ridge* visit Qingdao, two years after tensions over Taiwan[219]	E	Attraction
August	US Sudan Afghanistan Al-Qaeda	USN warships launch cruise missile attacks against Khost in Afghanistan and Al Shifa in Sudan; the former was believed to be the hiding place of Osama bin Laden, the latter was a pharmaceutical factory allegedly being used to manufacture chemical weapons. Both bombings were in response to the al-Qaeda attacks on the American embassies in Kenya and Tanzania earlier in the year[220]	D	Coercion

(Continued)

Date	Principal Actors	Description	Cable Classification	Composite Classification
August to February 2000	Australia Indonesia	Various RAN units support UN sanctioned peace enforcement operation in East Timor, under the banner of Op *Stabilise/Warden*[221]	P	Deterrence
September	UK Albania	The UK stations a warship off Albania for NEO if required[222]	P	Assistance/ Reassurance
September	China Japan	Chinese protesters land on the disputed Senkaku/Diaoyu Islands and clash with Japanese coastguard[223]	P	Coercion
September	UK West Indies	RN conducts disaster relief in St Kitts and Montserrat in wake of Hurricane *Georges*[224]	–	Assistance
October	NATO Greece Turkey	Greece and Turkey exercise together as part of the NATO exercise *Dynamic Mix*, the first time the two countries have done so for 13 years[225]	E	Co-operation
October	NATO Serbia	NATO's STANAVFORMED conducts presence operations in the Adriatic as demonstration of resolve against Serbian ethnic cleansing in Kosovo. The force is stood down after diplomatic protests[226]	P	Deterrence/ Reassurance
October	South Korea Russia	South Korean ships *Seoul* and *Taejon* visit Vladivostok on a goodwill port call[227]	E	Attraction
October to November	UK Estonia Russia	UK mine hunter conducts clearance of WWI and WWII mines off Estonia[228]	P/E	Assistance/ Attraction
November	France UK	France proposes co-operation over aircraft carrier development plans[229]	–	Co-operation
November	US Iraq	The US stations two carrier battle groups and two amphibious ready groups in the Gulf as a signal to Iraq to permit access to weapon inspectors[230]	P	Coercion
November	US UK Netherlands France Canada Honduras Nicaragua	Major multinational relief operations in and off coast of Honduras and Nicaragua after Hurricane Mitch[231]	–	Assistance

Date	Countries	Description		Category
December	Iran Oman	Omani officers accept an invitation to watch Iranian naval exercises. Iran had been trying to conduct joint exercises with US-Gulf allies for a decade[232]	—	Co-operation/ Attraction
December	US UK Iraq Int Community	Op *Desert Fox* takes place. It includes the most punishing air strikes against Iraq since the 1991 Gulf War. There are significant diplomatic protests worldwide[233]	D	Coercion
December	North Korea South Korea	A North Korean submarine violates South Korean waters and is sunk by the ROK Navy[234]	D	Picture Building/ Deterrence
1999				
January to March	UK Sierra Leone	UK stations warship off Sierra Leone to support government in fight against rebels[235]	P/C	Reassurance
January to April	UK Iraq Serbia	HMS *Invincible* deploys to the Gulf following 'diplomatic difficulties' with Iraq. It conducts maritime interdiction, air surveillance and enforcement of the no-fly zone. On returning to the UK it is diverted to the Ionian Sea to participate in Op *Allied Force* against Serbia[236]	D	Coercion
February	Sri Lanka LTTE	Tamil Tigers capture a Sri Lankan Navy patrol craft[237]	—	Coercion
February	US Albania	The US donates five patrol vessels to the Albanian coastguard under a PfP effort to counter drug trafficking[238]	—	Attraction
February	France Fiji	France assists Fiji by conducting maritime surveillance flights over its EEZ, using its naval aircraft based in New Caledonia[239]	E	Assistance/ Attraction
March	India Int community	India deploys the aircraft carrier *Viraat* to the Gulf for the first time as part of its diplomatic plan to increase its influence in the region[240]	E	Prestige/ Attraction
March	India Thailand Sri Lanka Bangladesh Indonesia Singapore Maldives Mauritius UAE Oman	In an ambitious series of exercises (*Milan*), India strives for 'professional interaction' with neighbouring states. The Western Fleet exercises off the Kochi coast with the Maldives, Mauritius, Sri Lanka, the UAE and Oman, whilst the Eastern Fleet operates in the Bay of Bengal with Sri Lanka, Thailand, Bangladesh, Indonesia and Singapore[241]	E	Co-operation/ Attraction/ Prestige

(Continued)

Date	Principal Actors	Description	Cable Classification	Composite Classification
March	India Sri Lanka LTTE	The Indian Navy and Coastguard intercept an supply ship transporting arms to the Tamil Tigers[242]	D	Co-operation/ Coercion
March	GCC Iran	The Gulf Co-operation Council states voice concern over Iranian naval exercises; they stage their own week-long naval exercise in response[243]	–	Co-operation/ Deterrence
March	North Korea South Korea	South Korea recovers a North Korean infiltration craft which sank after a gun battle in December 1998[244]	–	Picture Building/ Deterrence/ Coercion
March	NATO Serbia	Op *Allied Force* is launched, consisting of air and Tomahawk Land Attack Missile (TLAM) strikes on Serbia[245]	D	Coercion
March	Japan China	Discovery of a 'spy ship' off the Noto Peninsula[246]	E	Picture Building
April	India South African Development Community	The Indian Navy participates in *Blue Crane*, a peacekeeping exercise for the South African Development Community (no other non-SADC state is involved)[247]	E	Co-operation/ Attraction
April	Australia Vietnam	HMAS *Perth* and *Arunta* become the first Australian ships to visit Vietnam since the end of the Vietnam War, becoming a symbol of improving relationships and agents of furthering commercial ties[248]	E	Attraction
May	NATO Serbia	NATO's STANAVFORLANT prepares to deploy for embargo operations in the Adriatic, similar to *Sharp Guard* from 1993 to 1996. The force poises off Gibraltar[249]	P	Deterrence
May	New Zealand South Korea	New Zealand and South Korea conduct a joint anti-submarine exercise[250]	E	Co-operation
May	India Pakistan Dom Community	In the wake of the Kargil crisis, when Pakistani forces crossed the Line of Control in the disputed territory, India put its Navy on alert and altered the operations deployment plans for its Eastern and Western Fleets. This sent a signal that any 'misadventure' would be firmly dealt with. India claimed that its naval response had a definitive effect on the outcome of the crisis[251]	D	Deterrence

Date	Actors	Event		
May to August	Australia Solomon Islands	HMAS *Tobruk* contributes to the evacuation of foreign nationals from Solomon Islands[252]	D	Assistance
June	China	China bans USN ships from Hong Kong as part of a suspension of military contact following the bombing of the Chinese Embassy in Belgrade[253]	–	Coercion
June	US North Korea South Korea	Shots are exchanged between North and South Korean coastguard ships after North Korean vessel crosses the Northern Limit Line; in September North Korea announces that the line is invalid[254]	D	Coercion/Deterrence
June	US North Korea South Korea	The US deploys the USS *Constellation* carrier battle group and the USS *Peleliu* amphibious ready group to the Western Pacific in response to tensions between North and South Korea[255]	P/E	Deterrence/Reassurance
July	Philippines China	The Philippine Navy sink a Chinese fishing boat off the Spratley Islands following a collision; they express regret[256]	D/E	–
August	India Pakistan Dom Community	The Indian fleet poises off Karachi and India claims its presence hastens the end of the recent Kashmir border dispute[257]	P	Deterrence
August	South Korea North Korea Japan	Pyongyang protests when South Korea and Japan hold a joint SAR exercise in South Korean waters[258]	–	Co-operation/Deterrence
August	US Japan North Korea	The US sends two missile tracking ships to Japan following reports of North Korean ballistic missile tests[259]	–	Reassurance/Deterrence
August	Georgia US	Georgian and US coastguard vessels hold a joint assault exercise in the Black Sea[260]	E	Co-operation/Attraction
August	China US	China allows the first visit by USN ships to Hong Kong since the bombing of its Belgrade Embassy[261]	E	Attraction
October	US Canada Indonesia East Timor	The US deploys USS *Belleau Wood* and Canada deploys HMCS *Protecteur* to East Timor to help restore peace after much infrastructure is destroyed following vote to become independent from Indonesia[262]	P/E	Assistance/Reassurance

(Continued)

Date	Principal Actors	Description	Cable Classification	Composite Classification
October	India Int Community Dom Community	The Indian Navy conducts high profile anti-poaching and anti-illegal immigration operations in and near the Nicobar Islands[263]	–	Deterrence
November	South Korea Vietnam North Korea	Three South Korean warships visit Vietnam for the first time[264]	E	Attraction
November	UK Turkey	HMS *Ocean* provides assistance to Turkey following an earthquake[265]	–	Assistance
November	Russia Int Community	Russian Prime Minister Vladimir Putin announces that the Russian Navy will resume global deployments[266]	–	Prestige
2000				
February	France Argentina	The first French/Argentinian naval exercise takes place between the Mar Del Plata and Cape Horn. It involves the French helicopter carrier *Jeanne d'Arc*, the destroyer *Georges Leygues* and the Argentinian submarine *Salta* and frigate *Espora*[267]	E	Co-operation/ Attraction
February	France India	A French/Indian naval exercise in the Arabian Sea is the first Indian military exercise with a Western power since its nuclear tests in 1998[268]	E	Co-operation/ Attraction
February	US China	USS *John C. Stennis* carrier battle group visits Hong Kong. It is seen as a sign of improving relations between the two countries[269]	E	Attraction
February	UK France	HMS *Victorious* becomes the first UK ballistic nuclear deterrent submarine to visit France; it spends five days in Brest[270]	E	Attraction/ Co-operation
February	France Gulf States	French naval, air and ground forces conduct Ex *Pearl of the West* 2000, the largest exercise for France in the Gulf since the 1991 war[271]	E	Co-operation/ Attraction/ Prestige
February to March	Iran Int Community	Iran conducts Ex *Vahdat* 78 (Unity 78), a naval exercise in the Gulf, Gulf of Oman and Strait of Hormuz[272]	E	Prestige/ Deterrence

Date	Actors	Description		Purpose
March	UK Mozambique	The UK deploys an auxiliary vessel and Royal Marines to Mozambique to conduct humanitarian assistance following floods, under the banner of Op *Barwood*[273]	—	Assistance
March	China Japan	Chinese naval vessels train in the vicinity of the disputed Senkaku/Diaoyu Islands[274]	P/E	Deterrence
March to April	Fiji Tonga France	Following a military co-operation agreement earlier in the month, France rapidly plans and executes joint naval exercises with the Pacific countries[275]	E	Co-operation/ Attraction
March to April	UK US Canada Netherlands Colombia Venezuela	Six states conduct naval exercises together in the Caribbean[276]	E	Co-operation
March to September	Singapore Int Community	Singapore conducts its first round the world deployment to showcase its new LST, RSS *Endurance*. Port visits include New York, Hawaii, Mexico, Panama, Canada, the UK, France, Egypt and Saudi Arabia[277]	E	Prestige
April	India Thailand	Two Indian warships visit Bangkok and exercise with the Thai Navy; it is part of the Navy's theme for 2000: 'Building Bridges of Friendship'[278]	E	Attraction
May	Pakistan Saudi Arabia	Pakistan and Saudi Arabia conduct Ex *Naseem Al-Bahr* (Wind of the Sea) in the Arabian Sea. It is aimed at improving co-operation. Pakistani ships then visit Saudi Arabia, Bahrain, the UAE, Iran and Qatar[279]	E	Co-operation/ Attraction
May	India Sri Lanka LTTE	India and Sri Lanka conduct a joint naval exercise in the Bay of Bengal. There is speculation that there could be joint patrols and Indian assistance to prevent the Tamil Tigers trafficking arms by sea[280]	E	Co-operation
May	India Sri Lanka LTTE	The Indian Navy's Eastern Command is put on a war footing under Op *Jalinkas* as a signal of deterrence after the Tamil Tigers advance in Jaffna[281]	P/E	Deterrence/ Reassurance
May	US Sierra Leone	The USN deploys a patrol craft to Sierra Leone to conduct a NEO if required[282]	P	Reassurance
May to June	UK Sierra Leone UN	Op *Palliser*, a UK operation in support of the government of Sierra Leone when the capital, Freetown, was under attack from rebels. HMS *Illustrious*, *Ocean*, supporting frigates and auxiliaries are deployed[283]	D/P	Reassurance/ Deterrence/ Coercion

(Continued)

Date	Principal Actors	Description	Cable Classification	Composite Classification
June	Australia New Zealand Solomon Islands	Australia and New Zealand dispatch ships to conduct a NEO following a coup in the Solomon Islands[284]	P	Assistance/ Reassurance
June	Sri Lanka LTTE	Tamil Tigers sink two Sri Lankan fast attack craft off Vadamarachchi[285]	–	Coercion
August	Russia UK Norway	The Russian submarine *Kursk* sinks with the loss of all lives. The UK and Norway each send specialists to assist[286]	–	Co-operation/ Assistance/ Attraction
August	US China	USS *Chancellorville* pays a port visit to Qingdao as part of a resumption of US-Chinese military relations[287]	E	Attraction
August	China South Africa	The Chinese warship *Shenzen* and its auxiliary *Nancang* visit Simons Town[288]	E	Attraction
August	New Zealand Solomon Islands	New Zealand deploys HMNZS *Te Kaha* to the Solomon Islands after a request for a 'secure, neutral venue for peace talks'[289]	C	Attraction/ Prestige
September	US South Africa	USS *George Washington* visits Cape Town. It is the first visit by a USN carrier to South Africa since the 1960s; a possible response to the Chinese visit a month earlier[290]	E	Attraction/ Prestige
September	US Italy Turkey Russia Int Community	A joint submarine rescue exercise involving Turkey, Italy and the US takes place off Mersin Bay in Turkey; it follows the Russian submarine *Kursk* disaster in August[291]	E	Co-operation
September	Australia Fed States of Micronesia	Various RAN units provide surveillance support to the Federated States of Micronesia[292]	E	Co-operation/ Picture Building/ Attraction
October	US Yemen Int Community	USS *Cole* suffers a terrorist attack in Yemeni port of Aden[293]	D	Coercion

Date	Countries		Description	
October	UK Belize	–	HMS *Cardiff* is dispatched to Belize to provide support after Hurricane Keith[294]	Assistance
October	India China Vietnam Indonesia	E	An Indian naval task group pay goodwill visits to China, Vietnam and Indonesia[295]	Prestige/ Attraction
November to December	UK Sierra Leone Int Community	P/E	In Operation *Silkman*, an RN amphibious task group conducts a show of strength and beach landing near Freetown; the timing coincided with the end of a 30-day ceasefire and was aimed to deter rebels from outbreaks of violence[296]	Reassurance/ Deterrence
2001				
January	US Israel Turkey	E	The US, Israel and Turkey conduct a joint SAR exercise in the Mediterranean[297]	Co-operation/ Attraction
January	Russia Int Community	–	Russia announces one of its navy's longest deployments since Soviet break-up. The warship *Vinogradov* and support vessel *Panteleyev* will spend two months in the Indian and Pacific Oceans[298]	Prestige
February	US Algeria	E	USS *Mitscher* participates in an anti-submarine warfare exercise with Algeria[299]	Co-operation/ Attraction
February	US Taiwan China Marshall Islands	–	The US vetoes a visit by the Taiwanese 'friendship fleet' to the Marshall Islands under the Compact of Free Association. The Marshall Islands had established diplomatic relations with the Republic of China (Taiwan) in 1998[300]	Coercion
March	India Singapore	E	The Indian and Singaporean navies conduct a bilateral anti-submarine exercise[301]	Co-operation
April	Turkey Bulgaria Georgia Romania Russia Ukraine	–	An agreement is signed to establish BLACKSEAFOR, a naval force of the Black Sea countries to be used for SAR, environmental protection, mine countermeasures and goodwill visits[302]	Co-operation/ Attraction

(*Continued*)

Date	Principal Actors	Description	Cable Classification	Composite Classification
April	North Korea South Korea	A North Korean patrol boat violates South Korean territorial waters. South Korean ships intercept the vessel and escort it out. North Korea does not recognize the border or territorial waters of the South[303]	P	Coercion
April	China Australia Taiwan Int Community	PLAN vessels challenge Australian warships transiting the Taiwan Strait[304]	P	Coercion
April to May	India Indonesia	In a 'new chapter of cooperation' the Indian Navy assists Indonesia with a survey of Sabang[305]	E	Attraction/ Assistance
April to June	Australia Vanuatu	HMAS *Kanimbla* conducts disaster relief operations in Vanuatu following volcanic eruption on island of Lopevi[306]	–	Assistance
May	Taiwan China Int Community	The Taiwanese 'friendship fleet' returns to Taiwan after a 95-day deployment, visiting eight countries in the Pacific, Central and South America, all of which recognize Taiwan diplomatically[307]	E	Prestige/ Attraction
June	Singapore Asia-Pacific Community	Singapore hosts a mine countermeasures exercise, reinforcing its leading role in promoting multilateral military activity in the Asia-Pacific region. Participants include Australia, China, France, India, Indonesia, Japan, Malaysia, Papua New Guinea, Russia, South Korea, Thailand, the US, Vietnam, New Zealand and Canada[308]	E	Co-operation/ Attraction
June	Australia Indonesia	HMAS *Hawkesbury* and *Huon* becomes first RAN ships to visit major Indonesian port since operations in East Timor began[309]	E	Attraction
August	UK Oman Int community	Largest RN task group since Falklands conflict in 1982 sails for Ex *Saif Sareea* II	E	Attraction
August	China India	Reciprocating the Indian visit of the previous year, two Chinese warships visit Mumbai[310]	E	Attraction
August	India Bangladesh	India and Bangladesh conduct a SAR exercise[311]	E	Co-operation

Month	Actors	Event	Code	Category
September	US Int Community Dom Community	On the day of the terrorist attacks (9/11) in New York, the aircraft carrier USS *Enterprise* deploys to the Northern Arabian Gulf as a contingency force[312]	C/P	Deterrence/ Reassurance
September	South Africa US	South Africa refuses permission for the visit of a nuclear powered aircraft carrier, USS *Enterprise*, to Cape Town[313]	–	–
September	China Int Community	China increases its patrols of the South China Sea and Spratley Islands with three new patrol boats. The vessels belong to the PLAN but are marked as 'customs' to downplay their role[314]	E	Picture Building
October	UK Oman Int Community	Ex *Saif Sareea* II becomes a symbol of the global war on terror. An Omani Navy commodore becomes the maritime component commander in a UK Type 22 frigate[315]	E	Attraction/ Co-operation
October	Australia Int Community	HMAS *Warramunga* turns back illegal immigrants at Ashmore Reef. HMAS *Adelaide* fires warning shots across the bow of another vessel carrying illegal immigrants[316]	P	Deterrence/ Reassurance
October	South Korea China North Korea	South Korea pays its first naval goodwill visit to mainland China, led by the destroyer *Euljimundok*; there had been a previous visit to Hong Kong in 1998[317]	E	Attraction
November	US UK Afghanistan Int Community	The US and UK lead a coalition assault into Afghanistan from ships in the Indian Ocean[318]	D	Coercion/ Co-operation/ Reassurance
November	Japan Int Community	A Japanese warship is deployed to the Indian Ocean for 'data gathering'; other destroyers and mine countermeasures support vessels deploy for 'co-operation and support activities'[319]	P/E	Co-operation/ Picture Building
December	Nigeria South Africa	Nigeria and South Africa conduct joint anti-piracy patrols off the west coast of Africa[320]	P/E	Co-operation

(Continued)

Date	Principal Actors	Description	Cable Classification	Composite Classification
2002				
January	US Algeria	The US and Algeria conduct their fourth joint exercise in the Mediterranean[321]	E	Co-operation/ Attraction
February	France Tanzania Regional Community	France and Tanzania co-host a peace support exercise in Tanzania's Tanga Bay. France provides its amphibious ship *Sirocco*. Other states participating are Kenya, South Africa, the Seychelles, Madagascar, Malawi, Botswana, Lesotho, Mozambique, Zambia, Swaziland, Zimbabwe and Mauritius[322]	E	Co-operation/ Attraction
April	India US Int Community	Under the banner Op *Sagittarius*, the Indian Navy escort high-value vessels through the Strait of Malacca choke point as part of the US-led Op *Enduring Freedom* (the war on terror following the attacks of 11 September 2001)[323]	P/E	Co-operation/ Prestige
May	Germany Int Community	Germany assumes command of the international naval Task Force 150, operating around the Horn of Africa as part of the global war on terror[324]	–	Prestige/ Co-operation
May	India Mexico	At Mexican request, the Indian Navy escorts a sail training ship through the Strait of Malacca[325]	P/E	Co-operation/ Prestige
May	Taiwan China	Taiwan tests its first anti-ship missile, the Hsiung-Feng 2, with a reported range of 150 km[326]	–	Deterrence
May	India France	A joint Indian/French naval exercise is conducted in the Arabian Sea. The Indian defence minister visits the French flag ship *Charles de Gaulle*[327]	E	Co-operation/ Attraction
June	North Korea South Korea	Shots exchanged as North Korean patrol boats cross the Northern Limit Line and are intercepted by the South Korean Navy[328]	D	Coercion/ Deterrence
July	New Zealand Vietnam	RNZN ships *Te Mana* and *Endeavour* pay a goodwill visit to Ho Chi Minh City[329]	E	Attraction
July	Germany India	The German and Indian Navies conduct a PASSEX off Kochi[330]	E	Co-operation
August	Russia Int Community	Russia conducts the largest naval exercise in the Caspian Sea since the end of the Soviet Union; it involves 60 ships and 10,000 men[331]	E	Prestige

Month	Countries	Description		
August	Russia Int Community	Russia is forced to cancel a Black Sea Fleet exercise, reportedly because of fuel shortages. It was due to exercise with the French Navy and pay visits to France and Italy[332]	—	—
September	India Indonesia	India and Indonesia commence joint patrols of the Malacca Strait[333]	P/E	Co-operation
October	Japan Int Community	Japan's first post-WWII international fleet review is held in Tokyo Bay[334]	E	Attraction/Prestige
October	India Kuwait Oman Int Community	The Indian Navy's training squadron visit Kuwait and Oman[335]	E	Attraction
November	China Myanmar India	China commences building a major naval signals intelligence facility on Myanmar's Great Coco Island, near India's strategically important Andaman and Nicobar Islands[336]	—	Picture Building
December	US Yemen North Korea Spain	A Spanish warship, acting as part of Task Force 150, intercepts a ship carrying Scud missiles from North Korea to Yemen. However, after protests from Yemen the ship is allowed to proceed. The US Secretary of State then announces that Yemen had agreed not to pass the missiles to a third party[337]	P	—
2003				
January	India Sri Lanka LTTE	The Indian government announces that its Navy will provide logistical support to Sri Lanka in the fight against the Tamil Tigers at sea[338]	P	Co-operation/Attraction
January	US UK Iraq Int Community	US and UK naval assets begin to mass in the Arabian Gulf following Iraqi refusal to allow weapons inspectors access to sites required[339]	D	Coercion
February	France Int Community	The French carrier *Charles de Gaulle* and its task group of three frigates, one nuclear submarine and replenishment vessel sail for the eastern Mediterranean. The French political leadership had formally declared their opposition to military intervention in Iraq, but the deployment is viewed as a signal of quiet preparations for involvement[340]	E	Prestige/Coercion

(*Continued*)

Date	Principal Actors	Description	Cable Classification	Composite Classification
March	Iran India	Iran and India conduct joint naval exercises off Mumbai in an attempt to increase bilateral co-operation[341]	E	Co-operation/Attraction
March	US UK Iraq Int Community	The invasion of Iraq begins with an assault from the sea[342]	D	Coercion
March	UK Sierra Leone	The UK deploys HMS *Iron Duke* plus an auxiliary with Royal Marines embarked to Sierra Leone in support of the government when civil unrest was feared[343]	P/C	Reassurance/Deterrence
April	Russia Int Community	Russia commences a long-planned naval deployment to the Indian Ocean. The Defence Ministry claim that it is not connected with the US-led invasion of Iraq. It is the largest Russian deployment in a decade[344]	C/E	Prestige
April	Brunei Philippines	Brunei and the Philippines hold their first bilateral naval exercise, *Seagull 01–03*[345]	E	Co-operation
April	Russia Ukraine NATO	Russia and Ukraine conduct joint naval exercises, *Peace Fairway*, in the Black Sea. This follows a NATO announcement of a PfP exercise with Ukraine and involvement of STANAVFORMED planned for later in the year[346]	E	Co-operation/Attraction
May	Australia Solomon Islands	RAN delivers medical aid to Solomon Islands[347]	–	Assistance
May	India Sri Lanka	Indian Navy provides flood relief for Sri Lanka[348]	–	Assistance
May	India Russia	Indian and Russian navies conduct the first bilateral exercise between the two countries (Ex *Indra* 03)[349]	E	Co-operation
May	Canada Int Community	Canada reduces its naval footprint in the Persian Gulf, withdrawing one of its frigates after three months of a planned six-month deployment[350]	–	–
June	India African Union	The Indian Navy considers a request to provide maritime security for the African Union (AU) summit in Mozambique[351]	–	Attraction/Co-operation

Month	Actors	Description	Type	Function
June	Chile UK France Canada US	Ex *Teamwork South* 2003 takes place off the coast of northern Chile. It aims to improve interoperability between the participating forces, particularly when working under a UN mandate[352]	E	Co-operation
June to July	US ASEAN	A series of joint US-ASEAN naval exercises, *Carat* 03, takes place, aiming to improve interoperability[353]	E	Co-operation
July	US India Regional Community	The US and India conduct a SAR exercise off Chennai; there are observers from Madagascar, Sri Lanka, Mauritius and the Maldives[354]	E	Co-operation/Attraction
July	Greece Tunisia	The Greek and Tunisian navies conduct their first joint exercise, *Poseidon*[355]	E	Co-operation
July	US Fiji	USS *O'Kane* becomes the first USN warship to visit Fiji in three years following the overthrow of the government there in May 2000[356]	E	Attraction
July	India Mozambique AU Int Community	INS Ranjit and Suvarna deploy to Mozambique to provide maritime security for the AU summit in Maputo. Medicine was also delivered[357]	P/E	Deterrence/Attraction/Reassurance
August	Japan Russia	Japanese and Russian warships conduct bilateral anti-terrorism exercises in the Okhotsk Sea; the exercises are a departure from the normal SAR and are an attempt to strengthen ties[358]	E	Co-operation
August	US Liberia	In response to deteriorating conditions in Liberia, the US president authorizes deployment into the country's territorial waters to support UN and West African states to restore order and to provide humanitarian assistance[359]	C	Reassurance/Deterrence/Assistance
September	Taiwan China	Taiwan conducts large live-fire exercise involving ships, aircraft, troops and vehicles in an anti-amphibious scenario. However, the exercise suffered a series of mishaps including missed targets; Taiwan publicly blamed the presence of an unspecified third party 'spy ship' and a Chinese electronic warfare monitoring aircraft for the problems	P/E	Coercion/Deterrence
September	India Iran	The Indian and Iranian navies conduct a PASSEX off Bandar Abbas[360]	E	Co-operation

(Continued)

Date	Principal Actors	Description	Cable Classification	Composite Classification
October	Greece NATO	Greece withdraws the Hellenic Navy from participation in Op *Enduring Freedom*, citing costs and commitment in home waters[361]	–	–
November	US South Africa Int Community	The USN deploys its experimental catamaran HSV-2 *Swift* to South Africa; visits to West African ports will follow[362]	E	Attraction/ Assistance/ Co-operation
November	US Vietnam	USS *Vandergrift* becomes the first USN warship to visit Vietnam since the fall of Saigon in 1975; the visit follows a visit to Washington the previous week by the Vietnamese deputy defence minister for talks aimed at launching bilateral military relations[363]	E	Attraction
November	India China	Following a port visit to Shanghai, the Indian and Chinese navies conduct a joint SAR exercise[364]	E	Co-operation
November to December	India Seychelles	An Indian Navy survey vessel, INS *Nirdeshak*, conducts survey operations around the Seychelles[365]	E	Assistance/ Attraction
December	China Pakistan	The Chinese and Pakistani navies conduct their first ever bilateral exercise[366]	E	Co-operation/ Attraction
2004				
January	China Japan	Japanese patrol vessels allegedly attack Chinese fishing vessels in the vicinity of Senkaku/Diaoyu Islands[367]	P	Coercion/ deterrence
March	US Japan North Korea South Korea	The US announces that it will deploy an Aegis-equipped destroyer to the Sea of Japan to bolster ballistic missile defences[368]	P/E	Deterrence/ Reassurance
May to July	India Mozambique Int Community	INS *Savitri* and *Sujata* deploy to Mozambique to provide maritime security (Op *Farisha* 04) during a World Economic Forum meeting and a meeting of Afro-Pacific-Caribbean heads of state at Maputo. Simultaneously, medical treatment is given to 450 patients and naval training is given to the Mozambique Navy[369]	P/E	Co-operation/ Assistance/ Attraction

Month	Countries	Description		
June	US Argentina	During its commissioning voyage from Norfolk, VA to San Diego, CA, USS *Ronald Reagan* conducts exercises with South American navies. Of note, it includes 'touch and go' exercises with Argentinian Super Etendard aircraft, which have not been to sea since the scrapping of the Argentinian aircraft carrier *Veinticinco de Mayo* in 1997[370]	E	Prestige/ Co-operation
June	US Brunei Singapore	The US, Brunei and Singapore conduct a Co-operation Afloat Readiness and Training (*Carat*) exercise in South East Asia[371]	E	Co-operation
June	Iran UK	Iranian Navy seizes British sailors and marines in Royal Navy rigid inflatable boats in the Shatt al-Arab waterway, claiming they had entered Iranian territorial waters. They are released after two days[372]	D/P	Coercion
July	Singapore Malaysia Indonesia	Singapore, Malaysia and Indonesia commence joint patrols of the Strait of Malacca[373]	P/E	Co-operation
July	Russia Int Community	The ballistic submarine *Delta*-IV launches a satellite.[374]	–	Prestige
July	China Japan	A Chinese naval survey vessel and marine research ship operate within the Japanese EEZ off Senkaku/Diaoyu Islands[375]	P/E	Coercion
August	Russia Georgia Ukraine Bulgaria Romania Turkey	Georgia leads the BLACKSEAFOR for the first time, during a month-long cruise around the Black Sea[376]	–	Co-operation
September	UK Grenada Grand Cayman	HMS *Richmond* and RFA *Wave Ruler* divert to Grenada and Grand Cayman to provide disaster relief after Hurricane Ivan[377]	–	Assistance
September	Brazil Namibia	Brazil gifts patrol vessel to Namibia[378]	–	Assistance/ Attraction
October	Australia Russia	HMAS *Arunta* visits Vladivostok to support navy-to-navy talks and further diplomatic relations between two countries[379]	E	Attraction/ Co-operation

(Continued)

Date	Principal Actors	Description	Cable Classification	Composite Classification
October	Russia US Norway	Russia and the US conduct a bilateral naval exercise off the Norwegian coast and pay port visit to Stavanger[380]	E	Co-operation/ Attraction
October	South Korea US North Korea	The US alerts South Korea to the presence of two suspected North Korean submarines in its waters. Later, in an incident reported to be unrelated, a South Korean naval vessel sinks in bad weather[381]	P	Reassurance/ Deterrence
November	Brazil Argentina Uruguay US Spain	Brazil, Argentina, Uruguay, the US and Spain participate in the *Unitas* naval exercise in Uruguayan waters; SAR based[382]	E	Co-operation
November	Australia Kiribati	RAN conducts mission to destroy or remove thousands of pieces of WWII ordnance from island of Tarawa in Kiribati[383]	–	Assistance/ Attraction
November	China Japan	A submerged Chinese nuclear powered submarine violates Japanese territorial waters. China later apologizes, blaming a 'technical error'[384]	P/E	–
December	Indonesia Int Community	Numerous navies engage in disaster relief and humanitarian assistance in response to earthquake and tsunami on Sumatra[385]	–	Assistance
2005				
January	UK Int Community	RN deploys HMS *Invincible* and her task group on a three-month *Marstrike* 05 deployment to the Mediterranean and Gulf; the aim is to demonstrate the operational capability of the UK's maritime strike task group[386]	E	Prestige
January	China Vietnam	In a dispute over economic rights in the South China Sea, the PLAN seizes Vietnamese fishing vessels and detains their crews. This tactic continues for at least the next five years[387]	P/E	Deterrence
January	India Myanmar	INS *Sukanya* pays a goodwill visit to Rangoon[388]	E	Attraction

February	India Seychelles	India gifts fast attack craft to the Seychelles[389]	—	Attraction
May	US Azerbaijan Kazakhstan	US provides $100 million for the *Caspian Guard* initiative, helping the Caspian Sea littoral states to improve maritime surveillance and security in a strategically important region; it gives US business a foothold[390]	—	Attraction
July	Russia NATO	Russian ships *Moskva* and *Rytliviy* make port call to Naples whilst the commander of the Russian Black Sea Fleet meets with NATO commanders to discuss potential Russian co-operation with Op *Active Endeavour* in the Mediterranean[391]	E	Attraction
July to August	Israel Palestinian Auth Dom Community Int Community	Following the Disengagement Plan, the Israeli withdrawal from Gaza, the Israeli Navy deploy patrol vessels off the Gaza coastline to provide maritime protection for the withdrawing forces[392]	P	Reassurance/ Deterrence
August	China Russia	China and Russia hold a joint tri-service exercise, *Peace Mission* 2005, near Vladivostok in the Russian Far East, in Shandong Province and afloat[393]	E	Co-operation
August	China Int Community	Speculation mounts about China's aircraft carrier ambitions. The ex-Russian carrier *Varyag* is under repair in China and is seen being painted in Chinese military markings[394]	—	Prestige
August	Russia Japan	A JMSDF vessel is deployed to assist following an accident involving a Russian submarine off the Kamchatka peninsula[395]	—	Assistance
September	China Japan	Chinese naval vessels operate near the Kashi oil fields in order to demonstrate capability and protect maritime rights and interests in the disputed East China Sea[396]	P/E	—
September	Canada US	HMCS *Athabaskan*, *Ville de Quebec* and *Toronto* deploy to the Gulf Coast of the US to help relief efforts after Hurricane Katrina[397]	—	Assistance
September	India Sri Lanka LTTE	The first Indian-Sri Lankan naval special forces exercise takes place at Tangalle, Sri Lanka[398]	—	Co-operation
September	India Indonesia	The Indian and Indonesian navies conduct Op *Indindo Corpat*, a co-ordinated patrol of the international maritime boundary in the Andaman Sea[399]	P/E	Co-operation

(Continued)

Date	Principal Actors	Description	Cable Classification	Composite Classification
October	India Russia	The Indian and Russian navies conduct a joint exercise which includes anti-submarine warfare, maritime interdiction and boarding[400]	E	Co-operation
October	Singapore Malaysia	Singapore and Malaysia embark on their first joint military endeavour outside the FPDA (consists of Singapore and Malaysia, plus the UK, Australia and New Zealand). The first step is a joint submarine rescue capability[401]	E	Co-operation
November	Sweden Singapore	After a decade of relationship building (see February 1996 onwards), Singapore decides to buy Swedish submarines[402]	–	Attraction
November	Malaysia Int Community Dom Community	Following a rise in piracy in the Strait of Malacca, Malaysia establishes the Maritime Enforcement Agency as a symbol of its determination to focus on providing safe sea routes to international shipping[403]	–	Deterrence/ Reassurance
2006				
January to March	India Seychelles	India conducts surveys of Seychelles waters. The completed charts are presented to the vice president of the Seychelles in a ceremony[404]	E	Assistance/ Attraction/ Picture Building
February	Israel Palestinian Auth Int Community	Israel declares exclusion zone around the Tetis natural gas installation, 13 miles from its coast, and steps up naval patrols; the installation is critical to the Israeli economy and seen as a soft target for terrorist attack[405]	P/E	Deterrence
March	China US	The USN's Pacific Command proposes a series of officer exchanges between itself and the PLAN. If approved, it will be the first bilateral military contact between the two countries since a mid-air collision soured relations in 2001[406]	–	Co-operation
April	Nigeria Dom Community Int Community	Nigeria announces that it is developing an unmanned coastal surveillance capability; the move follows a series of attacks on Niger Delta oil installations in the preceding months[407]	–	Deterrence/ Picture Building
May	India Indonesia	The Indian warship *Rajput* becomes the first foreign warship on the scene after an earthquake in Indonesia; relief operations are conducted[408]	–	Assistance

Month	Actors	Description		
June	India Int Community	India demonstrates its Navy's global reach by deploying a four-ship task group to the Mediterranean. It visits Israel, Egypt, Greece, Turkey and Libya[409]	E	Prestige/Attraction
June	NATO Cape Verde Int Community	NATO conducts Exercise *Steadfast Jaguar* in Cape Verde. The exercise, which includes an amphibious assault and numerous aircraft carriers and other ships from member states is set to test NATO's Response Force in Africa. Cape Verde was keen to host the exercise and aspires to join the Alliance[410]	E	Reassurance/Co-operation
July	India Int Community Dom Community	On its return from the Mediterranean the Indian naval task group is diverted to Lebanon and conducts a NEO from Beirut; 2,280 Indian, Sri Lanka and Nepalese nationals are collected[411]	D	Assistance
July	US China	The PLAN accepts an invitation to observe a major US exercise, *Valiant Shield*, in seas off Guam. It is the largest US exercise in the Western Pacific since the Vietnam War[412]	–	Co-operation
July	Russia Japan	A Russian patrol boat fires on a Japanese fishing vessel, killing one crew member. Japan protests[413]	P	Deterrence
July	US NATO Ukraine Russia	Ex *Sea Breeze* 06, an attempt to improve NATO's relationship with Ukraine and encourage her to join the alliance is a diplomatic failure; Russia objects, the local population protest against the US-led force and the exercise does not take place as planned. Ultimately, Ukraine announces its decision not to rush into NATO membership[414]	E	Co-operation/Attraction/Coercion
July	Israel Hezbollah Lebanon Int Community	Israeli warship *Hanit* is sunk by an anti-ship missile fired by Hezbollah in Lebanon. The ship had been enforcing a blockade during the 2006 'war'[415]	D/P	Coercion
July to August	North Korea Japan US	North Korea conducts ballistic missile firing into Sea of Japan. US responds by deploying Aegis cruiser *Shiloh* to Yokosuka[416]	P	Coercion/Deterrence/Reassurance
July to August	UK Lebanon	UK conducts Op *Highbrow*, a NEO from Beirut, evacuating some 4,500 civilians including 1,300 in a single journey in HMS *Bulwark*[417]	D	Assistance

(Continued)

Date	Principal Actors	Description	Cable Classification	Composite Classification
August	Taiwan China	Taiwan completes the development of a supersonic anti-ship missile and overtly displays it on a *Cheng Kung* class frigate; local media reports that its purpose may be to strike at land targets in mainland China[418]	–	Deterrence
August	Russia Ukraine US NATO Int Community	The Russian-led BLACKSEAFOR conducts Ex *Black Sea Harmony*, just weeks after the failed US-led *Sea Breeze* exercise led by the US and NATO[419]	C/E	Attraction/ Co-operation
September	US China	China and the US conduct joint SAR exercise off San Diego[420]	E	Co-operation
October to November	UK Sierra Leone Int Community	The UK deploys an amphibious task group to West Africa in a show of support to the Sierra Leone government and to conduct capacity building and goodwill visits[421]	E	Reassurance/ Attraction
2007				
January	Nigeria Int Community Dom Community	The Nigerian Navy exercises its Eastern and Western Fleets, a total of four ships, in the strategically important Bight of Bonny; the exercise is believed to be a stepping stone to securing sea lines of communication in the Gulf of Guinea for crude oil exports[422]	E	Deterrence/ Reassurance
March	Iran UK	Iran's Revolutionary Guard detains 15 UK naval personnel from HMS *Cornwall* in the Arabian Gulf; Iran claims that the boat carrying the British servicemen and women was in its territorial waters. The personnel are shown on Iranian television[423]	P/E	Coercion
March to April	India Mauritius	INS *Sarvekshak* conducts surveys of Mauritius and presents the completed charts to the country's prime minister[424]	E	Assistance/ Attraction
April	US India Japan	The first US-Indo-Japanese naval exercise is conducted[425]	E	Co-operation

Date	Actors	Description		Category
April	China ASEAN	China publicly seeks a joint naval exercise with ASEAN. Previously, interaction between ASEAN states and China had been limited to bilateral naval exercises and port visits. The initiative is intended to help expand political and economic ties[426]	—	Attraction
April	India China	The Indian and Chinese navies exercise together[427]	E	Co-operation
April	India Russia	A joint Indian-Russian naval exercise takes place off Vladivostok[428]	E	Co-operation
April to May	India Maldives	India conducts EEZ patrols on behalf of the Maldives[429]	E	Assistance/ Picture Building
April to September	US Int Community	The US pilots its first Global Fleet Station deployment, using the high-speed vessel *Swift*. It visits seven Caribbean and Central American states and conducts training, exercises and seminars with target audiences[430]	E	Attraction/ Co-operation/ Prestige
May	India Int Community	A 17-ship exercise takes place in the Singapore Strait and the disputed South China Sea, with participants from India, the US, France, Japan, Malaysia, New Zealand, Singapore, Australia and China[431]	E	Co-operation/ Reassurance
May	India Pakistan Int Community	India test fires cruise missile from a Kilo class submarine. It is deemed to be a 'watershed' moment in Indian military development, allowing the country to join an exclusive club of states with that capability[432]	E	Prestige
June	US Int Community	The USN announces plans to send an amphibious ship to the Gulf of Guinea to act as a 'school house' for regional navies and to provide a persistent presence in the troubled area[433]	C/E	Attraction/ Co-operation
July	Syria Iran Israel US Int Community	Syria and Iran equip their fast attack craft with anti-ship missiles of the type used by Hezbollah to attack INS *Hanit* in 2006. The countries are believed to be demonstrating their ability to disrupt maritime communications in the eastern Mediterranean and Arabian Gulf[434]	E	Coercion/ Deterrence
July	US Vietnam	USS *Peleliu* of the Pacific Partnership Station visits Danang, making a 'watershed' in post-war US-Vietnamese military relations[435]	E	Attraction

(Continued)

Date	Principal Actors	Description	Cable Classification	Composite Classification
August	US UK	The USMC embarks its largest ever detachment of AV8B Harriers on to HMS *Illustrious*. It demonstrates the two countries' interoperability for strike missions[436]	E	Co-operation
August	Canada Int community	Canada deploys HMCS *Fredericton* (frigate). *Summerside* (patrol vessel) and *Corner Brook* (submarine) to the high north to exercise sovereignty of part of the Arctic Ocean (Operation *Nanook 07*) as climate change looks to open shipping routes[437]	—	—
August to September	India Int Community	India conducts a month-long series of bilateral exercises with Asian and Western navies in the Bay of Bengal and Gulf of Aden. They are aimed at 'constructive engagement' and increased 'domain awareness'; however, Chinese officials visit New Delhi to discuss the exercises which they believe may be aimed at 'containment' of China[438]	E	Co-operation/ Attraction
September	Argentina Chile	Argentina pulls its navy out of annual bilateral exercises with Chile due to financial constraints and the poor operational condition of its units. It brings into question the importance given to the Argentina-Chile relationship. The exercises had been held annually since 1998[439]	—	—
October	Sri Lanka LTTE	The Sri Lankan Navy claims success over the Tamil Tigers after destroying the 'final' rebel vessel being used to smuggle arms into the country[440]	—	Coercion
October	US UK Iran	USN and RN conduct Ex *Sandstone*, a joint anti-submarine exercise in the Northern Arabian Sea; the exercise is designed to send a signal to Iran that its submarine force should not attempt to interfere with Western vessels in the event of a conflict[441]	E	Deterrence/ Co-operation
November	UK Yemen	RN and Yemeni Navy and coastguard conduct joint operations in the Gulf of Aden as a deterrent to human trafficking between Somalia and Yemen[442]	E	Co-operation/ Deterrence
November	Malaysia Singapore Indonesia	Malaysia, Singapore and Indonesia conduct joint naval patrols of the Strait of Malacca to help contain piracy in the region[443]	P/E	Co-operation/ Deterrence

Date	Countries	Code	Event	Category
November	China / Japan	E	The first post-WWII visit by a Chinese warship to Japan takes place[444]	Attraction
November to December	UK / Ireland	E	Op *Wasp* sees the UK and Republic of Ireland conduct joint fisheries patrols in the Irish Sea[445]	Co-operation
December	UK / US	E	HMS *Campbeltown* and USS *Gunston Hall* conduct joint counter-piracy patrol off the Somali coast[446]	Co-operation/Deterrence
December	India / Vietnam	–	India attempts to strengthen its relations with Vietnam by offering spares for its ageing fleet of Soviet-era warships[447]	Attraction/Assistance
December	Russia / Japan	P	Russia seizes six Japanese vessels found to be fishing off Kunashiri island[448]	Deterrence
December to February	Russia / Int Community	–	Russia publicly announces plans to revive its global maritime capability after years of atrophy. It deploys its aircraft carrier *Admiral Kuznetsov* and escorts to the Mediterranean[449]	Prestige
2008				
January	UK / US / Yemen	C/E	RN, USN, Yemeni Navy and Yemeni coastguard conduct human trafficking deterrence patrols off the Yemeni coast under Op *Argo Idefix*[450]	Co-operation/Deterrence
January	France / UAE / Iran	–	France plans to establish a naval base in the UAE by 2009 in an attempt to reassure Gulf allies of its commitment following growing threat from Iran[451]	Reassurance/Attraction
January	India / Bangladesh	–	The Indian Landing Ship *Gharial* deploys to Bangladesh for relief operations following Cyclone Sidr[452]	Assistance
January	Japan / US / Int Community	P/E	Japan takes the political decision to revive its refuelling mission in the Indian Ocean, in support of US warships in the war on terror[453]	Co-operation
February	India / Pakistan	E	India tests its first nuclear-capable submarine launched missile; Pakistan warns that a new nuclear arms race may result[454]	Deterrence
February	US / Int Community	E	USN demonstrates its ability to shoot down a satellite for the first time. USS *Lake Erie* engaged the 'out-of-control' satellite at an altitude of 153 miles above the Pacific[455]	Coercion/Deterrence

(*Continued*)

Date	Principal Actors	Description	Cable Classification	Composite Classification
March	US Lebanon Syria	USN deploys the USS *Nassau* expeditionary strike group to the eastern Mediterranean in the wake of increasing political tensions between Lebanon and Syria[456]	P/C	Coercion
March	Sri Lanka LTTE	Sri Lankan Navy fast attack craft is sunk by Tamil Tigers following an engagement at sea[457]	–	Coercion
March	North Korea South Korea	Tensions rise between the two Koreas after the North carries out a test firing of an anti-ship cruise missile in the Yellow Sea[458]	E	Coercion
March to April	UK Dom Community	RFA *Lyme Bay* deploys to Tristan de Cunha to repair harbour wall at Calshot Harbour; without repairs the harbour would have become unusable[459]	–	Assistance/ Reassurance
April	Taiwan China	Taiwan conducts an amphibious exercises but decides not to sail its ships through the Taiwan Strait in order to avoid any 'misunderstanding' with China[460]	P	Deterrence/ Reassurance
April	UK Bahrain	RN and RFA help to form 'ring of steel' around Bahrain during Bahraini Grand Prix[461]	P/E	Deterrence/ Assistance
April to May	Spain UK Brazil El Salvador	RFA *Mounts Bay* joins Spanish amphibious task group, *Esparabas*, deploying to Brazil and El Salvador[462]	E	Co-operation/ Attraction
May	US Int Community	USN establishes the Africa Partnership Station and deploys it for naval diplomacy duties in the Gulf of Guinea[463]	E	Attraction/ Co-operation
May	UK India Myanmar Int Community	HMS *Westminster* and *Edinburgh* deploy to Burma to offer assistance following cyclone *Nargis*; Burmese military government decline support and ships depart. However, two Indian warships provide relief[464]	–	Assistance
May	UK Bangladesh	HMS *Echo* conducts collaborative surveying operations in Bangladeshi territorial waters[465]	–	Co-operation/ Assistance/ Picture Building

May	UK Iran Int Community	RN conducts an overt anti-submarine warfare exercise in the Indian Ocean (Ex *Phoenix*) to prove the capabilities of its helicopter-borne sonar, 2087; it demonstrates the UK's ability to counter submarines in demanding conditions at range from the UK[466]	E	Prestige/ Deterrence
May	India Brazil South Africa	In a sign that the relationship among some of the emerging powers is not confined to the economic, a trilateral Indian/Brazilian/South African naval exercise takes place off South Africa[467]	E	Co-operation/ Attraction
June	US Int Community	In BMD tests, USS *Lake Erie* successfully performs a terminal phase intercept of a ballistic target; it marks a leap forward in capability[468]	E	Deterrence
June	Japan China	JMSDF destroyer *Sazanami* becomes the first Japanese warship to visit a Chinese port since the end of the Second World War[469]	E	Attraction
July	Russia Norway Int Community	The Russian Federation deploys Northern Fleet warships into the Arctic for the first time since the end of the Cold War. They operate in the vicinity of Svalbard; Russia states that it does not recognize Norway's claim of a 200-mile EEZ in the Arctic[470]	C/E	Coercion/ Prestige
July	US Int Community	The USN re-establishes its Fourth Fleet in order to operate in the Caribbean and the waters off Central and South America and build 'multi-national coalitions'[471]	E	Co-operation/ Attraction
August	UK Netherlands France West Indies	UK, Dutch and French ships conduct joint counter-narcotics operations in the Caribbean as part of Op *Carib Venture*[472]	P/E	Deterrence/ Picture Building
August	India Int Community	Three Indian warships join the international counter-piracy effort off the Horn of Africa[473]	P/E	Co-operation/ Deterrence/ Reassurance/ Prestige
August	Russia Georgia Int Community	Russian ships of the Black Sea Fleet are involved in a 'skirmish' with Georgian vessels. Russia claims that the Georgian ships had violated their declared 'safety zone' off the coast of Abkhazia. One Georgian vessel is sunk and 30 sailors killed[474]	D	Coercion

(Continued)

Date	Principal Actors	Description	Cable Classification	Composite Classification
August	Russia Ukraine	The Ukraine president issues a decree that Moscow must give three days' warning if it wishes to sail the Black Sea Fleet from Sebastopol through Ukrainian waters[475]	–	Coercion
September	Malaysia Int Community	Malaysia deploys ships to join the anti-piracy effort off the Horn of Africa[476]	P/E	Co-operation/ Deterrence/ Reassurance/ Prestige
September	Russia Int Community	Russia deploys ships from the Baltic to the Gulf of Aden to join the international anti-piracy effort off the coast of Somalia[477]	P/E	Co-operation/ Deterrence/ Reassurance/ Prestige
October	India Indonesia Thailand	Indian, Indonesian and Thai warships conduct joint patrols[478]	P/E	Co-operation
October	Japan Dom Community US	There are local protests in the port of Yokosuka after the arrival of the nuclear-powered carrier USS *George Washington*; the ship replaced the conventionally powered USS *Kitty Hawk*[479]	E	Coercion
November	NATO UN Somalia	NATO provides naval escort for World Food Programme ships delivering aid to Somalia[480]	D/E	Deterrence/ Reassurance
November	India Pakistan LeT	A terrorist attack by Lashkar-e-Taiba (LeT), launched from the sea, kills 140 people and injures over 300 others in Mumbai[481]	C/E	Coercion
November	Russia Venezuela	Russian Navy warships *Pyotr* and *Admiral Chabanenko* visit Venezuela, coincident with a visit to the country by President Medvedev; it is the first Russian Navy visit to the Caribbean since the end of the Cold War. The visit is also rumoured to be linked to a potential sale of submarines to Venezuela[482]	E	Attraction

Date	Actors	Event		Functions
November	Iran Int Community	Iran projects its naval power in the Gulf, establishing an 'impenetrable defence line', with the launch of new fast attack craft and a midget submarine[483]	E	Deterrence/ Coercion
December	China Japan	Two Chinese oceanographic research ships enter Japanese territorial waters off Senkaku/Diaoyu Islands[484]	E	Coercion/ Picture Building
December	China Int Community	China commences its counter-piracy operations in the Gulf of Aden[485]	E	Co-operation/ Deterrence/ Reassurance/ Prestige
December to January 2009	Israel Hamas Dom Community	The Israeli Navy conducts Operation *Cast Lead*, a campaign against Hamas in the Gaza Strip, including support to ground troops and anti-smuggling patrols[486]	–	Deterrence/ Reassurance
2009				
January	Japan Int Community	Japan considers sending a destroyer to join the international counter-piracy effort off the Horn of Africa[487]	E	Co-operation/ Deterrence/ Reassurance/ Prestige
January	Russia Georgia Abkhazia Ukraine	The Georgian breakaway region of Abkhazia announces a plan to allow Russia to establish a naval base and an airfield on its territory; this would provide Moscow with access to the Black Sea other than from its disputed Crimea base[488]	–	Attraction/ Reassurance Coercion
February	North Korea South Korea US	USN increases its number of sorties of intelligence gathering Aegis ships after satellite imagery shows North Korean missile sites preparing to launch missiles[489]	–	Picture Building
February to August	UK Int Community	RN deploys its largest deployment to the Far East in a decade. During *Taurus* 09 the ships exercise with vessels of 13 states and visit numerous countries	–	Prestige/ Attraction/ Co-operation

(Continued)

Date	Principal Actors	Description	Cable Classification	Composite Classification
March	Japan, North Korea, South Korea	Japan deploys its Aegis destroyers *Kongou* and *Chokai* to the Sea of Japan in readiness for a North Korean missile launch. North Korea threatens war if its missiles are shot down. The missile launch takes place in April without incident[490]	P	Deterrence/Reassurance
March	US, China	USNS *Impeccable* is challenged by PLAN warships and civilian vessels when operating in China's EEZ south of Hainan Island; *Impeccable* leaves the scene but returns within days in the company of USS *Chung Hoon*[491]	P	Deterrence
April	Nigeria, MEND, Dom Community	The Nigerian Navy is attacked by armed militants from the Movement for the Emancipation of the Niger Delta (MEND); two sailors are killed and at least one gunboat seized. MEND had previously attacked oil installations[492]	–	Coercion
April	China, Int Community	China holds an International Fleet Review at Qingdao and displays its nuclear powered submarines for the first time[493]	E	Prestige
April	Seychelles, Int Community	The Seychelles becomes the first East African state to contribute to the Horn of Africa counter-piracy effort; the coastguard assist in two operations with a patrol aircraft and patrol vessel, PW *Andromache*. The president applauds his country's ability to work with international navies[494]	P	Co-operation/Deterrence/Prestige
May	MEND, Nigeria, Int Community	MEND warns oil companies to withdraw workers from the region or face 'imminent hurricane'[495]	–	Coercion
May	Iran, Int Community, Dom Community	Iran deploys two naval ships, the frigate *Alborz* and the auxiliary *Bushehr*, to conduct anti-piracy operations off Somalia[496]	P/E	Deterrence/Co-operation/Reassurance/Attraction
June	NATO, UN, Somalia	NATO provides naval escort for World Food Programme ships delivering aid to Somalia[497]	P/E	Reassurance/Deterrence

Date	Countries	Description		Category
June	US Libya	A US coastguard vessel, *Boutwell*, becomes the first American 'military' ship to visit Libya since President Ghadaffi seized power in 1969[498]	E	Attraction
June	Malaysia Indonesia	An Indonesian patrol vessel 'almost' fires on a Malaysian patrol vessel which violated Indonesian territorial waters in a disputed maritime zone to the east of Borneo[499]	D	Deterrence/ Coercion
July	GCC Int Community UN NATO	The Gulf Co-operation Council demand that the Red Sea be excluded from international arrangements on counter-piracy, stating instead that security there was 'the responsibility of the Arab countries overlooking it'. They determine to create an Arab naval force[500]	–	Prestige/ Coercion/ Co-operation/ Reassurance
July	Israel Iran Int Community	Israel deploys the attack submarine *Leviathan* and an accompanying corvette, *Hanit*, through the Suez Canal and into the Red Sea for the first time. It is believed to be a signal to Iran about regional intentions[501]	P/E	Deterrence
August	UK Somalia Puntland	During Op *Patch*, HMS *Cornwall* facilitates engagement between Somali officials and representatives of Puntland[502]	E	Assistance/ Prestige
August	India Maldives China	The Indian Navy strengthens its ties with the Maldives, augmenting its co-operation and security initiatives. The move is believed to be a counter to growing Chinese influence in the Indian Ocean[503]	–	Assistance/ Attraction/ Co-operation/ Deterrence
August	China US	China asks the US to end its maritime surveillance activities within the Chinese-claimed EEZ; the request was ostensibly to reduce the risk of naval confrontation[504]	–	Coercion/ Picture Building
October	Georgia Russia	Georgia deploys a coastguard vessel in territorial waters off the breakaway region of Abkhazia in an attempt at a 'naval blockade'. Russia responds by stating that its Black Sea Fleet will ensure lines of communication remain open[505]	D/P	Coercion
November	UK Commonwealth Trinidad and Tobago	HMS *Iron Duke* provides maritime security for Commonwealth Heads of Government meeting in Trinidad and Tobago[506]	E	Assistance/ Reassurance
November	North Korea South Korea	North and South Korean ships engage in 'firefight' in Yellow Sea off Daechung Island following the North's incursion into disputed waters[507]	D	Coercion/ Deterrence

(Continued)

Date	Principal Actors	Description	Cable Classification	Composite Classification
2010				
January	North Korea South Korea	In a supposed bid to strengthen its position ahead of talks with the South, North Korea fires artillery shells into its own territorial waters in the Yellow Sea near the disputed maritime Northern Limit Line. South Korea returned fire with 100 warning shots. The North then declared the area a 'no-sail zone'.[508]	C	Coercion
February	Canada Haiti Int Community	Canada deploys HMCS *Halifax* and *Athabaskan* to provide support to Haiti following January earthquake[509]	–	Assistance
February	India China	India increases its naval presence and surveillance activities around the Andaman and Nicobar islands in a counter to growing Chinese presence in the region[510]	E	Picture Building/ Deterrence
February to March	UK Haiti Int Community	RFA *Largs Bay* deploys to Haiti as part of Op *Panlake* relief effort[511]	–	Assistance
March	North Korea South Korea	North Korea attacked and sank the South Korean warship *Cheonan*; 46 lives are lost. North Korea denies responsibility[512]	D	Coercion
April	China Japan	Ten Chinese warships pass between Okinawa's main island and Miyako Island before heading into Pacific Ocean[513]	P	Coercion/ Prestige Attraction
April	Ukraine Russia	Ukraine agrees to extend the lease allowing the Russian Navy to operate from Sevastopol; the announcement is met with violent clashes in Ukraine[514]	–	
April to May	Iran Int Community	Iran conducts a series of naval exercises around the Strait of Hormuz. The exercises were stated to be aimed at securing Iranian shipping routes, but have alienated many GCC countries who see them as a challenge to their power in the region[515]	E	Coercion/ Deterrence
May	Israel Palestinian Authority Turkey Int Community	MV *Mari Marmara*, operated by a Turkey-based pressure group, attempts to break the Israeli blockade of Gaza. The Israeli Navy intercept and board the vessel and violence ensues. Nine people are killed and there is worldwide condemnation of the Israeli heavy-handed tactics[516]	D/C	Coercion

Date	Actors	Description		Category
June	Turkey Israel	Turkey cancels a planned naval exercise with Israel following the *Mari Marmara* incident[517]	—	—
July	China US ASEAN	China conducts an unprecedented military exercise in the South China Sea, involving ships and aircraft from all three of its fleets. This came after US Secretary of State Hillary Clinton stated earlier that month at the ASEAN Regional Forum that 'the US has a national interest in freedom of navigation, open access to Asia's maritime commons, and respect for international law in the South China Sea'[518]	E	Deterrence
July	North Korea South Korea US	North Korea denounces a combined US-South Korean naval exercise, stating that it is a 'major danger to the security of the region'[519]	—	Coercion/ Co-operation
August	Iran Int Community	Iran publicly unveils four new mini-submarines at Bandar Abbas[520]	—	Prestige/ Coercion
August	South Africa Mozambique	South African Navy ships exercise with Mozambique and conduct joint security patrols of territorial waters[521]	—	Co-operation
August to September	UK Argentina Brazil Int Community	Whilst the runway in the Falkland Islands is being resurfaced, HMS *Ocean* deploys to the South Atlantic and pays a visit to Brazil and West Africa. Though she does not physically reach the Falklands, she demonstrates British capability and commitment to Argentina	P	Deterrence/ Attraction/ Reassurance
September	China Japan	A Chinese trawler is detained after it rammed into two Japanese coastguard vessels in a disputed area of the East China Sea[522]	P	Deterrence
September to October	Malaysia China Int Community	Malaysia conducts a two-week 'maritime domain awareness' exercise in the Strait of Malacca and then declares the security of the South China Sea a 'top priority.'[523]	E	Deterrence/ Picture Building
November	UK West Indies	HMS *Manchester* conducts disaster relief and humanitarian assistance in St Lucia and Turks and Caicos in wake of Hurricane Tomas[524]	—	Assistance
November	North Korea South Korea US	North Korea fires 170 artillery shells at the island of Yeonpyeong killing four people; the firing is believed to be in response to a South Korean Navy live firing exercise in the nearby disputed region of the Yellow Sea; the USN deploys the aircraft carrier USS *George Washington* to the Yellow Sea in support of South Korea[525]	D/P	Coercion/ Deterrence/ Reassurance
November to December	UK France	RN nuclear submarine HMS *Tireless* deploys to Indian Ocean with French carrier battle group (Op *Agapanthe*)[526]	E	Co-operation

Control: chronological survey of naval diplomacy 1960–64 and 1980–84

Date	Principal Actors	Description	Cable Classification	Composite Classification
1960				
January	US Int Community	The US bathyscaphe *Trieste* reaches a record-breaking depth of 35,800 feet in the Marianas Trench.[527]	–	Prestige
April to May	Netherlands Indonesia New Guinea	To deter attacks by Indonesia on New Guinea, the Netherlands government announce despatch of carrier *Karel Doorman* and two destroyers. No attacks are made, but reactions from Indonesia are damaging and those from third parties are adverse.[528]	P	Deterrence
May	Cuba US	A Cuban cutter fires on the US submarine *Sea Poacher* in the San Nicholas Channel.[529]	D	Deterrence
May	US Int Community	The nuclear powered US submarine *Triton* completes the first submerged circumnavigation of the globe; it takes 84 days.[530]	–	Prestige
July	US Congo Reg Community	USN carrier *Wasp* arrives off coast to evacuate US citizens and, while there, delivers fuel to UN forces.[531]	P	Assistance
July	US USSR Int Community	US submarine *George Washington* conducts the first test firing of Polaris ballistic missiles from a submerged boat. It demonstrates American capability.[532]	E	Prestige/ Deterrence
August	US USSR Int Community	US submarine *Seadragon* is the first ever to surface at the North Pole. The crew play baseball on the polar ice.[533]	E	Prestige
November	US Cuba Guatemala	After armed uprisings allegedly inspired by Cuba against the governments of Guatemala and Nicaragua, the carrier USS *Shangri-La* and US destroyers patrolled the Caribbean coasts of these countries until December 'to prevent intervention on the part of Communist-directed elements'.[534]	P	Deterrence/ Reassurance
November	US USSR Int Community	US submarine *George Washington*, which had test fired Polaris missiles earlier in the year, sails for the first nuclear deterrent patrol.[535]	P	Deterrence

1961				
April	US Cuba	C	Visible presence offshore of US fleet encourages a group of Cuban exiles organized by the CIA to attempts the overthrow of Castro. Receiving no actual naval support the bid fails.[536]	–
June to July	UK Iraq Regional Comm	P	After Iraq claims sovereignty over Kuwait on 25 June and make menacing troop movements, Britain responds to Kuwaiti appeal for help by landing marines from HMS *Bulwark*. These are reinforced by tanks, troops and, ultimately, 45 warships (including two aircraft carriers). Ground forces replaced by Arab League troops in October and Iraq recognizes Kuwaiti independence in October 1963. Iraqi aggression successfully deterred by quick British response.[537]	Deterrence/ Reassurance
July	France Tunisia	P	After initial bombardment by aircraft from the carrier *Arromanches*, the cruisers *Colbert*, *Bouvet* and *Chevalier-Paul* force the entrance to the Lake of Bizerta and, with the help of French troops, break the Tunisian blockade of the Bizerta naval base complex and re-establish French control.[538]	Coercion?
November	US Dominican Republic	P	Visible presence offshore of US fleet (including carriers *Franklin D. Roosevelt* and *Valley Forge* with 1,800 marines on board) enable President Kennedy's representative to secure the expulsion of the Trujillos (the family of the late dictator) and the establishment of a government acceptable to the US[539]	Coercion
November	UK Kenya	–	HMS *Victorious* (later *Centaur*) and helicopters, plus amphibious ship *Striker* with Royal Marines embarked provide humanitarian assistance after severe flooding in Kenya.[540]	Assistance
1962				
January	Indonesia Netherlands	C	Indonesian motor torpedo boats try to land infiltrators into New Guinea but are caught by the Netherlands Navy, who sink one and put the rest to flight.[541]	–
January	UK Iraq Kuwait	P	HMS *Centaur* is deployed to Kuwait to act as a deterrent against Iraqi aggression.[542]	Deterrence/ Reassurance

(*Continued*)

Date	Principal Actors	Description	Cable Classification	Composite Classification
May	US North Vietnam Laos Thailand	Carrier covers landing of US marines in Thailand, an operation intended to demonstrate US readiness to intervene if communists push their military success in Laos too far.[543]	E/P	Deterrence/ Reassurance
May	US USSR	US aircraft carrier *Wasp* leads a force of eight ships into the Baltic. It is the largest American deployment into these waters since the end of World War II.[544]	E/P	Deterrence/ Coercion
July	US UK SEATO China	US, UK and SEATO naval forces exercise together and conduct a 'show of force' in the South China Sea.[545]	E/P	Co-operation/ Deterrence
August to May 1963	United Nations Pakistan Indonesia	Pakistan operates nine vessels as part of the UN Temporary Executive Authority, one of the 'first generation' peacekeeping missions, following the Indonesian invasion of West New Guinea.[546]	–	Deterrence/ Reassurance
October	US USSR Cuba	The US imposes an air and naval blockade on Cuba following the discovery of the construction of 'offensive military' facilities by the Soviet Union. The ensuing Cuban missile crisis becomes a defining moment of the Cold War.[547]	D	Coercion
1963				
February	France Brazil	French destroyer *Tartu* sent to fishing grounds off north-east coast of Brazil after three French lobster boats had been seized by Brazilian warships 60 miles off the coast. Brazil countered with a cruiser, five destroyers and two corvettes, *Tartu* was soon withdrawn and the effect of these moves is open to question.[548]	C/E	Coercion/ Deterrence
February	US Dominican Republic	US aircraft carrier *Boxer* anchors off Santo Domingo ready to send helicopters to rescue Vice President Johnson in case of trouble during the latter's visit. Nothing happens.[549]	P/D	Deterrence

Date	Countries		Description	Category
April	US UK Haiti	C	US task force cruises off Haiti to protect US nationals in case of conflict between Haiti and Dominican Republic, perhaps also to intervene if government of Haiti is overthrown, but crisis blows over. A British destroyer and frigate also stand by US, but not British, nationals are subsequently evacuated.[550]	Deterrence/ Reassurance
August	Cuba UK	D/P	Two Cuban warships land a party on a British island in the Bahamas to seize 19 Cuban refugees and two fishing boats. Investigation by HMS *Londonderry* reveals that the normally uninhabited island had been used by Cuban exiles based in the US as a launching pad for their attacks on Cuba. Steps were taken to discourage the use of British territory for this purpose.[551]	—
October	US Haiti Cuba	—	USS *Lake Champlain, Liddle* and *Muliphen* undertake disaster relief operations in Haiti following Hurricane *Flora*. Cuba refuses an offer of US assistance.[552]	Assistance
December	USSR Albania Regional Community	—	Following a deterioration in relations, Albania ejects Soviet Navy from its base in the country. Over the subsequent years the USSR then attempts to find a suitable alternative in the Mediterranean.[553]	—
December	US Iran	—	The US destroyer *Strong* and Iranian ship *Babr*, with medical teams embarked, conduct a joint 17-day mission at three Iranian ports to provide medical support to local people.[554]	Co-operation/ Assistance
1964				
January	UK US Zanzibar	D	After the Zanzibar government is overthrown by coup d'état, USS *Manley*, HMS *Owen* and *Rhyl* and RFA *Hebe* with one company of infantry evacuate US and some British nationals.[555]	Assistance/ Reassurance
January	UK Uganda Kenya Tanganyika	D	During mutinies in three former colonies in East Africa, the governments' request British help and three carriers (*Albion, Centaur* and *Victorious*) are deployed with other warships and RFAs as well as two marine commando and army units. The incident ends swiftly with no British losses and two mutineers killed. Population reassured.[556]	Assistance/ Reassurance

(Continued)

Date	Principal Actors	Description	Cable Classification	Composite Classification
January to March	UK Turkey Cyprus	To reinforce their threat of armed intervention, failing the adoption of satisfactory measures for the protection of Turkish minority in Cyprus, the Turkish fleet conducts overt manoeuvres.[557]	P	Reassurance/ Coercion
February	US Cuba	Four Cuban fishing vessels are seized off the coast of Florida by the US. In response, Cuba cuts off the water supply to the Guantanamo naval base.[558]	P	Coercion
March	US Brazil	A USN task force prepares to deploy to Rio de Janeiro to offer support to the rebels during the Brazilian 'general's coup' against the president. It was not needed and stood down.[559]	C	Coercion/ Assistance
April	US USSR	The Soviet oceanographic research ship *Sergei Vavilov* visits Boston. It is the first Soviet ship to visit since the end of World War II.[560]	E	Co-operation
April to May	US Int Community Regional Community	USN deploys the 'Concord Squadron' to the Indian Ocean to conduct a six-week goodwill tour of Africa and the Middle East.[561]	E	Attraction
August	US North Vietnam	US destroyers on patrol in the Gulf of Tonkin are attacked by North Vietnamese torpedo boats.[562]	P	Coercion/ Deterrence
September	UK Indonesia	Indonesian threats result in a British naval task group exercising freedom of the seas in the Lombok Strait.[563]	E	Deterrence/ Reassurance
1980				
February	UK St Kitts	HMS *Rhyl* stands by the island of St Kitts, to be on hand during an election.[564]	C	Reassurance/ Deterrence
April	US Iran	Helicopters from USS *Nimitz* in Arabian Sea attempt to rescue US hostages from the embassy in Tehran. Mechanical failures force the operation to be abandoned.[565]	D	–
May	Bahamas Cuba UK	The Bahamian Defence Force Ship *Flamingo* is sunk by Cuban aircraft whilst taking a Cuban fishing vessel into custody for illegal fishing. HMS *Eskimo* and support ship are sailed from St Vincent in case of escalation.[566]	D/P	Coercion/ Reassurance
August	Libya Italy	A Libyan submarine and frigate drive the Italian floating oil rig *Saipen* II from disputed waters of Medina Bank.[567]	P	Coercion

August	UK St Lucia Cayman Islands	HMS *Glasgow* administers disaster relief in St Lucia and HMS *Scylla* assists in the Cayman Islands after Hurricane Allen.[568]	–	Assistance
October	UK Iran Iraq	British warships are diverted to the Gulf to start the *Armilla* Patrol for the protection of merchant shipping during war between Iran and Iraq.[569]	P	Reassurance/Deterrence
November	UK Turks and Caicos	HMS *Active* remains in the vicinity of the Turks and Caicos following civil unrest.[570]	C/E	Reassurance/Deterrence
1981				
May	UK Bermuda	HMS *Cardiff* stands by to assist in Bermuda following civil unrest and a general strike.[571]	C/E	Reassurance/Assistance
April	USSR Cuba	A squadron of five Soviet ships pays an official goodwill visit to Cuba.[572]	E	Attraction/Reassurance
June	UK Algeria	A merchant tanker (Shell) is stopped and diverted by Algerian gunboats; HMS *Dido* is sent to assist but the incident ends without intervention.[573]	P/E	Coercion/Reassurance
August	US Libya	Aircraft from carrier USS *Nimitz* shoot down two oncoming Libyan aircraft while task force is in Gulf of Sirte to emphasize US rejection of Libyan claim that Gulf is their territorial waters. The dispute persists.[574]	P	Coercion
August	Iran Denmark	The Iranian Navy seize Danish ship carrying explosives to Iraq. The start of a long campaign against neutral shipping in the Gulf.[575]	D	–
August	USSR Int Community	The new Soviet aircraft carrier, *Kiev*, makes its maiden voyage to the Baltic.[576]	E	Prestige
August	US Int Community	USN leads Exercise *Ocean Venture* in the Atlantic. It involves 250 ships from the US, UK, Argentina, Brazil, Colombia, Uruguay, Venezuela, the Netherlands, Canada, West Germany, Portugal, France, Denmark and Spain. Norway refuses to join the exercise because it involves so many non-NATO members. The USSR denounces the exercise as 'sabre rattling'.[577]	–	Co-operation/Deterrence
September	USSR Poland	During a period of political disaffection in Poland, the Soviet naval exercise *Zapad* culminates in the landing of 6,000 troops and marines on the Baltic coast close to the Polish border.[578]	E	Coercion

(*Continued*)

Date	Principal Actors	Description	Cable Classification	Composite Classification
1982				
April	Argentina UK	After an initial foray into South Georgia by an Argentinian scrap merchant, an Argentine naval task force lands troops to seize Port Stanley in the Falkland Islands. Initially successful, but leads to war and defeat for Argentina.[579]	D	Coercion
April	Italy Egypt Israel	Italian warships patrol the Strait of Tiran as part of the Multinational Force and Observers monitoring military disengagement in Sinai.[580]	–	Co-operation/ Deterrence/ Reassurance
February	USSR Italy	The Italian submarine *Leonardo da Vinci* detects a Soviet *Victor I* Class submarine in Italian waters off the naval base at Taranto. The submarine was tracked for 18 hours before it left Italian territorial waters.[581]	–	Picture Building
May	US Cuba	In Exercise *Ocean Ventura*, US Navy lands 400 marines at their enclave in Guantanamo Bay and evacuates 300 Americans. Cubans call it an 'intimidating show of strength'.[582]	E	Deterrence
September	USSR USA Japan China	Soviet Backfire bomber aircraft are detected over the Sea of Japan and Soviet air and naval forces surge in the area when aircraft carrier USS *Enterprise* transits North Pacific. The action is seen to be a sign of Soviet concern over US carrier-based air power in the Far East.[583]	C/E	Deterrence/ Reassurance
December	US USSR Lebanon Regional Comm	Fourteen US warships are deployed off the Lebanese coast and carry out exercises to demonstrate US resolve.[584]	E	Coercion
1983				
January	Argentina Brazil	Argentine patrol boat turns back a Brazilian naval survey vessel from the Beagle Channel in assertion of a disputed territorial claim.[585]	P	Coercion

February	US Libya Sudan Egypt	Following a request by the Egyptian presence for a show of force, the USN aircraft carrier *Nimitz* poises just outside Libyan waters. Egypt accuses Libya of planning to invade Sudan; Libya denies the accusation.[586]	P	Deterrence/ Reassurance
February to April	UK Int Community	The *Caribtrain 83* deployment led by HMS *Invincible* visits and conducts exercises with Portugal, the US, the Bahamas and Belize, including exercises designed to demonstrate British ability to reinforce in a crisis.[587]	E	Co-operation/ Prestige
March	USSR India	Soviet aircraft carrier *Minsk* visits India to reinforce the bilateral 'security alliance'.[588]	E	Attraction
April	Norway USSR	An unknown submarine, believed to be Soviet, is detected in Hardanger Fjord in Norway. The Norwegian Navy fires on the submarine and the defence minister states that it will be destroyed if it fails to surface.[589]	–	Picture Building/ Deterrence
April	Spain UK	Three Spanish warships arrive in Algeciras Bay to express indignation of visit of HMS *Invincible* (with HRH the Duke of York on board) to Gibraltar.[590]	E	–
August	South Korea North Korea	South Korean warships sink a North Korean ship allegedly engaged in spying.[591]	D	Deterrence
August	UK New Zealand Mauritius	One British and one New Zealand frigate with supporting auxiliary are diverted to the British Indian Ocean Territory after incursions by Mauritian vessels.[592]	P	Deterrence/ Reassurance
August	US USSR Nicaragua	A US destroyer stops a Soviet flagged freighter in international waters; the vessel was bound for Nicaragua. The action was an attempt to demonstrate US intent to prevent the shipment of arms to the Communist government in Nicaragua.[593]	D	Coercion
August	US Chad Libya	The US State Department accuse Libya of 'blatant intervention' in the civil war/insurgency in Chad. USS *Eisenhower* is dispatched and anchors close to Libyan waters as a visible symbol of American intent.[594]	P/E	Deterrence/ Reassurance
September to December	US UK Grenada	In Operation *Urgent Fury* a US naval task force lands troops, in spite of indignant protest by the British prime minister, to occupy the island of Grenada and replace a left-wing government by one more acceptable to the US.[595]	D	Coercion

(Continued)

Date	Principal Actors	Description	Cable Classification	Composite Classification
November	UK Egypt	HMS *Hermes*, with 40 Cdo embarked, pays a goodwill visit to Alexandria and exercises with Egyptian forces.[596]	E	Co-operation/ Attraction
December	US Lebanon Syria	Syrian forces in Lebanon fire on US aircraft, provoking an air strike on Syrian positions near Beirut from the carriers USS *Independence* and *John F. Kennedy*. Two US aircraft are lost in the operation. In turn, Lebanese Druze and Shia militias attack US Marine positions in the city.[597]	P	Deterrence
1984				
January	UK Australia	HMS *Invincible* is refused permission to visit Sydney after the British government refused to comment on whether or not she was carrying nuclear weapons.[598]	E	–
January	USSR Cuba Int Community	Soviet warships visit Havana.[599]	E	Attraction/ Reassurance
February	NATO USSR	NATO conducts its largest amphibious exercise in the Norwegian Arctic, involving 150 ships, 300 aircraft and 25,000 personnel.[600]	E	Prestige/ Deterrence/ Co-operation
February	USSR Sweden NATO	Soviet submarine activity is detected operating close to the Swedish naval base at Karlskrona.[601]	–	Picture Building
February	UK Lebanon	During unrest and civil war, 5,000 civilians are evacuated to Cyprus from Lebanon by British ships.[602]	P	Reassurance
February	US Italy Lebanon	US and Italian ground forces are evacuated from Lebanon. Seven warships led by the Italian *Vittorio Veneto* escort the withdrawing forces. USN warships provide naval gunfire support to the Army in southern Beirut.[603]	D	Reassurance/ Deterrence
March	USSR US	The USSR deploys an additional aircraft carrier, *Novorossiyk*, to its Pacific Fleet in response to the USN's deployment of Tomahawk cruise missiles in the region.[604]	E	Deterrence

March	US Japan	USN and JMSDF conduct their first joint mine countermeasures exercise in 13 years. The exercise takes place between Honshu and Shikoku Islands.[605]	E	Co-operation
March	US South Korea North Korea	The annual US-South Korea *Team Spirit* exercise takes place.[606]	P/E	Co-operation/ Deterrence
March	USSR Vietnam US	The Soviet Navy operates a sizeable force of 20 surface ships and four submarines from Cam Ranh Bay. It is judged to be an attempt to gain influence in the region to the detriment of the US.[607]	C/E	Attraction
March	France Spain	French patrol boats attack and capture two Spanish trawlers in the Bay of Biscay.[608]	D	Deterrence
March to May	US Nicaragua	The US conducts covert mining of Nicaraguan harbours during the peak coffee exporting season.[609]	–	Coercion
April	USSR US	Soviet carrier *Minsk* fires flares at the US destroyer (*Harold Holt*) trailing her in the South China Sea.[610]	E	Deterrence/ Coercion
April	USSR Int Community	The USSR stages a major naval exercise in the Norwegian Sea; it is seen as a show of strength.[611]	E	Prestige/ Deterrence
May	Japan US Australia New Zealand Canada	Japan joins the Rim of the Pacific (RIMPAC) joint naval exercise for the first time.[612]	E	Co-operation
May	Iran Iraq GCC	Iran attacks Saudi Arabian and Kuwaiti oil tankers in the Gulf in order to force GCC states to pressure Iraq into ending its attacks on Iranian oil exports.[613]	P	Coercion
June	US USSR UK France Iran Iraq Regional Community	Combined East-West naval powers manifest their concern at the maritime repercussions of the Iran-Iraq war by keeping warships in the Persian Gulf.[614]	C	Deterrence/ Coercion/ Reassurance

(*Continued*)

Date	Principal Actors	Description	Cable Classification	Composite Classification
June	Australia US Int Community	Australia sends destroyer *Brisbane* to work with USN in the North West Indian Ocean; it is seen as a response to the Iran-Iraq war spilling over into the maritime domain.[615]	E	Co-operation
June	East Germany USSR Bulgaria Romania	The East German training ship *Wilhelm Pieck* makes goodwill visits to Romanian, Bulgarian and Soviet Black Sea ports.[616]	E	Attraction
June	Egypt USSR	The Egyptian destroyer *El Fateh* pays a four-day goodwill visit to the Soviet Black Sea Fleet. There were Egyptian, Iraqi and UAE cadets on board.[617]	E	Attraction
July	China Vietnam Reg Community	PLAN reinforces Paracel Island garrison and conducts naval exercises in the area. The sovereignty of the South China Sea islands are disputed by Vietnam.[618]	P	Deterrence/Coercion
July	US Libya	The US Sixth Fleet enters the Gulf of Sirte in order to exercise freedom of navigation; Libya, which claims the Gulf to be part of its territorial waters calls the US action 'provocative'.[619]	P/E	Deterrence/Coercion
August	Egypt Kuwait	Four Kuwaiti gunboats visit Egypt. It is the first military contact between the two countries since, like most Arab states, Kuwait broke diplomatic relations with Egypt after the Camp David Treaty with Israel.[620]	E	Attraction
August	UK US France Egypt	An international effort commences to clear the Gulf of Suez and southern Red Sea of mines from the 1973 Arab-Israeli War. Egypt had asked the UK, US and France for assistance in the matter.[621]	P	Assistance/Reassurance/Co-operation
August	US Colombia Ecuador Peru Brazil Paraguay Uruguay Venezuela	The US conducts naval training with South American counterparts in the latest in the *Unitas* series of exercises.[622]	E	Co-operation/Attraction

September	UK / Iran	The UK releases three Iranian auxiliary ships from British shipbuilding yards, embargoed since 1980.[623]	–	Attraction
September	Japan / USSR	Following discovery of seabed tracks, Japan claims that USSR has been operating mini-submarines in its territorial waters. The area is in one of the straits through which the Soviet Pacific Fleet must pass to reach open ocean.[624]	–	Picture Building
September	US / Libya	Libyan armed forces are placed on alert as US Sixth Fleet continues to operate in the Gulf of Sirte.[625]	P/E	Deterrence
October	Canada / Thailand	Canadian warships visit Bangkok in an attempt to strengthen ties between the two countries.[626]	E	Attraction
November	Sri Lanka / India / LTTE	Sir Lanka increases naval patrols of the strait between India and Sri Lanka in order to prevent shipment of arms to Tamil separatists.[627]	–	Deterrence
November	US / Reg Community	USN deploys three ships to West Africa to build relationships with littoral states.[628]	E	Attraction
December	Australia / Indonesia	Australia and Indonesia conduct a joint naval exercise, *New Horizon*, off Darwin.[629]	E	Attraction/ Co-operation
December	US / Israel	USS *Dwight D. Eisenhower* leads US and Israeli naval exercises; they are a sign of relaxation in the strained relations between the two countries following the 1982 Israeli invasion of Lebanon.[630]	E	Co-operation/ Attraction

Notes

1 Cable, James, *Gunboat Diplomacy 1919–1991: Political Applications of Limited Naval Force, 3rd Ed.* (Basingstoke: Macmillan, 1994), p. 213; *Jane's Defence Weekly* [*JDW*] 15, No. 2 (1991): p. 40.

2 Benbow, Tim. *British Uses of Aircraft Carriers and Amphibious Ships: 1945–2010.* Corbett Paper 9. (Shrivenham: The Corbett Centre for Maritime Policy Studies, King's College London, 2012), p. 40.

3 US. Congressional Research Service. Grimmett, R. *Instances of Use of US Armed Forces Abroad, 1798–2010.* RL41677. (Washington, DC: CRS, 2011), p. 15; *JDW* 15, No. 4 (1991): p. 101.

4 Australia. Royal Australian Navy. *Database of Royal Australian Navy Operations, 1990–2005.* Working Paper No. 18. (Canberra: Sea Power Centre, 2005); Benbow, *British Uses of Aircraft Carriers and Amphibious Ships*, p. 40.

5 *JDW* 15, No. 7 (1991): p. 207.

6 Ibid., p. 214.

7 *JDW* 15, No. 6 (1991): p. 168.

8 Australia, *RAN Operations Database*.

9 *JDW* 15, No. 13 (1991): p. 467.

10 US. Center for Naval Analyses. Siegel, Adam. *To Deter, Compel, and Reassure in International Crises: The Role of U.S. Naval Forces.* CRM 94–193. (Alexandria, VA: CNA, 1995), p. 19.

11 Australia. Australian Fisheries Management Agency. www.afma.gov.au/managing-our-fisheries/compliance-activities/illegal-foreign-fishing/ (accessed 15 August 2013).

12 *JDW* 15, No. 16 (1991): p. 631.

13 Australia, *RAN Operations Database*.

14 Japan. 'Defense of Japan.' Japanese Defense White Paper 2011. www.mod.go.jp/e/publ/w_paper/2011.html (accessed 23 May 2013).

15 Australia, *RAN Operations Database*.

16 UK. Royal Navy. *Royal Navy Operations 1970–2013.* (Portsmouth: Naval Historical Branch, 2013).

17 *JDW* 15, No. 22 (1991): p. 903.

18 Cable, *Gunboat Diplomacy, 3rd Ed.*, p. 213.

19 *JDW* 16, No. 4 (1991): p. 131.

20 *JDW* 16, No. 8 (1991): p. 297.

21 *JDW* 16, No. 12 (1991): p. 500.

22 Australia, *RAN Operations Database*.

23 *JDW* 16, No. 10 (1991): p. 395.

24 Ibid., p. 396.

25 *JDW* 16, No. 11 (1991): p. 449.

26 *JDW* 16, No. 13 (1991): p. 558.

27 *JDW* 16, No. 14 (1991): p. 586.

28 *JDW* 16, No. 16 (1991): p. 705.

29 *JDW* 16, No. 17 (1991): p. 747.

30 UK, *RN Operations 1970–2013*.

31 *JDW* 16, No. 21 (1991): p. 1003.

32 UK, *RN Operations 1970–2013*.

33 *JDW* 16, No. 23 (1991): p. 1081.

34 *JDW* 17, No. 3 (1992): p. 71.

35 Global Security. 'Native Fury.' www.globalsecurity.org/military/ops/native-fury.htm. (accessed 15 August 2013); *JDW* 17, No. 10 (1992): p. 375.

36 *JDW* 17, No. 13 (1992): p. 503.

37 Ibid., p. 513.

38 *JDW* 17, No. 17 (1992): p. 686.

39 *JDW* 17, No. 19 (1992): p. 791.
40 Ibid., p. 796.
41 *JDW* 17, No. 21 (1992): p. 882.
42 Benbow, *British Uses of Aircraft Carriers and Amphibious Ships*, p. 41.
43 *JDW* 17, No. 24 (1992): p. 1011.
44 *JDW* 17, No. 26 (1992): p. 1123.
45 UK, *RN Operations 1970–2013*.
46 Ibid.
47 *JDW* 18, No. 1 (1992): p. 12.
48 Siegel, *To Deter, Compel, and Reassure*, p. 20.
49 *JDW* 18, No. 2 (1992): p. 11.
50 *JDW* 18, No. 3 (1992): p. 7.
51 Ibid., p. 14.
52 *JDW* 18, No. 4 (1992): p. 7.
53 *JDW* 18, No. 7 (1992): p. 16.
54 Ibid., p. 19.
55 UK, *RN Operations 1970–2013*.
56 *JDW* 18, No. 9 (1992): p. 6.
57 *JDW* 18, No. 10 (1992): p. 34.
58 *JDW* 18, No. 13 (1992): p. 6.
59 *JDW* 18, No. 14 (1992): p. 12.
60 *JDW* 18, No. 17 (1992): p. 8.
61 *JDW* 18, No. 18 (1992): p. 6.
62 *JDW* 18, No. 19 (1992): p. 5.
63 *JDW* 18, No. 24 (1992): p. 5.
64 Siegel, *To Deter, Compel, and Reassure*, p. 28.
65 Australia, *RAN Operations Database*.
66 *JDW* 19, No. 3 (1993): p. 12.
67 Benbow, *British Uses of Aircraft Carriers and Amphibious Ships*, p. 41.
68 *JDW* 19, No. 13 (1993): p. 11.
69 Australia, *RAN Operations Database*.
70 UK, *RN Operations 1970–2013*.
71 Australia, *RAN Operations Database*.
72 *JDW* 19, No. 19 (1993): p. 11.
73 Russia. 'Chronology of the Three Centuries of the Russian Fleet.' http://rusnavy.com/history/kron.htm (accessed 5 November 2013); *JDW* 19, No. 25 (1993): p. 17.
74 Grimmett, *Use of US Armed Forces Abroad*, pp. 16–17.
75 Kin, Taeho. 'Korean Perspectives on PLA Modernization and the Future East Asian Security Environment.' In Pollack, Jonathan & Yang, Richard (Eds.). *In China's Shadow*. (Westport, CT: Rand, 1998), p. 54.
76 *JDW* 20, No. 12 (1993): p. 15.
77 UK, *RN Operations 1970–2013*.
78 *JDW* 20, No. 16 (1993): p. 6.
79 Grimmett, *Use of US Armed Forces Abroad*, pp. 16–17.
80 *JDW* 20, No. 25 (1993): p. 9.
81 Australia, *RAN Operations Database*.
82 *JDW* 21, No. 3 (1994): p. 11.
83 *JDW* 21, No. 7 (1994): p. 14.
84 Ibid., p. 8.
85 *JDW* 21, No. 10 (1994): p. 4.
86 *JDW* 21, No. 18 (1994): p. 5.
87 *JDW* 21, No. 19 (1994): p. 8.
88 *JDW* 21, No. 21 (1994): p. 1.
89 *JDW* 21, No. 22 (1994): p. 6.

90 *JDW* 21, No. 24 (1994): p. 11.
91 *JDW* 21, No. 25 (1994): p. 4.
92 Ibid., p. 13.
93 *JDW* 21, No. 26 (1994): p. 5.
94 Ibid., p. 10.
95 Australia, *RAN Operations Database*.
96 *JDW* 22, No. 1 (1994): p. 6.
97 *JDW* 22, No. 2 (1994): p. 4.
98 Ibid., p. 12.
99 *JDW* 22, No. 7 (1994): p. 6.
100 *JDW* 22, No. 8 (1994): p. 4.
101 Ibid., p. 5.
102 *JDW* 22, No. 9 (1994): p. 6.
103 Global Security. '7th Fleet.' www.globalsecurity.org/military/agency/navy/c7f.htm (accessed 15 August 2013).
104 *JDW* 22, No. 13 (1994): p. 12.
105 Australia, *RAN Operations Database*.
106 *JDW* 22, No. 14 (1994): p. 2.
107 UK, *RN Operations 1970–2013*; Siegel, *To Deter, Compel, and Reassure*, p. 28; *JDW* 22, No. 15 (1994): p. 3.
108 *JDW* 22, No. 17 (1994): p. 5.
109 Ibid., p. 19.
110 *JDW* 22, No. 19 (1994): p. 11.
111 Ibid., p. 12.
112 Canada. 'Royal Canadian Navy.' Background Summaries: Recent Operations Overview. www.navy.forces.gc.ca/cms/4/4-a_eng.asp?id=460 (accessed 3 June 2013).
113 Lanteigne, Marc. *Chinese Foreign Policy: An Introduction, 2nd Ed.* (Abingdon: Routledge, 2013), p. 136.
114 *JDW* 23, No. 2 (1995): p. 9.
115 Australia, *RAN Operations Database*.
116 UK, *RN Operations 1970–2013*.
117 Ibid.
118 *JDW* 23, No. 5 (1995): p. 5.
119 *JDW* 23, No. 9 (1995): p. 12.
120 Australia, *RAN Operations Database*.
121 *JDW* 23, No. 9 (1995): p. 15.
122 *JDW* 23, No. 11 (1995): p. 6.
123 *JDW* 23, No. 17 (1995): p. 6.
124 UK, *RN Operations 1970–2013*.
125 Australia, *RAN Operations Database*.
126 *JDW* 23, No. 23 (1995): p. 6.
127 *JDW* 23, No. 24 (1995): p. 16.
128 *JDW* 24, No. 1 (1995): p. 13.
129 Ibid., p. 15.
130 *JDW* 24, No. 6 (1995): p. 23.
131 Australia, *RAN Operations Database*.
132 UK, *RN Operations 1970–2013*.
133 Porch, Douglas. 'The Taiwan Strait Crisis of 1996: Strategic Implications for the United States Navy.' *US Naval War College Review* 52, No. 3 (1999): p. 18.
134 *JDW* 24, No. 9 (1995): p. 4.
135 *JDW* 24, No. 14 (1995): p. 18.
136 Ibid., p. 22.
137 Porch, 'The Taiwan Strait Crisis', p. 18.
138 *JDW* 24, No. 22 (1995): p. 18.

139 *Jane's Navy International (JNI)* 101, No. 1 (1996): p. 5.
140 Porch, 'The Taiwan Strait Crisis', p. 18.
141 *JDW* 25, No. 1 (1996): p. 6.
142 *JDW* 25, No. 2 (1996): p. 3.
143 *JDW* 25, No. 3 (1996): p. 14.
144 UK, *RN Operations 1970–2013*.
145 *JDW* 25, No. 6 (1996): p. 5.
146 Arapoglou, Stergios. *Dispute in the Aegean Sea the Imia/Kardak Crisis.* Master's Thesis. US Air Command and Staff College, Maxwell, 2002, p. 17.
147 *JDW* 25, No. 8 (1996): p. 3.
148 *JDW* 25, No. 9 (1996): p. 13.
149 *JDW* 25, No. 13 (1996): p. 13.
150 UK, *RN Operations 1970–2013*.
151 *JDW* 25, No. 19 (1996): p. 4.
152 Ibid., p. 17.
153 *JDW* 25, No. 24 (1996): p. 23.
154 UK, *RN Operations 1970–2013*.
155 *JDW* 26, No. 1 (1996): p. 21.
156 Japan, Defense White Paper 2011.
157 Ibid.
158 *JDW* 26, No. 11 (1996): p. 23.
159 *JDW* 26, No. 13 (1996): p. 3; *JNI* 101, No. 8: p. 5.
160 Global Security. 'Senkaku/Diaoyutai Islands.' www.globalsecurity.org/military/world/war/senkaku.htm (accessed 17 June 2013); Japan, Defense White Paper 2011.
161 *JDW* 26, No. 18 (1996): p. 17.
162 UK, *RN Operations 1970–2013*.
163 *JDW* 27, No. 2 (1997): p. 3.
164 UK, *RN Operations 1970–2013*; Benbow, *British Uses of Aircraft Carriers and Amphibious Ships*, p. 44.
165 Australia, *RAN Operations Database*.
166 *JDW* 27, No. 9 (1997): p. 13.
167 UK, *RN Operations 1970–2013*.
168 *JDW* 27, No. 10 (1997): p. 6.
169 *JDW* 27, No. 16 (1997): p. 13.
170 *JDW* 27, No. 18 (1997): p. 13.
171 Ibid., p. 15.
172 *JDW* 27, No. 19 (1997): p. 18.
173 Ibid.
174 *JDW* 27, No. 20 (1997): p. 13.
175 *JDW* 27, No. 22 (1997): p. 13.
176 UK, *RN Operations 1970–2013*.
177 Ibid.
178 *JDW* 28, No. 5 (1997): p. 14.
179 *JDW* 28, No. 9 (1997): p. 20.
180 Ibid., p. 30.
181 Australia, *RAN Operations Database*.
182 *JDW* 28, No. 15 (1997): p. 3.
183 *JDW* 28, No. 17 (1997): p. 5.
184 Ibid., p. 17.
185 UK, *RN Operations 1970–2013*.
186 Ibid.
187 *JDW* 28, No. 19 (1997): p. 27.
188 *JDW* 28, No. 20 (1997): p. 14.
189 *JDW* 28, No. 21 (1997): p. 23.

190 *JDW* 28, No. 22 (1997): p. 14.
191 *JDW* 29, No. 1 (1998): p. 13.
192 Ibid., p. 17.
193 *JDW* 29, No. 2 (1998): p. 5.
194 *JDW* 29, No. 3 (1998): p. 13.
195 Benbow, *British Uses of Aircraft Carriers and Amphibious Ships*, p. 45; *JDW* 29, No. 4 (1998): p. 4.
196 UK, *RN Operations 1970–2013*.
197 *JDW* 29, No. 9 (1998): p. 14.
198 *JDW* 29, No. 12 (1998): p. 4.
199 *JDW* 29, No. 14 (1998): p. 20.
200 *JDW* 29, No. 15 (1998): p. 23.
201 *JDW* 29, No. 16 (1998): p. 14.
202 Ibid., p. 21.
203 *JDW* 29, No. 19 (1998): p. 6.
204 Ibid., p. 12.
205 *JDW* 29, No. 20 (1998): p. 6.
206 Australia, *RAN Operations Database*.
207 *JDW* 29, No. 23 (1998): p. 13.
208 *JDW* 29, No. 24 (1998): p. 5.
209 Ibid., p. 6.
210 Ibid., p. 11.
211 Ibid., p. 14.
212 Australia, *RAN Operations Database*.
213 Japan, Defense White Paper 2011.
214 *JDW* 29, No. 26 (1998): p. 19.
215 *JDW* 30, No. 1 (1998): p. 6.
216 *JDW* 30, No. 4 (1998): p. 5.
217 Ibid., p. 18.
218 Ibid., p. 10.
219 *JDW* 30, No. 5 (1998): p. 6.
220 Ghosh, P. K. 'Revisiting Gunboat Diplomacy: An Instrument of Threat or Use of Limited Naval Force.' *Strategic Analysis* 26, No. 11 (2001): p. 2014; US. Congressional Research Service. Ploch, L. *Africa Command: U.S. Strategic Interests and the Role of the U.S. Military in Africa*. RL34003. (Washington, DC: CRS, 2011), p. 34.
221 Australia, *RAN Operations Database*.
222 UK, *RN Operations 1970–2013*.
223 Global Security. 'Senkaku/Diaoyutai Islands.'
224 UK, *RN Operations 1970–2013*.
225 *JDW* 30, No. 15 (1998): p. 13.
226 UK, *RN Operations 1970–2013*.
227 *JDW* 30, No. 17 (1998): p. 10.
228 UK, *RN Operations 1970–2013*.
229 *JDW* 30, No. 18 (1998): p. 3.
230 *JDW* 30, No. 20 (1998): p. 3.
231 UK, *RN Operations 1970–2013*.
232 *JDW* 30, No. 23 (1998): p. 18.
233 Grimmett, *Use of US Armed Forces Abroad*, p. 20.
234 Japan, Defense White Paper 2011.
235 UK, *RN Operations 1970–2013*.
236 Benbow, *British Uses of Aircraft Carriers and Amphibious Ships*, p. 47.
237 *JDW* 31, No. 9 (1999): p. 16.
238 *JDW* 31, No. 10 (1999): p. 21.
239 Ibid., p. 29.

240 India. *MOD Annual Report 1999–2000*, p. 31.
241 Ibid.
242 Ibid., p. 28.
243 *JDW* 31, No. 10 (1999): p. 37.
244 *JDW* 31, No. 12 (1999): p. 14.
245 *JDW* 31, No. 13 (1999): p. 3.
246 Japan, Defense White Paper 2011.
247 India. *MOD Annual Report 1999–2000*, p. 29.
248 Stevens, David. *The Royal Australian Navy*, Vol. 3. (Oxford: Oxford University Press, 2001), p. 281.
249 *JDW* 31, No. 18 (1999): p. 5.
250 *JDW* 31, No. 19 (1999): p. 6.
251 Global Security. '1999 Kargil Conflict.' Global Security. www.globalsecurity.org/military/world/war/kargil-99.htm (accessed 14 June 2013); India. *MOD Annual Report 1999–2000*, p. 28.
252 Australia, *RAN Operations Database*.
253 *JDW* 31, No. 22 (1999): p. 15.
254 Japan, Defense White Paper 2011.
255 *JDW* 31, No. 26 (1999): p. 3.
256 *JDW* 32, No. 4 (1999): p. 12.
257 *JDW* 32, No. 6 (1999): p. 13.
258 *JDW* 32, No. 4 (1999): p. 13.
259 *JDW* 32, No. 7 (1999): p. 15.
260 *JDW* 32, No. 8 (1999): p. 10.
261 Ibid., p. 15.
262 Grimmett, *Instances of Use of US Armed Forces Abroad, 1798–2010*, p. 21; Canada, *Background Summaries*.
263 India. *MOD Annual Report 1999–2000*, p. 29.
264 *JDW* 32, No. 18 (1999): p. 14.
265 Benbow, *British Uses of Aircraft Carriers and Amphibious Ships*, p. 48.
266 *JDW* 32, No. 22 (1999): p. 5.
267 *JDW* 33, No. 6 (2000): p. 9.
268 Ibid., p. 15.
269 *JDW* 33, No. 7 (2000): p. 24.
270 *JDW* 33, No. 8 (2000): p. 6.
271 *JDW* 33, No. 9 (2000): p. 8.
272 *JDW* 33, No. 10 (2000): p. 23.
273 UK, *RN Operations 1970–2013*.
274 Global Security. 'Senkaku/Diaoyutai Islands.'
275 *JDW* 33, No. 12 (2000): p. 14.
276 *JDW* 33, No. 13 (2000): p. 8.
277 Ibid., p. 19.
278 India. *MOD Annual Report 2000–2001*, p. 33.
279 *JDW* 33, No. 19 (2000): p. 15.
280 *JDW* 33, No. 21 (2000): p. 3.
281 India. *MOD Annual Report 2000–2001*, p. 33.
282 Ploch, *Africa Command*, p. 35.
283 UK, *RN Operations 1970–2013*; Benbow, *British Uses of Aircraft Carriers and Amphibious Ships*, pp. 48–49.
284 *JDW* 33, No. 24 (2000): p. 12.
285 Ibid.
286 *JDW* 34, No. 8 (2000): p. 4.
287 *JDW* 34, No. 5 (2000): p. 4.
288 *JDW* 34, No. 8 (2000): p. 5.

289 Ibid., p. 18.
290 *JDW* 34, No. 6 (2000): p. 19.
291 *JDW* 34, No. 11 (2000): p. 5.
292 Australia, *RAN Operations Database*.
293 Grimmett, *Instances of Use of US Armed Forces Abroad, 1798–2010*, p. 22.
294 UK, *RN Operations 1970–2013*.
295 India. *MOD Annual Report 2000–2001*, p. 34.
296 UK, *RN Operations 1970–2013*; Benbow, *British Uses of Aircraft Carriers and Amphibious Ships*, p. 49.
297 *JDW* 35, No. 2 (2001): p. 3.
298 Strategy Page. 'February 6, 2001.' StrategyWorld.com. www.strategypage.com/qnd/russia/articles/20010206.aspx (accessed 15 August 2013).
299 *JDW* 35, No. 7 (2001): p. 16.
300 *JDW* 35, No. 9 (2001): p. 5.
301 India. *MOD Annual Report 2001–2002*, p. 6.
302 *JDW* 35, No. 15 (2001): p. 9.
303 *JDW* 35, No. 16 (2001): p. 18.
304 *JDW* 35, No. 19 (2001): p. 5.
305 India. *MOD Annual Report 2001–2002*, p. 28.
306 Australia, *RAN Operations Database*.
307 *JDW* 35, No. 21 (2001): p. 14.
308 *JDW* 35, No. 26 (2001): p. 13.
309 Australia, *RAN Operations Database*.
310 India. *MOD Annual Report 2001–2002*, p. 35.
311 Ibid., p. 38.
312 Benbow, *British Uses of Aircraft Carriers and Amphibious Ships*, p. 50.
313 *JDW* 36, No. 12 (2001): p. 24.
314 *JDW* 36, No. 13 (2001): p. 11.
315 *JDW* 36, No. 17 (2001): p. 4.
316 Ibid., p. 14.
317 *JDW* 36, No. 18 (2001): p. 30.
318 Benbow, *British Uses of Aircraft Carriers and Amphibious Ships*, p. 50. Whilst this incident may be interpreted as a prelude to war, it is included here as an example of *limited* naval force.
319 Japan, Defense White Paper 2011.
320 *JDW* 36, No. 23 (2001): p. 17.
321 *JDW* 37, No. 4 (2002): p. 15.
322 *JDW* 37, No. 10 (2002): p. 16.
323 India. *MOD Annual Report 2002–2003*, p. 26.
324 *JDW* 37, No. 21 (2002): p. 5.
325 India. *MOD Annual Report 2002–2003*, p. 27.
326 *JDW* 37, No. 22 (2002): p. 14.
327 Ibid.
328 Japan, Defense White Paper 2011.
329 *JDW* 38, No. 2 (2002): p. 14.
330 India. *MOD Annual Report 2002–2003*, p. 28.
331 *JDW* 38, No. 7 (2002): p. 9.
332 *JDW* 38, No. 9 (2002): p. 9.
333 *JDW* 39, No. 23 (2003): p. 12.
334 Japan, Defense White Paper 2011.
335 India. *MOD Annual Report 2002–2003*, p. 26.
336 *JDW* 39, No. 1 (2003): p. 12.
337 *JDW* 38, No. 25 (2002): p. 2.
338 *JDW* 39, No. 3 (2003): p. 13.
339 Benbow, *British Uses of Aircraft Carriers and Amphibious Ships*, p. 52.

340 *JDW* 39, No. 6 (2003): p. 4.
341 The Times of India. 'Indo-Iranian Naval Exercises to Begin Today.' 9 March 2003. http://articles.timesofindia.indiatimes.com/2003-03-9/india/27267982_1_exercises_ warships_bilateral_ties (accessed 15 August 2013).
342 Benbow, *British Uses of Aircraft Carriers and Amphibious Ships*, p. 52; Ploch, *Africa Command*, p. 35.
343 Benbow, *British Uses of Aircraft Carriers and Amphibious Ships*, p. 54.
344 *JDW* 39, No. 15 (2003): p. 6.
345 Ibid., p. 16.
346 *JDW* 39, No. 17 (2003): p. 3.
347 Australia, *RAN Operations Database*.
348 India. *MOD Annual Report 2003–2004*, p. 45.
349 Ibid., p. 45.
350 *JDW* 39, No. 21 (2003): p. 9.
351 *JDW* 39, No. 22 (2003): p. 14.
352 *JDW* 40, No. 4 (2003): p. 8.
353 *JDW* 40, No. 1 (2003): p. 17.
354 India. *MOD Annual Report 2003–2004*, p. 43.
355 *JDW* 40, No. 4 (2003): p. 12.
356 Ibid., p. 15.
357 India. *MOD Annual Report 2003–2004*, p. 40.
358 *JDW* 40, No. 6 (2003): p. 15.
359 Ploch, *Africa Command*, p. 35.
360 India. *MOD Annual Report 2003–2004*, p. 49; *JDW* 40, No. 11 (2003): p. 4.
361 *JDW* 40, No. 15 (2003): p. 11.
362 *JDW* 40, No. 20 (2003): p. 19.
363 *JDW* 40, No. 21 (2003): p. 18.
364 India. *MOD Annual Report 2003–2004*, p. 45.
365 Ibid., p. 42.
366 China. 'China's National Defense in 2010.' Information Office of the State Council of the People's Republic of China, 31 March 2011. www.china.org.cn/government/ whitepaper/2011-03/31/content_22263510.htm (accessed 30 October 2012).
367 Global Security. 'Senkaku/Diaoyutai Islands.'
368 *JDW* 41, No. 13 (2004): p. 18.
369 India. *MOD Annual Report 2004–2005*, p. 46.
370 *JDW* 41, No. 26 (2004): p. 11.
371 Ibid., p. 15.
372 UK, *RN Operations 1970–2013*.
373 Japan, Defense White Paper 2011.
374 Russia. 'Chronology of the Russian Fleet.'
375 Global Security. 'Senkaku/Diaoyutai Islands.'
376 *JDW* 41, No. 32 (2004): p. 11.
377 UK, *RN Operations 1970–2013*.
378 *JDW* 41, No. 39 (2004): p. 28.
379 Australia, *RAN Operations Database*.
380 *JDW* 41, No. 40 (2004): p. 14.
381 *JDW* 41, No. 43 (2004): p. 16.
382 *JDW* 41, No. 46 (2004): p. 10.
383 Australia, *RAN Operations Database*.
384 Japan, Defense White Paper 2011; *JDW* 41, No. 47 (2004): p. 15.
385 UK, *RN Operations 1970–2013*; *JDW* 42, No. 2 (2005): pp. 3–4.
386 *JDW* 42, No. 4 (2005): p. 11.
387 McVadon, Eric A. 'China's Navy Today: Looking toward Blue Water.' In Erickson, Andrew, Goldstein, Lyle & Lord, Charles (Eds.). *China Goes to Sea: Maritime Transformation in Comparative Historical Perspective*. (Annapolis: Naval Institute

Press, 2009), p. 388; Wong, Edward. 'Vietnam Enlists Allies to Stave Off China's Reach.' *New York Times*, 4 February 2010. www.nytimes.com/2010/02/05/world/asia/05hanoi.html?_r=0 (accessed 17 June 2013).

388   India. *MOD Annual Report 2005–2006*, p. 34.

389   Ibid., p. 39.

390   *JDW* 42, No. 21 (2005): p. 12.

391   *JDW* 42, No. 30 (2005): p. 11.

392   *JDW* 42, No. 29 (2005): p. 17.

393   *JDW* 42, No. 33 (2005): p. 15.

394   Ibid., p. 7.

395   Japan, Defense White Paper 2011.

396   Smith, Paul J. 'The Senkaku/Diaoyu Island Controversy: A Crisis Postponed.' *US Naval War College Review* 66, No. 2 (2013): p. 39.

397   Canada, *Background Summaries*.

398   India. *MOD Annual Report 2005–2006*, p. 38.

399   Ibid., p. 37.

400   Ibid., p. 38.

401   *JDW* 42, No. 43 (2005): p. 14.

402   *JDW* 42, No. 46 (2005): p. 10.

403   *JDW* 42, No. 50 (2005): p. 13.

404   India. *MOD Annual Report 2006–2007*, p. 30.

405   *JDW* 43, No. 7 (2006): p. 20.

406   *JDW* 43, No. 11 (2006): p. 7.

407   *JDW* 43, No. 15 (2006): p. 17.

408   India. *MOD Annual Report 2006–2007*, p. 32.

409   Ibid., p. 31.

410   *JDW* 43, No. 26 (2006): p. 18.

411   India. *MOD Annual Report 2006–2007*, p. 32.

412   *JDW* 43, No. 27 (2006): p. 18.

413   Japan, Defense White Paper 2011.

414   Sanders, Deborah. 'US Naval Diplomacy in the Black Sea: Sending Mixed Messages.' *US Naval War College Review* 60, No. 3 (2007): pp. 61–72.

415   Cordesman, Anthony, Sullivan, George & Sullivan, William. *Lessons of the 2006 Israeli-Hezbollah War*. Significant Issues Series Vol 29, No. 4. (Washington, DC: Center for Strategic & International Studies, 2007), p. 131; *JDW* 43, No. 30 (2006): p. 18.

416   Japan, Defense White Paper 2011; *JDW* 43, No. 28 (2006): p. 5.

417   UK, *RN Operations 1970–2013*; Benbow, *British Uses of Aircraft Carriers and Amphibious Ships*, p. 55.

418   *JDW* 43, No. 32 (2007): p. 5.

419   Gorenburg, Dmitry. 'Ten Years of BlackSeaFor: A Partial Assessment.' http://russiamil.wordpress.com/tag/black-sea-harmony/ (accessed 19 February 2013).

420   Japan, Defense White Paper 2011.

421   Benbow, *British Uses of Aircraft Carriers and Amphibious Ships*, p. 56.

422   *JDW* 44, No. 5 (2007): p. 16.

423   *JDW* 44, No. 14 (2007): p. 13.

424   India. *MOD Annual Report 2007–2008*, p. 30.

425   Ibid., p. 32; Japan, Defense White Paper 2011.

426   *JDW* 44, No. 17 (2007): p. 14.

427   *JDW* 44, No. 23 (2007): p. 15.

428   India. *MOD Annual Report 2007–2008*, p. 33.

429   Ibid., p. 31.

430   Sohn, Kathi A. 'The Global Fleet Station: A Powerful Tool for Preventing Conflicts.' *US Naval War College Review* 62, No. 1 (2009): p. 48.

431 India. *MOD Annual Report 2007–2008*, p. 32.
432 *JDW* 44, No. 21 (2007): p. 15.
433 *JDW* 44, No. 24 (2007): p. 10.
434 *JDW* 44, No. 30 (2007): p. 18.
435 Lucius, Robert, E. 'Pacific Partnership Visits Vietnam.' *US Naval War College Review* 60, No. 4 (2007): p. 125.
436 *JDW* 44, No. 32 (2007): p. 5.
437 *JDW* 44, No. 33 (2007): p. 8.
438 *JDW* 44, No. 32 (2007): p. 15; *JDW* 44, No. 35 (2007): p. 14.
439 *JDW* 44, No. 50 (2007): p. 31.
440 *JDW* 44, No. 42 (2007): p. 14.
441 *JDW* 44, No. 47 (2007): p. 4.
442 UK, *RN Operations 1970–2013*.
443 *JDW* 47, No. 50 (2007): p. 20.
444 Japan, Defense White Paper 2011.
445 UK, *RN Operations 1970–2013*.
446 Ibid.
447 *JDW* 45, No. 1 (2008): p. 15.
448 Japan, Defense White Paper 2011.
449 Russia. 'Chronology of the Russian Fleet'; *JDW* 44, No. 50 (2007): p. 4.
450 UK, *RN Operations 1970–2013*.
451 *JDW* 45, No. 4 (2008): p. 7.
452 India. *MOD Annual Report 2008–2009*, p. 36.
453 *JDW* 45, No. 3 (2008): p. 4.
454 *JDW* 45, No. 10 (2008): p. 6.
455 *JDW* 45, No. 13 (2008): p. 8.
456 *JDW* 45, No. 11 (2008): p. 18.
457 *JDW* 45, No. 14 (2008): p. 17.
458 *JDW* 45, No. 15 (2008): p. 20.
459 UK, *RN Operations 1970–2013*.
460 *JDW* 45, No. 17 (2008): p. 20.
461 UK, *RN Operations 1970–2013*.
462 Ibid.
463 Ploch, *Africa Command*, p. 20.
464 UK, *RN Operations 1970–2013*.
465 Ibid.
466 *JDW* 45, No. 19 (2008): p. 7.
467 India. *MOD Annual Report 2008–2009*, p. 37.
468 *JDW* 45, No. 24 (2008): p. 8.
469 *JDW* 45, No. 27 (2008): p. 14.
470 *JDW* 45, No. 30 (2008): p. 12.
471 Ibid., p. 14.
472 UK, *RN Operations 1970–2013*.
473 India. *MOD Annual Report 2008–2009*, p. 33.
474 Russia. 'Chronology of the Russian Fleet.'
475 *JDW* 45, No. 35 (2008): p. 10.
476 *JDW* 45, No. 37 (2008): p. 6.
477 Russia. 'Chronology of the Russian Fleet.'
478 India. *MOD Annual Report 2008–2009*, p. 38.
479 *JDW* 45, No. 40 (2008): p. 20.
480 UK, *RN Operations 1970–2013*.
481 *JDW* 45, No. 49 (2008): p. 5.
482 Russia. 'Chronology of the Russian Fleet'; *JDW* 45, No. 49 (2008): p. 10.
483 *JDW* 45, No. 49 (2008): p. 18.

484   Japan, Defense White Paper 2011.
485   China. 'China's National Defense in 2010'; *JDW* 46, No. 1 (2009): p. 6.
486   *JDW* 47, No. 10 (2010): p. 23.
487   *JDW* 46, No. 4 (2009): p. 5.
488   *JDW* 46, No. 5 (2009): p. 13.
489   *JDW* 46, No. 8 (2009): p. 6.
490   *JDW* 46, No. 11 (2009): p. 17; *JDW* 46, No. 16 (2009): p. 5.
491   Dutton, Peter. 'Three Disputes and Three Objectives: China and the South China Sea.' *US Naval War College Review* 64, No. 4 (2011): p. 54.
492   *JDW* 46, No. 16 (2009): p. 19.
493   *JDW* 46, No. 17 (2009): p. 15.
494   *JDW* 46, No. 19 (2009): p. 19.
495   *JDW* 46, No. 20 (2009): p. 17.
496   *JDW* 46, No. 22 (2009): p. 18.
497   UK, *RN Operations 1970–2013.*
498   *JDW* 46, No. 23 (2009): p. 39.
499   *JDW* 46, No. 27 (2009): p. 17.
500   Ibid., p. 18.
501   *JDW* 46, No. 28 (2009): p. 16.
502   UK, *RN Operations 1970–2013.*
503   *JDW* 46, No. 34 (2009): p. 14.
504   *JDW* 46, No. 36 (2009): p. 32.
505   *JDW* 46, No. 41 (2009): p. 14.
506   UK, *RN Operations 1970–2013.*
507   Foster, Peter. 'North and South Korea Warships Exchange Fire.' *Daily Telegraph*, 10 November 2009; Japan, Defense White Paper 2011.
508   *JDW* 47, No. 5 (2010): p. 5.
509   Canada, *Background Summaries.*
510   *JDW* 47, No. 7 (2010): p. 6.
511   UK, *RN Operations 1970–2013.*
512   Kim, Duk-Ki. 'The Republic of Korea's Counter-Asymmetric Strategy.' *US Naval War College Review* 65, No. 1 (2012): p. 55.
513   *JDW* 47, No. 14 (2010): p. 6; Japan, Defense White Paper 2011.
514   *JDW* 47, No. 18 (2010): p. 5; Russia. 'Chronology of the Russian Fleet.'
515   *JDW* 47, No. 19 (2010): p. 18.
516   US. Congressional Research Service. Migdalovitz, C. *Israel's Blockade of Gaza, the Mavi Marmara Incident, and Its Aftermath.* R41275. (Washington, DC: CRS, 2010); *JDW* 47, No. 23 (2010): p. 11.
517   *JDW* 47, No. 24 (2010): p. 16.
518   Pedrozo, Paul. 'Beijing's Coastal Real Estate: A History of Chinese Naval Aggression.' *Foreign Affairs*, 15 November 2010. www.foreignaffairs.com/articles/67007/raul-pedrozo/beijings-coastal-real-estate (accessed 22 November 2010).
519   *JDW* 47, No. 30 (2010): p. 15.
520   *JDW* 47, No. 33 (2010): p. 16.
521   *JDW* 47, No. 35 (2010): p. 17.
522   Pedrozo, 'Beijing's Coastal Real Estate.'
523   *JDW* 47, No. 42 (2010): p. 26.
524   UK, *RN Operations 1970–2013.*
525   *JDW* 47, No. 48 (2010): pp. 5, 11.
526   UK, *RN Operations 1970–2013.*
527   Polmar, Norman. *Chronology of the Cold War at Sea, 1945–1991.* (Annapolis: Naval Institute Press, 1998), p. 66.
528   Cable, *Gunboat Diplomacy, 3rd Ed.*, p. 188.
529   Polmar, *Chronology of the Cold War at Sea*, p. 67.

530 Ibid.

531 Cable, *Gunboat Diplomacy, 3rd Ed.*, p. 188; Benbow, *British Uses of Aircraft Carriers and Amphibious Ships*, p. 9.

532 Polmar, *Chronology of the Cold War at Sea*, p. 67.

533 Ibid.

534 Cable, *Gunboat Diplomacy, 3rd Ed.*, pp. 188–189.

535 Polmar, *Chronology of the Cold War at Sea*, p. 68.

536 Cable, *Gunboat Diplomacy, 3rd Ed.*, p. 189; Ciment, J. & Hill, K. (Eds.). *Encyclopedia of Conflicts Since World War II*, Vol. 1. (Chicago: Fitzroy Dearborn, 1999), pp. 507–512.

537 Benbow, *British Uses of Aircraft Carriers and Amphibious Ships*, p. 9. Cable, *Gunboat Diplomacy, 3rd Ed.*, p. 189.

538 Ibid.

539 Ibid.

540 Benbow, *British Uses of Aircraft Carriers and Amphibious Ships*, p. 10.

541 Cable, *Gunboat Diplomacy, 3rd Ed.*, p. 190.

542 Benbow, *British Uses of Aircraft Carriers and Amphibious Ships*, p. 10.

543 Cable, *Gunboat Diplomacy, 3rd Ed.*, p. 190; Polmar, *Chronology of the Cold War at Sea*, p. 73.

544 Ibid., p. 74.

545 Benbow, *British Uses of Aircraft Carriers and Amphibious Ships*, p. 10.

546 Ramsbotham, Oliver & Woodhouse, Tom. *Encyclopedia of International Peacekeeping Operations*. (Santa Barbara, CA: ABC-CLIO, 1999), pp. 93, 172–173.

547 Gavin, Francis J. (Ed.). *The New York Times Twentieth Century in Review: The Cold War*. (Chicago: Fitzroy Dearborn, 2001), pp. 388–399.

548 Cable, *Gunboat Diplomacy, 3rd Ed.*, pp. 190–191.

549 Ibid.

550 Ibid.

551 Ibid.

552 Polmar, *Chronology of the Cold War at Sea*, p. 80.

553 Dismukes, Bradford & McConnell, James (Eds.). *Soviet Naval Diplomacy*. (New York: Pergamon Press, 1979), p. 20; Miller, David. *The Cold War: A Military History*. (London: John Murray, 1998), p. 181.

554 Polmar, *Chronology of the Cold War at Sea*, p. 81.

555 Cable, *Gunboat Diplomacy, 3rd Ed.*, p. 192.

556 Benbow, *British Uses of Aircraft Carriers and Amphibious Ships*, p. 11; Cable, *Gunboat Diplomacy, 3rd Ed.*, p. 192.

557 Cable, *Gunboat Diplomacy, 3rd Ed.*, p. 192.

558 Polmar, *Chronology of the Cold War at Sea*, p. 82.

559 Ciment & Hill, *Encyclopedia of Conflicts Since World War II*, Vol. 1, p. 334.

560 Polmar, *Chronology of the Cold War at Sea*, p. 83.

561 Ibid.

562 Cable, *Gunboat Diplomacy, 3rd Ed.*, pp. 192–193; Gavin, *The New York Times Twentieth Century in Review: The Cold War*, p. 431.

563 Benbow, *British Uses of Aircraft Carriers and Amphibious Ships*, p. 11.

564 UK, *RN Operations 1970–2013*.

565 Cable, *Gunboat Diplomacy, 3rd Ed.*, p. 206.

566 UK, *RN Operations 1970–2013*.

567 Cable, *Gunboat Diplomacy, 3rd Ed.*, p. 206.

568 UK, *RN Operations 1970–2013*.

569 Cable, *Gunboat Diplomacy, 3rd Ed.*, p. 206; Benbow, *British Uses of Aircraft Carriers and Amphibious Ships*, p. 17.

570 UK, *RN Operations 1970–2013*.

571 Ibid.

572 *RUSI News Sheet* 3 (1981): p. 6.
573 UK, *RN Operations 1970–2013*.
574 Cable, *Gunboat Diplomacy, 3rd Ed.*, p. 206; Benbow, *British Uses of Aircraft Carriers and Amphibious Ships*, p. 17.
575 Cable, *Gunboat Diplomacy, 3rd Ed.*, p. 207.
576 *Jane's Defence Review* 2, No. 6 (1981): p. 499.
577 *RUSI News Sheet* 7 (1981): p. 2; *RUSI News Sheet* 6 (1983): p. 6.
578 Cable, *Gunboat Diplomacy, 3rd Ed.*, p. 207; *RUSI News Sheet* 8 (1981): p. 5.
579 Cable, *Gunboat Diplomacy, 3rd Ed.*, p. 207; UK, *RN Operations 1970–2013*.
580 Ramsbotham & Woodhouse. *Encyclopedia of International Peacekeeping Operations*, p. 173.
581 *JDR* 3, No. 3 (1982): p. 231.
582 Cable, *Gunboat Diplomacy, 3rd Ed.*, p. 207.
583 *JDR* 4, No. 2 (1983): p. 131.
584 Cable, *Gunboat Diplomacy, 3rd Ed.*, p. 207.
585 Ibid.
586 *RUSI News Sheet* 25 (1983): p. 2.
587 Benbow, *British Uses of Aircraft Carriers and Amphibious Ships*, p. 18.
588 *JDR* 4, No. 6 (1983): p. 557.
589 *RUSI News Sheet* 27 (1983): p. 1.
590 Cable, *Gunboat Diplomacy, 3rd Ed.*, pp. 207–208.
591 Ibid., p. 208.
592 UK, *RN Operations 1970–2013*.
593 *RUSI News Sheet* 31 (1983): p. 4.
594 Ibid., p. 3.
595 Cable, *Gunboat Diplomacy, 3rd Ed.*, p. 208; UK, *RN Operations 1970–2013*.
596 *RUSI News Sheet* 34 (1983): p. 3.
597 *RUSI News Sheet* 35 (1983): p. 1.
598 *JDW* 1, No. 1 (1984): p. 15.
599 *JDW* 1, No. 2 (1984): p. 61.
600 *JDW* 1, No. 7 (1984): p. 267.
601 *JDW* 1, No. 19 (1984): p. 765.
602 UK, *RN Operations 1970–2013*.
603 *RUSI News Sheet* 37 (1984): p. 1.
604 *JDW* 1, No. 8 (1984): p. 307.
605 Ibid., p. 311.
606 Ibid., p. 313.
607 *JDW* 1, No. 10 (1984): p. 389.
608 Cable, *Gunboat Diplomacy, 3rd Ed.*, p. 208.
609 *RUSI News Sheet* 39 (1984): p. 1.
610 Cable, *Gunboat Diplomacy, 3rd Ed.*, p. 208; *JDW* 1, No. 14 (1984): p. 547.
611 *RUSI News Sheet* 39 (1984): p. 2.
612 *JDW* 1, No. 17 (1984): p. 677.
613 *JDW* 1, No. 20 (1984): p. 811.
614 Cable, *Gunboat Diplomacy, 3rd Ed.*, p. 206.
615 *JDW* 1, No. 22 (1984): p. 901.
616 *JDW* 1, No. 24 (1984): p. 1013.
617 *JDW* 1, No. 25 (1984): p. 1059.
618 *JDW* 2, No. 1 (1984): p. 7.
619 *JDW* 2, No. 5 (1984): p. 176.
620 Ibid., p. 177.
621 *JDW* 2, No. 6 (1984): p. 211; UK, *RN Operations 1970–2013*.
622 *JDW* 2, No. 7 (1984): p. 268.

623 *JDW* 2, No. 8 (1984): p. 307.
624 *JDW* 2, No. 10 (1984): p. 435.
625 *JDW* 2, No. 11 (1984): p. 483.
626 *JDW* 2, No. 16 (1984): p. 723.
627 *JDW* 2, No. 17 (1984): p. 760.
628 *JDW* 2, No. 19 (1984): p. 870.
629 *JDW* 2, No. 22 (1984): p. 1015.
630 Ibid., p. 1095.

Index